PARLIAMENTS AND COALITIONS

COMPARATIVE POLITICS

Comparative Politics is a series for students, teachers, and researchers of political science that deals with contemporary government and politics. Global in scope, books in the series are characterized by a stress on comparative analysis and strong methodological rigour. The series is published in association with the European Consortium for Political Research. For more information visit www.ecprnet.eu

The Comparative Politics series is edited by Professor David M. Farrell, School of Politics and International Relations, University College Dublin and Kenneth Carty, Professor of Political Science, University of British Columbia

OTHER TITLES IN THIS SERIES

The Challenges of Intra-Party Democracy
Edited by William P. Cross and Richard S. Katz

When Citizens Decide
Lessons from Citizen Assemblies on Electoral Reform
Patrick Fournier, Henk van der Kolk, R. Kenneth Carty, André Blais, and Jonathan Rose

Platform or Personality?
The Role of Party Leaders in Elections
Amanda Bittner

Political Leaders and Democratic Elections
Edited by Kees Aarts, André Blais, and Hermann Schmitt

The Politics of Party Funding
State Funding to Political Parties and Party Competition in Western Europe
Michael Koβ

Designing Democracy in a Dangerous World
Andrew Reynolds

Democracy within Parties
Candidate Selection Methods and
Their Political Consequences
Reuven Y. Hazan and Gideon Rahat

Party Politics in New Democracies
Edited by Paul Webb and Stephen White

Intergovernmental Cooperation
Rational Choices in Federal Systems and Beyond
Nicole Bolleyer

The Dynamics of Two-Party Politics
Party Structures and the Management of Competition
Alan Ware

Cabinets and Coalition Bargaining
The Democratic Life Cycle in Western Europe
Edited by Kaare Strøm, Wolfgang C. Müller, and Torbjörn Bergman

Politics at the Centre
The Selection and Removal of Party Leaders in the Anglo Parliamentary Democracies
William P. Cross and André Blais

Parliaments and Coalitions

The Role of Legislative Institutions in Multiparty Governance

LANNY W. MARTIN

GEORG VANBERG

Great Clarendon Street, Oxford, OX2 6DP,
United Kingdom

Oxford University Press is a department of the University of Oxford.
It furthers the University's objective of excellence in research, scholarship,
and education by publishing worldwide. Oxford is a registered trade mark of
Oxford University Press in the UK and in certain other countries

First published 2011
First published in paperback 2013

Impression: 1

British Library Cataloguing in Publication Data
Data available

ISBN 978–0–19–960788–4 (Hbk.)
ISBN 978–0–19–967478–7 (Pbk.)

Printed by the MPG Printgroup, UK

To *Dean*
and
To *Julia and Sophie*

Acknowledgments

We first started to think about the potential role of legislative institutions in resolving the tensions in coalition governance more than seven years ago, resulting in articles that appeared in the *American Journal of Political Science* (2004) and the *American Political Science Review* (2005). These earlier works convinced us of the need for more comprehensive study of the legislative process across parliaments with a variety of institutions. While extending our theoretical framework to systems with more or less powerful legislative institutions was relatively straightforward, collecting the data required to test the argument proved to be a more time-consuming exercise. This book is the result of these efforts.

In completing this manuscript, we have benefited from the generous feedback of colleagues and friends who have commented on the project and drafts of this book at various stages. In particular, we would like to thank Torbjörn Bergman, Sona Golder, Peter Kurrild-Klitgaard, Bing Powell, Lars Schoultz, Jürg Steiner, John Stephens, Michael Thies, and Milada Vachudova. Aaron Brunier, Martin Hansen, Robert Klemmensen, and Arjan Schakel assisted with data collection. We would also like to thank seminar participants at the University of Mannheim, the Comparative Politics Working Group at UNC-Chapel Hill, and Texas A&M University.

We also benefited greatly from the financial support of several institutions. The Center for European Studies at the University of North Carolina at Chapel Hill and Rice University provided support for data collection in Ireland. Most importantly, the National Science Foundation generously funded several grants (SES-0241536, SES-0241466, SES-0451893, and SES-0452036) that supported the bulk of data collection for this project.

Bing Powell has had a defining intellectual influence on both of us. He served as our dissertation advisor at the University of Rochester, and we became comparativists under his guidance. He is not only a leading scholar of democratic governance but also an exceptional teacher and mentor. We are proud to have been his students, and we hope that his influence is apparent in this book.

Finally, we would like to acknowledge the patient and loving support of our families, who put up with long absences during data collection in Europe, and cheerfully endured extended visits during the writing phase. More importantly, Dean, Julia, and Sophie remind us of what is truly important in life. Without them, we could not have completed this book. As a small sign of our gratitude, it is dedicated to them.

Contents

List of Figures

List of Tables

1

Introduction

On March 25, 2009, the grand coalition of Christian Democrats (CDU/CSU) and Social Democrats (SPD) introduced a "Bill for Improved Protection of Children" in the German Bundestag. In the wake of several highly salient, tragic cases of abuse and neglect, the coalition partners had reached a broad agreement that safeguards against the mistreatment of children should be strengthened. The draft bill prepared in the Ministry for Family, Seniors, Women, and Youth (headed by Minister Ursula von der Leyen of the CDU/CSU) made it easier for medical professionals to share concerns about suspected abuse without parental consent, provided for greater centralization and sharing of data across relevant agencies, and expanded the investigatory powers of child welfare officials. The cabinet reviewed the minister's draft, and the Social Democratic ministers voted with their Christian Democratic colleagues to send the bill to the legislature.[1] Despite this auspicious start for a bill dealing with what might appear to be a non-controversial issue—after all, who would oppose attempts to combat child abuse?—the bill quickly encountered obstacles in the Bundestag. During the first reading, when the bill was referred to committee for more detailed deliberation, Caren Marks, the leading Social Democratic legislator on women's and children's issues, announced:

> The majority of child welfare experts criticize this draft bill. In light of such critiques, we cannot just look the other way . . . The SPD faction takes this kind of targeted criticism very seriously. We will scrutinize this bill in all of its details during the legislative process. (BT Debate, April 23, 2009, p. 23, 622)

Marks' announcement turned out to be no idle threat. The bill was referred to the Committee on Family, Seniors, Women, and Youth as well as the Health, Domestic Policy, and Legal Affairs committees. In the committee deliberations, differences between the coalition partners soon became manifest. The SPD insisted that the CDU/CSU draft was too focused on enforcement and did not pay sufficient attention to preventive measures. The CDU/CSU resisted broadening the scope of the bill. By the end of May, negotiations had reached an impasse. The minister withdrew the bill, announcing that the government would not seek to implement a new policy prior to the legislative elections scheduled for September 2009. Not

[1] See Tagesschau, January 21, 2009.

surprisingly, each party publicly blamed the other for the failure, with Christian Democrats complaining that the SPD had torpedoed the bill in an "irresponsible and cynical" manner for election purposes, and SPD charging that the draft bill was an expression of a "control fetish" that "would not advance the protection of children."[2]

Certainly, this episode is not typical. For most coalition governments, most of the time, legislative initiatives do not end in disaster. But the story powerfully illustrates the central puzzle that is at the heart of this book. How do multiparty governments confront the challenges of joint policymaking, and what allows them to do so successfully?

Answering this question is not merely of academic interest. In many of the world's democracies, multiparty government is the norm. Since the end of World War II, coalitions have comprised roughly 70 percent of governments in European political systems (Gallagher *et al.*, 2005: 401). Even the United Kingdom—the traditional stronghold of single-party government—witnessed the formation of a two-party coalition following the May 2010 parliamentary elections. To the extent that economic and social outcomes in these countries are shaped by governmental policy, the quality of democracy as experienced by large numbers of citizens is therefore tied intimately to the ability of multiparty governments to make and to implement policy.

To understand how coalitions deal with the challenges of joint governance, we must first have a better understanding of the nature of these challenges. We argue that there are three features of multiparty government that conspire to create the tensions evident in the German example. The first, and perhaps most obvious, is that coalition governance requires parties with divergent preferences to agree on joint policy initiatives: that is, coalition politics requires *compromise*.[3] On any given issue, only one position or policy can typically be implemented. A government cannot adopt two income tax codes, regulatory policies, etc. When a coalition wishes to legislate in a particular area, it is therefore necessary to work out a mutually agreeable policy among its members—agreeable in the sense that no party prefers to leave the coalition rather than support the policy that is about to be implemented. For issues that are salient and anticipated during the negotiations that precede formation of a government, understandings on compromises may be reached as part of coalition negotiations. Sometimes, such agreements may be written directly into the coalition contract that parties sign prior to taking office

[2] See Tagesschau, June 29, 2009.

[3] Critics might object that it is not obvious that coalition government implies compromise on any given policy—perhaps coalition partners simply "divvy up" issue areas and give free rein to each partner in their domains. In fact, this is the logic of the prominent "portfolio allocation approach" of Laver and Shepsle (1996). We return to this issue in the next chapter. For now, we will simply proceed on the (hopefully substantively plausible) assumption that genuine compromise is a general feature of multiparty governance.

(Müller and Strøm, 2008).[4] For other issues, particularly those that arise during the course of a government's life, and therefore could not have been settled in coalition negotiations, compromises must be struck as these issues emerge. In either case, mutual accommodation is central to multiparty governance.[5] The second feature is the importance of *delegation* in modern policymaking. For reasons we explore in more detail below, coalition partners are typically forced to entrust cabinet ministers and bureaucracies with substantial authority over policy. The task of drafting statutes is dominated by ministers, supported by a staff of civil servants. As a result, control over the initial formulation of policy is primarily in the hands of a particular political party. The final—and perhaps most important—feature is that while they make policy *jointly*, parties that participate in coalition are held to account *separately*. Each coalition party must compete for votes under its own label.

A central thrust of our argument is that it is the combination of these three elements—compromise, delegation, and electoral competition—that makes coalition government qualitatively different from single-party government and gives rise to the tensions evident in the opening example. Compromise is not unique to coalition government, of course. *All* politics involves compromise. But because coalition government requires agreement among separate political entities (rather than, say, among members of the same political party), the pressures of electoral competition—to which individual parties are subject at regularly scheduled intervals—can make reaching and enforcing compromises more difficult. Parties must be concerned about the potential of being "punished" at the ballot box for appearing to be overly accommodating in their dealings with their coalition partners.[6]

In the face of such competition, delegation of authority to ministers becomes problematic because it implies that ministers will be tempted to undermine coalition compromises and to promote policies that (at least appear to) favor their own party at the expense of their coalition allies. Other coalition partners, in turn, have good reason to resist such attempts given that they may well be held responsible for government policy. The result is what one might call the *dilemma of coalition*

[4] Coalition contracts tend to cover a variety of issues, ranging from procedures for conducting policy negotiations, to the appointment process for cabinet members, to substantive policy agreements. See Müller and Strøm (2008) for more detail.

[5] For some scholars, the fact that coalition government requires compromise among several parties rather than providing full authority to one party holds normative appeal (e.g., see Lijphart, 1999; Powell, 2000). We do not focus on this normative issue, although our argument has implications for it, which we address in the final chapter.

[6] Recent work by Bawn and Rosenbluth (2006) on "long" and "short" coalitions is grounded in the same logic. They argue that fiscal restraint is more difficult to achieve under coalition than single-party government because budgetary agreements that require cross-party agreements are more difficult to reach and sustain in the face of electoral competition than agreements that are party-internal (as under single-party government). See also Rogowski and Kayser (2002).

governance: To govern successfully, coalition partners must be able to overcome the inherent tension between their *collective* interest in mutual accommodation and their *individual* incentives to pursue their particular policy objectives. This, then, is the puzzle we address in this book: How do coalition governments deal with the tensions of joint policymaking? Why are spectacular instances of failure—like the episode surrounding the German child protection bill—the exception rather than the rule? What are the mechanisms that allow coalitions to govern successfully, and how and when are these mechanisms used?

As the title of this book—*Parliaments and Coalitions*—reflects, our answer to this puzzle focuses on the role of legislative institutions in allowing multiparty governments to confront—and resolve—these tensions. If appropriate legislative institutions are present, coalition parties can "keep tabs on their partners" (Thies, 2001) through parliamentary review of ministerial proposals. This does not imply that parliaments are the *only* institutions that parties use for this purpose (e.g., see Müller and Strøm, 2000; Thies, 2001; Strøm *et al.*, 2008). As will become clear, executive institutions also play a key conflict resolution role, and interact with the legislative process in significant ways. In making this argument, the book contributes to, and highlights the connections between, two areas of inquiry that have largely developed in isolation from one another: *legislative studies* and *coalition theory*.

Most immediately, our results suggest that common perceptions of European legislatures are, at best, incomplete. With a few notable exceptions (Kim and Loewenberg, 2005; Martin and Vanberg, 2004, 2005; Carroll and Cox, 2010), the prevailing view among political scientists over the last few decades has been that parliaments play a marginal role in the policymaking process in parliamentary systems. While parliaments sustain the cabinet, and must formally consent to the adoption of legislation, scholars have argued that they exercise little influence on the formulation of policy. Instead, policy is created at the ministerial and cabinet levels, and then largely "rubber-stamped" by a government's support coalition. Gallagher *et al.* (2005: 62)—in a leading textbook on European politics—summarize this view well:

> A common theme in studies of European politics has been the 'decline of parliaments,' which have everywhere, according to some perceptions, lost to the grasping hands of governments the power they supposedly possessed in the late nineteenth century. By the middle of the twentieth century, it was generally agreed that governments acted while parliaments just talked.

Our argument and our empirical examination of legislation in five parliamentary democracies—Denmark, France, Germany, Ireland, and the Netherlands—challenge this conventional wisdom. While it is true that most legislative activity revolves around cabinet bills, drafted by a minister, we demonstrate that—when appropriate legislative institutions are present—the parliamentary process can play a central role in allowing coalition parties to "police the bargain" that is at the heart of coalition government, and to shape the policies that are ultimately adopted. As a result, legislatures are institutions of far greater significance to policy outcomes than scholars have generally appreciated. Moreover, we conclude that the importance of legislatures arises from the impact that legislative review has on the relationships between, and the relative power of, parties *within* government. It does not derive from the interactions between government and opposition that have traditionally been highlighted in research on legislative politics (e.g., see Strøm, 1990*b*; Powell, 2000).[7]

Second, the book contributes to deepening our understanding of coalition governance. Given the ubiquity of multiparty governments, and the centrality of interparty bargaining, it is not surprising that the study of coalitions has had a long and fruitful history in political science. Coalition theory has emerged as a major topic of inquiry in comparative politics, and scholars have made considerable progress in understanding the processes of coalition formation, the allocation of ministries across parties, and coalition termination.[8] However, scholars have paid much less attention to the policymaking process that unfolds between these "book-end" events of a coalition's life. This is ironic because what researchers—and, more importantly, citizens—ultimately care about are presumably not the identities of ministers or parties at the cabinet table, but the substantive policy outputs that governments implement. Indeed, it is probably no exaggeration to say that the immense interest scholars have expressed in coalition participation is rooted in the belief that knowing *who* is in government tells us something about what types of public policy outcomes to expect.

Over the past few years, a new direction in coalition theory has begun to explore the policymaking process under coalition government more directly, and we hope to contribute to this literature.[9] Taking this step in pushing coalition theory along is important for at least two reasons. As the opening story to this chapter suggests, and as we explain in greater detail in the next chapter, policymaking under coalition government differs in significant ways from policymaking under single-party government. To reiterate an earlier point, the fact that coalition government requires *separate* political units (parties) to make *joint* policy gives rise to dynamics and tensions that are more muted, or even absent, under single-party government. To understand how policy is made, and what policy outputs are to be expected from a multiparty coalition, it is therefore necessary to develop

[7] At the same time, our argument does not diminish the potential importance of government–opposition interactions in the legislative process. We explore these interactions in the empirical analyses in Chapters 5 and 6.

[8] The literature on these topics is vast. For good general reviews, see Laver and Schofield (1990), Strøm and Nyblade (2007), Martin and Stevenson (2001), Verzichelli (2008), Warwick and Druckman (2001), Warwick (1994).

[9] Recent contributions that examine the policymaking process under coalition government include studies by Heller (2001), Thies (2001), Kim and Loewenberg (2005), Carroll and Cox (2010), Strøm *et al.* (2008), and our own work (Martin and Vanberg 2004, 2005, 2008).

an account of the policymaking process under such governments. Who is able to shape policy? Under what conditions are they able to do so, and when will they choose to exercise their influence? How do the different institutional arrangements we observe across parliamentary systems condition the answers to these questions?

Understanding the policymaking process under coalition government also has implications for the formation and dissolution of coalitions. To the extent that political parties, represented by their leaders, care about policy outputs and outcomes—which they are likely to do if only for instrumental reasons (Strom, 1990*a*; Müller and Strøm, 1999)—*expectations* about how the policymaking process will unfold under alternative coalitions that could be formed should influence coalition negotiations, and hence formation. Put differently, bargaining over the formation of a coalition government is endogenous to anticipations of the policies that a new cabinet is likely to adopt once it is installed. This is, of course, not a new insight, and it has been implicit in much coalition theory. The seminal contribution of Laver and Shepsle's portfolio allocation theory (Laver and Shepsle, 1996) is to place this issue at the heart of a theory of coalition formation. We return to their argument in more detail in the next chapter. For now, we simply note that a more nuanced, complete understanding of the process of policymaking should allow further progress in explaining coalition formation and termination as well.

To make our argument, we proceed in several steps. In Chapter 2, we develop a theory of coalition policymaking that highlights why such policymaking poses a challenge, and explains how policymaking will unfold as parties counteract attempts by their partners to renege on the coalition bargain. In Chapter 3, we provide a detailed account of the institutional conditions under which parties can use the legislative process to manage the tensions of policymaking in multiparty governments. We also introduce the five parliamentary chambers that we focus on empirically (the Danish Folketing, the Dutch Tweede Kamer, the German Bundestag, the French Assemblée Nationale, and the Irish Dáil), and place them in a comparative context by presenting a general assessment of the strength of parliaments across sixteen European democracies. In Chapter 4, we describe an original data set that details the legislative histories of approximately 1,300 government bills across these parliaments. In Chapters 5 and 6, which constitute the empirical core of the book, we demonstrate how and under what conditions parliaments play a significant role in scrutinizing and shaping government legislation. We also discuss how coalitions can use cabinet and legislative institutions jointly as solutions to the problems of governance. Along the way, we evaluate, and provide novel evidence for, a number of other theoretical arguments that have been developed in the coalition literature over the past few decades, including those concerning the importance of cabinet-level institutions, such as junior ministers (Müller and Strøm, 2000; Thies, 2001), and the influence of opposition parties (Strøm, 1990*b*; Powell,

2000), as well as the special nature of minority governments (Strøm, 1990*b*). In the final chapter, we consider the positive and normative implications of our findings for our understanding of coalition government, the role and importance of legislative institutions, and the nature of democratic governance more generally.

2

Coalition Governance and Delegation

One of the most distinctive features of contemporary parliamentary government is that policymaking involves—and requires—a significant amount of delegation. The scope of public policy in advanced democracies is enormous, covering issues such as taxation, health care, defense, education, economic regulation, environmental protection, old-age pensions, energy policy, communications, financial regulation, and foreign affairs, to name only a few. Drafting legislation that effectively promotes a given policy goal in these areas typically requires detailed technical knowledge: Policymakers must solve a "means-ends" problem in determining *how* to achieve a desired result. They need to know which alternative policies can achieve a given end, which policies are (and are not) feasible, what consequences (intended and unintended) alternative policies may have, and what their associated costs are likely to be. In short, the problem of obtaining *information* represents a central challenge for effective policymaking.

Consider the following example. One of the most salient, and controversial, items in the coalition agreement signed by the Social Democrats and Greens to form a government in Germany in 1998 was the decision to eliminate German reliance on nuclear power and to shut down all nuclear reactors in the country. Although the desired outcome appears clear and simple, writing a policy that achieves that goal poses a complex problem. How can nuclear reactors be shut down and dismantled safely? What alternative sources of energy can be substituted? How feasible are these alternatives, and how can a transition be achieved technically? How costly will it be? What are the legal aspects of trying to eliminate nuclear power, which is largely produced by private companies with long-established property rights and contracts? What will be the economic consequences of a transition, and how can possible detrimental effects be minimized? Over what time frame can this goal be achieved? Not surprisingly, the coalition contract itself was vague on all of these issues. Crafting a policy to realize the end goal of eliminating nuclear power posed a daunting challenge requiring substantial technical knowledge and delicate trade-offs. The parties were simply not in a position to present a specific policy as part of (relatively brief) coalition negotiations.

One consequence of the growing importance of technical expertise in policymaking has been an increasing reliance on institutions and individuals who are able to supply specialized knowledge. As was already evident to Bagehot in the late nineteenth century, the authority to draft legislation in many parliamentary systems has increasingly been delegated from members of parliament to the cabinet, supported by the corresponding government ministries (Bagehot, 1872; Bryce, 1921; Wheare, 1963; Cox, 1987). One powerful indicator of this trend is the fact that the legislative process in parliamentary systems, by and large, revolves around cabinet-sponsored bills. Not only do the vast majority of bills considered in parliamentary systems originate in the cabinet, but once introduced, most of these bills are adopted. Private-member bills that do not enjoy the blessing of the cabinet play a fairly marginal role in the legislative process (see Anderweg and Nijzink, 1995: 171). The dominance of cabinet-sponsored legislation is, of course, one of the reasons for the widely shared view among scholars that parliaments are largely irrelevant for policymaking, particularly where party discipline is high.

More importantly for our purposes, delegation does not stop with the cabinet. While the introduction of a government bill generally requires the collective assent of the cabinet, bills themselves are typically not crafted by cabinet members in a joint effort (Laver and Shepsle, 1994, 1996). Cabinets are relatively small institutions, ranging from roughly fifteen people in most cases to approximately thirty ministers when a cabinet is unusually large. Each minister faces a high workload, being responsible for overseeing a government ministry that develops and implements government policy. Although cabinet members can, and do, work collectively to develop a general understanding and agreement on the broad outlines of coalition policy, it is often impossible to draft specific legislative proposals collectively. Ministers do not command the necessary technical expertise across the wide range of issues that come before the cabinet.

Instead, the development of legislative proposals—the precise wording and content of bills—is generally left to the minister under whose jurisdiction a particular policy proposal falls (aided, of course, by civil servants in the respective ministry).[1] Indeed, it is part of a minister's "job" in preparing a draft bill to become sufficiently informed on the technical aspects of a policy to generate proposals that are feasible and achieve the government's purpose. Gallagher *et al.* (2005: 56) describe this process, and its consequences for the influence of ministers:

> The cabinet does not and cannot simply sit around in a meeting and make policy in a vacuum. Real-world policy-making on complex issues involves the cabinet's accepting, rejecting, or amending specific and detailed policy proposals that are presented to it, based on extensive and often very technical

[1] Naturally, the relationships between ministers and their civil servants—parodied in the famous BBC series *Yes, Minister*—raise additional problems of delegation from which we abstract here. See Huber and Shipan (2002) for a principal–agent approach to delegation between governments and bureaucracies.

> documentation. Only the government department with responsibility for the policy area in question has the resources and expertise to generate such a proposal. Thus, only the minister in charge of the relevant department is in a position to present the policy proposal at cabinet, giving him or her a privileged position in the policy area in question.

The final sentence in this characterization raises an important issue, which is at the heart of our argument. While delegation provides undoubted benefits—most importantly, the infusion of expertise into the policymaking process—it also has potential drawbacks. Because ministers enjoy an "informational advantage" vis-à-vis their peers, other cabinet members may find it difficult to challenge or to amend legislative proposals outside their jurisdiction that are brought before the cabinet. This has several important implications for the practice of multiparty governance.

2.1 POLICY-SIGNALING

When all members of the cabinet agree on desired policies, the discretion enjoyed by ministers is not problematic—each minister will act as a "perfect agent" for the collective interests of the government. But where differences over policy exist, the same may not be true. As the delegation literature has established more generally (Epstein and O'Halloran, 1994, 1999; Huber and Shipan, 2002), delegation carries with it the risk that "agents" (in our case, ministers) will increasingly act in ways that frustrate the goals of their "principals" (in our case, their coalition partners) as their preferences diverge. This is especially true in the context of coalition government. To see why, consider what the "preferences" of parties represent.

Perhaps the most obvious, perpetual, and challenging task confronting political parties in established democracies is the need to attract financial and electoral support.[2] In this sense, the "policy preferences" of parties as organizations are, at least in part, derived from the underlying concerns of the constituents to whom the party must be attentive. Individual politicians may be interested in influencing policy, and they are likely to have a taste for winning office, but to achieve either, they must be responsive to the preferences of those whose support they are seeking to achieve their personal goals (Mayhew, 1974; Strom, 1990*a*; Müller and Strøm, 1999).[3]

[2] Indeed, the need to do so offers a central normative justification for democratic governance, since it provides the mechanism that induces political parties—as represented by party leaders—to be sensitive to the interests and concerns of the constituents they have decided to target.

[3] As parties attempt to identify and attract such support, they generally "carve up" the relevant ideological space in a political system, and rely on separate (although occasionally overlapping)

To attract votes and resources, parties need to convince potential supporters that they are effective agents in promoting policies that address the issues that constituents care about (perhaps even that the party is the *most* effective agent available). Not surprisingly, parties exert tremendous effort to convince potential supporters of this fact. Election campaigns, political commercials, public appearances, speeches, and distribution of literature represent the most obvious examples of their constant attempts to "make a case" to target audiences.[4]

For parties that are part of a coalition, making a case to voters involves an additional challenge. Coalitions govern jointly, but at election time, partners must compete for votes separately.[5] To put the matter differently, unlike under single-party government, where one party controls *both* the levers of power and competes under its own label, parties under coalition government are *jointly responsible* for policymaking but must secure citizen support *separately*. To the extent that a party will be judged on the basis of the government's policy record, party leaders must worry about the potential implications of compromise positions adopted as part of coalition bargaining that may be unpalatable to their supporters.

This dynamic is exacerbated by the fact that supporters have some reason to be skeptical about the vigor with which party leaders represent their interests once in coalition. Party leaders who join a coalition, either as members of the cabinet, or as backbenchers of a government party in parliament, enjoy *office-holding* benefits. For many professional politicians, these perks—gaining a seat at the cabinet table, or even just being a member of the governing coalition in parliament—will be tempting. They represent, after all, the achievement of the upper echelons of their profession. These benefits do not accrue to regular party members outside parliament nor to the financial and electoral supporters of the party. As a result, there exists what economists typically refer to as a *moral hazard* problem in the relationship between party leaders and the remainder of the party's supporters. All have a collective interest in placing the party in a position to influence policy, which is generally enhanced by membership in the cabinet.

constituencies for support. Some parties attempt to develop broad appeal to wider audiences; others are "niche" parties that pursue smaller constituencies with particular preferences (Meguid, 2008). In part, of course, the nature of the party system, and the strategies pursued by individual parties, are a function of the political environment in which parties must compete, defined by the potential divisions of interests among citizens and the electoral rules that specify how votes are translated into seats. In the presence of multiple cleavages or distinct interests, proportional representation rules tend to encourage a proliferation of parties with narrowly targeted appeals, while single-member district plurality rules will typically discourage narrow targeting and instead encourage the formation of broad-based coalitions of interests under one party's label (Cox, 1997).

[4] For example, in other work we have demonstrated that as elections draw nearer, parties engage in longer parliamentary speeches when it is in their interest to demonstrate to voters that the party has acted as a faithful agent of the voters on an issue, suggesting that parties do adjust the way in which they communicate with their target audiences (Martin and Vanberg, 2008).

[5] Coalition partners can (and do), of course, cooperate in election campaigns, and they may even announce pre-electoral coalitions that declare intentions to form a joint government (see Golder 2006).

But party leaders consume additional benefits of holding government office—prestige, ministerial salaries, a fancy office, etc.—that other party members do not share. Consequently, leaders are likely to be *more eager* to join a cabinet than their followers and, perhaps more importantly, may be willing to agree to larger policy concessions in order to secure (or maintain) a seat at the cabinet table. Party supporters may grow suspicious that party leaders, in an effort to "play nice" to secure the private benefits of holding office for themselves, may not vigorously represent the party's policy interests in negotiations. Laver and Schofield (1990: 24) summarize this potential tension:

> The general rule is that the rank-and-file, more concerned with ideology and less in line for the other spoils of office, tend to resent the policy compromises necessary to enter coalition and hence to oppose them. The parliamentary leaders, at least some of whom will become cabinet ministers, are more inclined to see the virtue of policy compromises if these increase the chance of the party going into government.

The danger that supporters will blame party leaders—and potentially punish the party electorally—for an excessive willingness to compromise is particularly high in areas in which constituents believe the party is in a strong position to affect policy. After all, the greater the direct control of the party's leaders over a policy area, the more reason supporters have for expecting the party to deliver on its promises. Most obviously, this is the case in policy areas that fall under the jurisdiction of the ministerial portfolios the party controls. For example, Social Democratic party activists and supporters will expect to see tangible evidence that a Social Democratic labor minister is working to deliver employment policies they favor. They are unlikely to be impressed if they perceive the party as bending too much to the interests of its coalition partners.

Party leaders obviously face strong incentives to counteract the perception that they are "selling out" in pursuit of their personal ambitions. They need to convince supporters—both in the process of negotiating a coalition, and during the life cycle of the government—that they are representing the concerns of constituents as effectively as possible, given the constraints of participating in coalition government. Some research suggests that such a dynamic can play out during the coalition formation process. Luebbert (1986: 52), for example, argues that even if party leaders reach agreement relatively quickly, the desire to convince supporters of the party's efforts on their behalf can lead them to feign drawn-out negotiations. Leaders delay announcing their agreement in hopes that delay suggests to supporters that the party is holding out for maximal concessions from its partners.

Naturally, the need to convince supporters that the party is an effective advocate does not diminish once a coalition takes office. If anything, it may become more pressing as a government begins to make policy decisions. Parties in coalition are therefore likely to be under pressure to pursue opportunities during the policymaking process that will allow them to claim (with some plausibility) that they have "fought the good fight" by making serious (and public) efforts to move policy in directions favored by their constituents, and to argue that they agreed only reluctantly to unpalatable coalition compromises under duress from their coalition partner(s). We refer to the policymaking activities that party leaders undertake to create the impression that they are working hard on their supporters' behalf—which we conceptualize as a specific form of "position-taking" (Mayhew, 1974)—as "policy-signaling."

2.2 THE DILEMMA OF COALITION GOVERNMENT

The drafting and introduction of legislation provides a particularly prominent avenue for policy-signaling. After all, legislation is directly tied to the policy choices of government. The unveiling of a legislative proposal by a minister is a salient event that usually generates significant media attention and provides an opportunity to hold press conferences and to make statements to party activists. Parties can point to their legislative initiatives in election campaigns and communications with key constituencies. That is, writing legislation that favors the party's goals, and perhaps even incorporates draft language adopted from suggestions by support groups, provides tangible evidence of the party's efforts, and is therefore an attractive way to curry favor. Huber (1996: 274) has emphasized this point more generally with respect to the legislative process:

> [Coalition] parties must reach policy agreements and vote together on a wide range of issues, and they must then campaign against each other for votes in the next election. This obviously creates problems for voters and parties alike. Voters face the problem of assessing which parties are responsible for which policy outcomes and of determining the policy positions of political parties on various issues. Parties face the problem of communicating information about issue positions and political responsibility to the voters.... Consequently, the legislative process is important not only as channel by which policies are chosen but also as a forum for communicating information to voters about issue positions.

In short, parties face strong incentives, through the ministries they control, to use their privileged position in the legislative process to engage in "policy-signaling" by drafting and introducing bills that are likely to be greeted favorably by the constituents whose support they are attempting to win. Naturally, such bills may often run counter to the preferred policies of *other* members of the coalition—especially in issue areas in which the coalition partners' preferences are heterogeneous. To the extent that such draft bills are the building blocks of coalition policy, this presents an obvious source of tension.

Unfortunately, even if other members of a coalition recognize that a minister is attempting to "take a position" by introducing a bill that is skewed toward her party's position, there may be very little they can do to prevent this or to modify a draft bill on the spot. The privileged position of the minister in drafting legislation derives from the fact that she enjoys an informational advantage. Other ministers may realize that a draft bill deviates from their legitimate expectations regarding coalition compromises; however, they do not have the same level of information about feasible policy alternatives, nor are they likely to know how to draft the technical statutory language to implement an alternative policy even if they could identify it. As Laver and Shepsle (1996: 32) put it:

> Given the intense pressure of work and lack of access to civil service specialists in other departments, it seems unlikely that cabinet ministers will be able successfully to poke their noses very deeply into the jurisdictions of their cabinet colleagues. This implies that members of the cabinet will have only very limited ability to shape the substance of policy emanating from the department of a ministerial colleague, an assumption that has received empirical support from a number of country specialists.

Consider an example. Suppose a minister, charged with devising a policy that will realize an agreement the parties have reached, introduces a draft bill that appears to some of her colleagues to deviate from the agreement in ways that favor the minister's position. When challenged, the minister argues that, although the bill does not conform to her coalition partners' expectations, it approximates the coalition agreement as much as possible, given the various feasibility constraints that must be dealt with. No better alternative is available. This claim may be hard for other cabinet ministers to evaluate in light of the informational advantage enjoyed by the minister. Suppose other ministers become convinced that their cabinet colleague is using her privileged position to bias policy in directions she favors. It may still be impossible for them to amend the bill in cabinet. Even if they know what they would ultimately *like* to achieve, they will typically lack the necessary technical knowledge to draft appropriate legislative language.[6]

An important consequence of this incentive structure is that policymaking under coalition government is under constant threat: Compromises are at the center of multiparty government, but coalition members have persistent incentives not to make—and not be perceived to make—concessions that depart too far from the party's stated platform. Once an agreement has been reached among coalition members, realizing this agreement requires intervention by ministers, whose job is to draft, and to implement, policies that achieve the agreed-upon

[6] Certain institutions in the cabinet may help them in this regard (see, e.g., Anderweg and Timmermans, 2008), and we later explore the influence of one of them—the position of the junior minister.

compromise. Because these ministers (and the parties they represent) are under pressure to push—or at least be *seen* to push—policies that can serve as signals to their constituents that the party is an effective proponent of their interests, such implementation is problematic. Ministers may try to use the discretion they enjoy by drafting bills that bias policy in their party's favor. Doing so advances their own party's preferred policies. More importantly, it serves as a potential signal to the party's supporters that leaders are representing their interests vigorously and are not just enjoying the spoils of office. How do parties in coalition respond to these tensions?

2.3 CONTROLLING MINISTERIAL DISCRETION

One prominent answer, which lies at the heart of Laver and Shepsle's influential portfolio allocation approach (Laver and Shepsle, 1996), assumes that parties largely resign themselves to the inevitability of ministerial subterfuge, or at least do not count on being able to rein in ministers belonging to other parties reliably. Instead, party leaders accept that once cabinet positions have been distributed, ministers become "dictators" in the policy areas that fall under their jurisdiction. In negotiating over coalitions, parties will therefore assume that—at least as a worst-case scenario—ministers will implement their (and their constituents') most preferred policy in the areas they control.

In the context of traditional spatial models with separable preferences, this implies that only the lattice points created by the dimension-by-dimension intersections of the parties' ideal points are feasible policy outputs. Figure 2.1 provides a graphical illustration, familiar from Laver and Shepsle's work. Two parties, A and B, engage in coalition negotiations in a two-dimensional policy space. Each party is characterized by an ideal point (its most preferred policy), and prefers policies that are closer to its ideal point to those that are further away.[7] For each party, the circular indifference curve through the point *SQ* indicates all policies preferred by the party to the status quo. The intersection of the two indifference curves indicates all policy positions that *both* parties prefer to the status quo. If a coalition between parties A and B allocates the ministry controlling dimension 1 to Party B and the ministry controlling dimension 2 to Party A, ministers, as policy dictators, will use their discretion to implement their most preferred policy in the dimension they control. This implies that Party B's minister implements policy x_B in dimension 1 and Party A's minister implements policy y_A in dimension 2. The

[7] In Figure 2.1, the ideal point of Party A is given by $x_A y_A$ while the ideal point of Party B is given by $x_B y_B$.

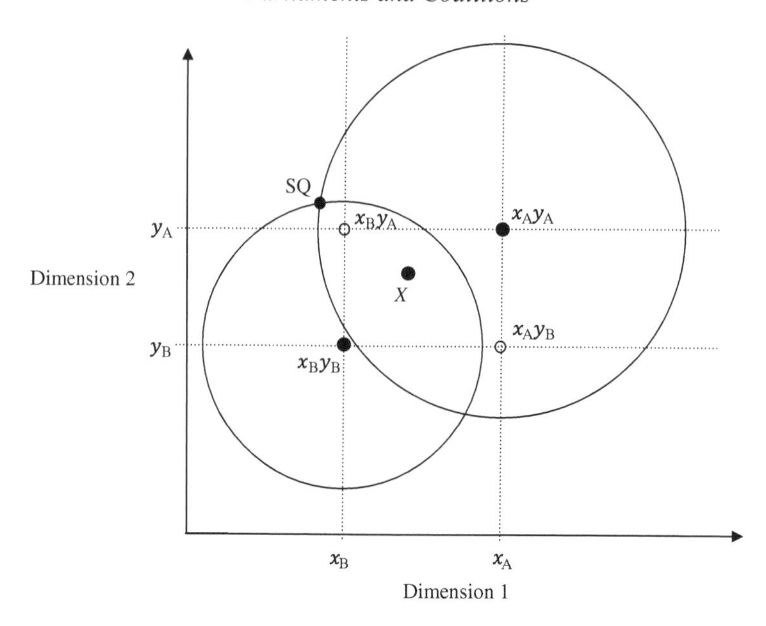

FIGURE 2.1 Ministerial Autonomy Equilibrium

aggregate result of this portfolio allocation is therefore the policy output $x_B y_A$. Because the resulting policy is preferred by both parties to the status quo, this is a potentially viable coalition.[8] (In contrast, the allocation in which Party A receives the dimension 1 ministry and party B receives the dimension 2 ministry is not a viable coalition: The resulting policy output is $x_A y_B$, which party B does not prefer to *SQ*.)

The appeal of this approach is that the resulting "coalition policy" is self-enforcing, and therefore incentive-compatible: Each minister is expected to carry out those policies that he or she prefers within his or her jurisdiction. In this sense, parties can "count on" the policies predicted by the approach to be implemented. "Genuine" coalition compromises, by which we mean policy outputs in which each party trades some moderation in policy areas it controls for moderation by

[8] It is important to note that the primary goal of Laver and Shepsle's analysis is not to provide an accurate depiction of cabinet decision-making. Rather, their goal is to construct a theory of coalition formation that takes account of party expectations about the ultimate policy outputs implied by particular coalition choices. That is, their aim is to make the process of coalition negotiation endogenous to expectations about the policy consequences of forming particular coalitions. This is a seminal contribution, and the "portfolio approach" serves as a stylized model of cabinet decision-making in order to generate these expectations. Applied to the current example, the approach predicts that the parties will agree to allocate the ministry that controls dimension 1 to party B and the ministry that controls dimension 2 to party A since both parties prefer $x_B y_A$ to *SQ*, but do not prefer $x_A y_B$ to *SQ*.

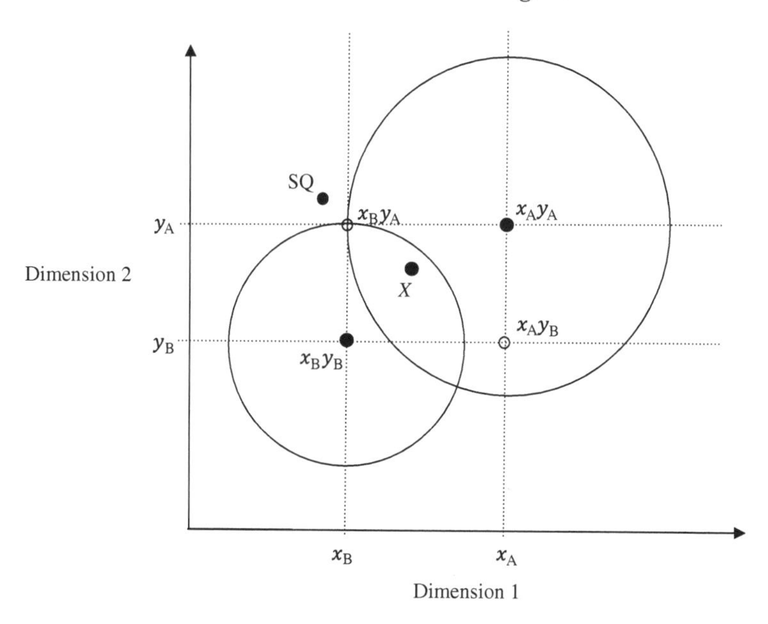

FIGURE 2.2 Coalition Compromises as Pareto Improvements

the other party in other areas, generally do not have this same "self-enforcing" quality. For example, in Figure 2.1, achieving the compromise policy *X* requires each minister to implement a policy in his or her dimension that is more moderate than he or she prefers.

Nevertheless, as has been pointed out in previous research (Thies, 2001; Martin and Vanberg, 2004), parties face strong incentives to try to pursue such compromise policies. Generally, *all* members of a coalition will prefer some genuine policy compromise to the lattice points that emerge from providing ministers with full policy autonomy in their jurisdictions. Consider Figure 2.2, which replicates the example of Figure 2.1. Drawing the parties' indifference curves through the lattice point $x_B y_A$—the "portfolio allocation" policy that results if party A controls dimension 2 and party B controls dimension 1—indicates that there exist a large number of compromise policies (including the agreement *X*) that are preferred by both parties to the policy that results if a B party minister implements x_B in her dimension and an A party minister implements x_A in his dimension. Importantly, *all* of these policy outputs require each minister to adopt policies in the dimension she controls that depart from her own most preferred position and accommodate the preferences of her partner (that is, after all, the meaning of compromise). In short, ministerial government is, at least with respect to policy outputs, Pareto-inefficient: Parties typically would prefer to implement policies that require moderation by all parties.[9]

The key problem confronting multiparty governments is that, given the strong policy-signaling incentives confronting ministers as they draft policies, reaping the benefits of mutually beneficial compromises requires mechanisms that allow parties to make *reliable* implementation of compromise possible despite the constant temptation confronting each coalition partner to deviate from such agreements. In other words, it requires a means by which parties can "keep tabs" on their partners (Thies, 2001).

2.4 MODELING SCRUTINY AND CHANGE

In the next chapter, we turn to the legislative process as an institutional device that coalition parties can employ to counteract ministerial discretion. Before considering a concrete institutional solution, it is useful to pursue a more general treatment. Suppose monitoring of ministers is possible, and coalition partners can modify ministerial initiatives that deviate too drastically from acceptable compromise positions. How would we expect coalition politics to play out if this is the case? When is potential ministerial drift a problem, and when will coalition partners attempt to counteract it? To answer these questions, we *assume* for the purposes of this section that a "monitoring mechanism" is available, that is, that parties have means (which they can employ at some cost) to scrutinize, and potentially change, ministerial draft bills.

We present a simple model designed to capture the interactions between coalition partners in light of the three features discussed above—the need for compromise, the necessity of delegation, and the reality of electoral competition. The goal is to investigate the consequences of the dilemma confronting multiparty government in a clear, intuitive manner, and to characterize its implications for coalition politics. How will multiparty government play out if parties confront these competing incentives? Will compromises be implemented successfully? Will ministers attempt to stray from the coalition bargain and engage in "policy-signaling"? Will ministerial proposals be scrutinized and amended, or will they simply be accepted? Would we expect different interactions over different types of issues?

[9] This result is not an artifact of separable preferences. It can be readily demonstrated that even with non-separable preferences, and differential weights attached to different dimensions, there are generally compromise policies that are preferred by all parties to the equivalent of the lattice points in the Laver–Shepsle model (i.e., those points at which the induced ideal points of all parties coincide).

Consider the following game, which takes place between two players, a *Minister* and a *Partner*. To simplify, we assume that the minister, who prepares legislation, has a choice of introducing one of two bills. She can either introduce a moderate bill (*M*) or a radical bill (*R*). Naturally, "real-world" policymaking is much more complex, but this simplification allows us to capture in an intuitive and tractable manner the distinction between a bill that is perceived to reflect an implicit or explicit compromise position among the coalition partners, and a bill that is perceived to violate such an agreement at the expense of the coalition partner. That is, the moderate bill approximates a compromise position between the coalition partners that is consistent with the spirit of the coalition bargain, whereas a radical proposal is slanted toward the minister's preferences in a manner that appears, at least on first inspection, to be inconsistent with the spirit of the coalition compromise.

To capture the informational advantage enjoyed by the minister, we assume that there are two possible "states of the world." In the "normal" state, both bills are feasible; that is, both bills can be implemented. In this environment, the radical bill represents an attempt by the minister to deviate from the coalition bargain and to take advantage of the need to delegate in drafting policy. In the "constrained" state, the moderate bill is not feasible—only the radical bill can be implemented. As a result, in this environment, the radical bill does not indicate that the minister is attempting to abuse her power. The nature of the policy environment is simply such that the coalition compromise cannot be implemented, and the feasible alternative happens to favor the minister. For example, technical or legal reasons may prevent a particular approach or make certain outcomes unachievable or prohibitively costly. The minister's privileged access to information implies that she can distinguish between these states; that is, she knows which policies are feasible. The partner, on the other hand, cannot do so without investing resources to acquire more information.

This information structure allows us to capture the dilemma confronting a coalition partner faced with a ministerial draft bill. If the minister's proposal appears, on first inspection, to violate the spirit of coalition, the partner faces some uncertainty. Perhaps the minister is attempting to abuse her discretion to introduce a bill that is unfavorable to her coalition partners and advances her own interests. But it is also possible that the minister is simply facing a constrained environment and is introducing a bill that is as close to the coalition compromise as is feasible—the best available policy just happens to favor the minister's position.[10] How should a coalition partner react? Should the party invest resources in

[10] This modeling choice assumes that in the constrained environment, the feasible bill is preferred by the minister. This is an innocuous assumption that focuses our attention on the relevant case in which a deviation from the coalition bargain is seen to favor the minister's side, and thus arouses the suspicions of coalition partners. If the constrained environment favors the partner's position, the monitoring problem we are concerned with does not arise.

scrutinizing and potentially amending the ministerial draft? Or should it simply acquiesce?

We assume that the policymaking process unfolds in the following manner:

1. Nature determines the policymaking environment. The environment is constrained with probability $Pr(Constrained) = p$, where $p \in (0, 1)$.
2. The minister observes the policymaking environment and introduces a draft bill $b \in \{M, R\}$.
3. The partner observes the bill introduced by the minister, and forms beliefs about the policymaking environment. She can agree to the minister's bill or scrutinize it, that is, $a_P \in \{Agree, Scrutinze\}$.
4. If the partner agrees, the minister's draft bill is passed and the game ends.
5. If the partner scrutinizes, she learns the state of the policymaking environment. In the constrained environment, the radical bill is implemented, because it is the only feasible bill. In the normal environment, the partner can insist that the minister's proposal be amended to reflect the coalition bargain, and the moderate bill is implemented.

The preferences of the players capture the substantive considerations outlined in the discussion above. We assume both players care about the policy that is ultimately implemented. To capture preference divergence between the coalition partners, we assume that the policy payoff to the minister of implementing the radical bill is $U_M^{Policy}(R) = X$, while the payoff to the moderate bill is $U_M^{Policy}(M) = 0$. For the coalition partner, the payoff to the radical bill is $U_P^{Policy}(R) = -X$, while the payoff to the moderate bill is $U_P^{Policy}(M) = 0$. Thus, as X increases, the preference divergence between the two partners increases.[11]

As discussed above, parties face electoral incentives to use the policymaking process to make statements that can appeal to their activists and to convince potential voters that they are working for their interests. Ministerial draft bills provide an important opportunity to do so. We capture this feature by assuming that, in addition to the policy payoffs of the policy that is ultimately adopted, the minister receives a position-taking benefit from the bill introduced. Let $b \in \{M, R\}$ denote the bill introduced by the minister. Then $U_M^{Position}(b) = \beta U_M^{Policy}(b)$, where $\beta > 0$. As β increases, the electoral incentives confronting the minister to claim the position-taking benefits of introducing the radical bill—even if she does not ultimately expect it to be implemented—grow.

We also assume that the process of scrutinizing and potentially amending ministerial drafts imposes costs. Given the informational advantage a minister

[11] This specification assumes that the preferences of the partners are symmetric about the compromise position. This assumption is convenient (because it reduces the number of parameters in the model), but the results reported below hold if the compromise imposes asymmetric burdens on the partners.

possesses, a coalition partner must expend resources to scrutinize ministerial policy proposals to determine the consequences the bill is likely to have, to identify feasible alternatives, and to draft the necessary statutory language. Thus, we assume that to scrutinize the bill offered by the minister, the coalition partner must pay a cost of $c > 0$.[12]

The process of scrutiny and amendment can also impose costs on the minister. If a ministerial draft bill is amended, resources have been devoted to developing a proposal that is not converted into law. We can think of these as opportunity costs. There are also potential reputation costs to ministers who are seen to be ineffective if bills are subjected to extended scrutiny and change. Finally, the perception by coalition partners that a minister has abused her role in the policy process by drafting legislation that is inconsistent with the coalition agreement is likely to have a negative impact on the relationship between the coalition partners. To capture these considerations, we assume that if the minister's draft bill is amended, she suffers a cost of $L > 0$.[13]

Both the minister and the partner have four pure strategies available. The minister can make her choice of bill contingent on her knowledge of the policymaking environment. Specifically, the minister's strategy set is given by

$$S_M = \{(R|N; R|C), (R|N; M|C), (M|N; R|C), (M|N; M|C)\} \tag{2.1}$$

where the notation $(A|N; B|C)$ indicates that the minister will propose bill "A" if the policymaking environment is normal and bill "B" if the policymaking environment is constrained. For the minister, only the first and third strategies are relevant: In the constrained environment, only the radical bill is feasible. As a result, the minister has a dominant strategy to introduce this bill and to reap the position-taking benefits of doing so.

The partner has four strategies available, in which her decision to scrutinize ministerial proposals is contingent on the bill that the minister introduces:

$$S_P = \{(S|R; S|M), (S|R; A|M), (A|R; S|M), (A|R; A|M)\} \tag{2.2}$$

Only the second and fourth strategies are relevant. Given the minister's strategies, a moderate bill will only be introduced when it is feasible, and the partner cannot expect to "do better" than to accept this bill without expending the effort to scrutinize the bill.

[12] One way to interpret the ministerial autonomy model (Laver and Shepsle, 1996) is to assume that these costs are prohibitively high, given the expected damage of ministerial subterfuge (see the equilibrium in Proposition 1 below.) A critical part of the argument we develop here is that the institutional structure of the policy-making process shapes these costs, and that coalition partners will be able to effectively scrutinize ministerial draft bills under certain conditions.

[13] See the Appendix for a game tree.

2.4.1 Equilibrium

To solve the model, we look for an equilibrium, that is, we consider those states in which each player is doing as well as he can, given how the other player behaves, and given what he believes about the policymaking environment.[14] Specifically, the minister's choice about which bill to introduce is optimal, given her expectations about the level of scrutiny she will face from her coalition partner, and the policy and position-taking incentives she confronts. For the partner, it implies that the partner uses the bill introduced by the minister to draw inferences about which policies are feasible, and to engage in optimal scrutiny and amendment of ministerial proposals. Because the minister will introduce a moderate bill only in the normal policymaking environment, it is immediate that the partner knows that the environment is normal if the minister introduces this bill. Let the partner's belief that the policymaking environment is constrained when the minister introduces the radical bill be given by $\gamma = Pr(C|R)$. The model has three equilibria, which capture three different modes of coalition interactions.

Proposition 1 (Ministerial Autonomy). *For* $X \leq \frac{c}{1-p}$, *the strategy profile* $s^* = (R|N; R|C), (A|R; A|M)$ *constitutes a PBE of the game. In this equilibrium, the partner's belief that the environment is constrained when the minister introduces the radical bill is given by* $\gamma = p$. *The minister always introduces the radical proposal and the partner always accepts the minister's proposal without scrutinizing it.*

We refer to this equilibrium as the "ministerial autonomy" equilibrium because it evokes the spirit of Laver and Shepsle's model (1996). In this equilibrium, ministers are free to implement their preferred policy—the policies that are introduced and passed are not compromise positions between the partners. Coalition partners accept such ministerial "drift" despite knowing that there is, with likelihood $(1 - p)$, a policy available that they prefer, and that would more closely approximate a compromise position. However, given the costs of scrutiny, and the expected impact of ministerial drift, the coalition partner chooses simply to acquiesce in the proposal. Not surprisingly, this equilibrium exists *only* for issues on which the preference divergence between the partners (X) is sufficiently small: As soon as the preferences of the coalition partners diverge sufficiently, thereby raising the costs of ministerial drift, ministerial autonomy can no longer be sustained.[15]

[14] In technical terms, the appropriate solution concept for this model is *Perfect Bayesian Equilibrium* (PBE), which requires that the players' strategies are sequentially rational, given their beliefs, and that the players' beliefs are derived from Bayes' Rule wherever possible. See the Appendix for formal proofs of the equilibria.

[15] The degree of preference divergence that is consistent with ministerial autonomy depends in sensible ways on the cost of scrutiny and on the likelihood that the environment is constrained. The more resources are required to scrutinize ministerial draft bills, the larger preference divergence can

Proposition 2 (Coalition Squabbles). *For $\frac{c}{1-p} < X < \frac{L}{\beta}$, the following strategy profile constitutes a PBE of the game: The minister always introduces the radical bill in the constrained environment. In the normal environment, she introduces the radical proposal with probability $\pi = \frac{cp}{(1-p)(X-c)}$. The partner never scrutinizes the moderate bill. She scrutinizes the radical bill with probability $\mu = \frac{(1+\beta)X}{L+X}$. In this equilibrium, the partner's belief that the environment is constrained when the minister introduces the radical bill is given by $\gamma = \frac{p}{p+(1-p)\pi}$.*

This equilibrium exists when the preference divergence between the partners is more significant than under ministerial autonomy, but not "too large." In equilibrium, ministers sometimes—but not always—(ab)use their discretion to introduce a radical bill when the coalition compromise is feasible. Partners, in turn, engage in selective scrutiny: They "spot-check" ministerial proposals when they appear to be out of line with the coalition bargain, but they do not do so all of the time. In other words, coalition politics has become more contentious: Ministers sometimes engage in attempts to "take a position" through controversial proposals, and coalition partners sometimes engage in efforts to "check" ministerial drift.

Proposition 3 (Maximal Position-Taking). *For $X \geq \max\left[\frac{c}{1-p}; \frac{L}{\beta}\right]$, the strategy profile $s^* = (R|N; R|C), (S|R; A|M)$ constitutes a PBE of the game. In this equilibrium, the partner's belief that the environment is constrained when the minister introduces the radical bill is given by $\gamma = p$. The minister always introduces the radical proposal and the partner always scrutinizes. In the normal environment, the proposal is amended and the moderate proposal is implemented.*

We refer to this equilibrium as the "maximal position-taking" equilibrium. This equilibrium emerges when the preference divergence between the coalition partners has become even more significant. Given that the partners disagree strongly about the issue at hand, coalition politics results in a game of "position-taking" and "modification." The coalition partner always scrutinizes the radical proposal on the chance that the minister is attempting to skew policy in her favor in violation of the coalition bargain. Nevertheless, although she knows that she will face scrutiny, and will ultimately be unable to implement the radical proposal if the moderate bill is feasible, the minister always introduces the radical bill. She does so because faithful adherence to the coalition agreement is costly, and she prefers to capture the position-taking benefits she can derive from introducing the radical bill.

become before ministerial autonomy can no longer be sustained. Similarly, the larger the likelihood that the environment is constrained, the greater the preference divergence that is consistent with ministerial autonomy.

2.4.2 *Empirical Implications*

Figure 2.3 illustrates the three equilibria in "preference divergence space." The extent of policy disagreement between the coalition partners (X) is plotted along the horizontal axis. The vertical axis indicates the weight placed by the minister on position-taking benefits (β). This two-dimensional space is a "preference divergence space" in the sense that it captures the two features of the coalition interaction that drive potential conflict between the partners: The extent to which the parties differ on the policy to be implemented, and the extent to which they face incentives to "take a position." As either parameter increases, the potential for disagreement among the partners—specifically, the minister's incentives to pursue the radical proposal—grow.

The graph clearly reveals the intuition behind the equilibria. On the left-hand side of the figure, where policy divergence (X) is low, the ministerial autonomy equilibrium prevails. The policy preferred by the minister (the "radical" bill) is sufficiently close to the moderate policy (given the costs of scrutiny) that the partner is willing to accept ministerial "drift" without interference. Once policy divergence crosses the $\frac{c}{1-p}$ threshold, the situation changes. In the top-right part of the figure, only the maximal position-taking equilibrium is possible. In the bottom-right part of the figure, we find the mixed strategy, coalition squabbling equilibrium. The progression from one equilibrium to the other makes

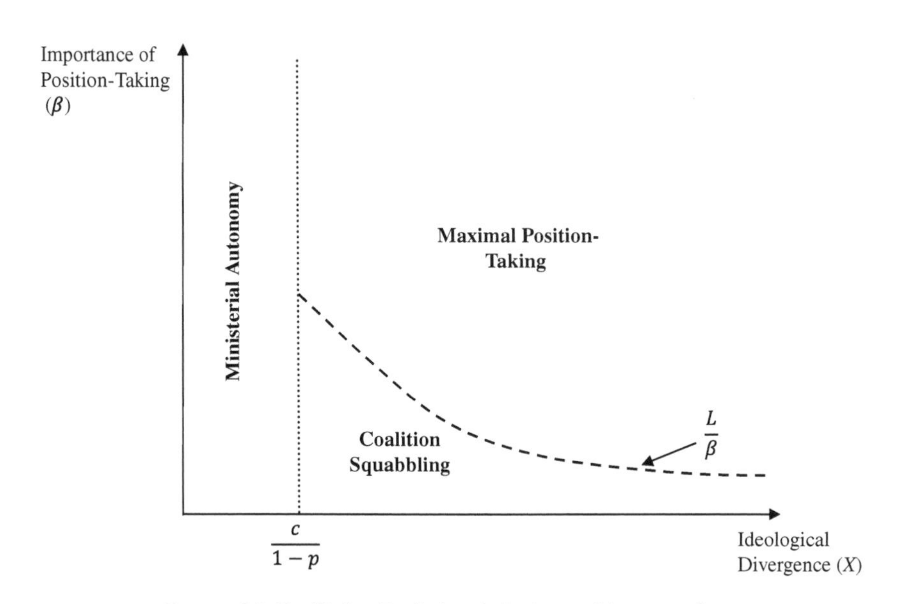

FIGURE 2.3 Equilibrium Predictions in Preference Divergence Space

intuitive sense: The distinction between the two equilibria concerns the extent (or frequency) of ministerial "drift." In the squabbling equilibrium, the minister will sometimes—but not always—propose the radical bill when the moderate one is feasible. In the maximal position-taking equilibrium, on the other hand, she will *always* introduce the radical bill. The reason for the minister's increasing willingness to be confrontational is that the benefit to introducing the radical bill—even if it is ultimately not implemented—increases; that is, the position-taking benefits have grown stronger. The figure clearly demonstrates this dynamic: Holding constant the level of policy divergence (X), we switch from the squabbling to the maximal position-taking equilibrium when the position-taking incentives (β) become sufficiently large.

This simple model suggests that the potential for scrutiny and amendment of ministerial draft bills—a possibility we have simply *assumed* in the model, but which we explore in great detail in the next chapter—plays an important role in coalition politics. The policy-signaling incentives confronting ministers, coupled with the need to delegate drafting authority to them, generate a dynamic in which ministers will attempt to undermine coalition compromises by "playing to their audiences" with the draft bills they introduce. Where the damage of such ministerial drift is sufficiently serious, coalition partners take advantage of amendment opportunities to "pull back" proposals by particular ministers. In other words, the possibility of reining in ministerial drift is an important tool for coalition partners, and it becomes increasingly important as the preferences of the partners diverge.

To evaluate the extent to which this dynamic is actually at play, we require empirical implications of the argument that are potentially observable. Two of the most important implications concern the degree of scrutiny to which ministerial bills are subjected, and the extent to which these draft proposals are altered by coalition partners. The model provides clear expectations about both scrutiny and the extent of change, and these expectations accord well with intuition. The following two hypotheses, which provide the foundation for the empirical work in Chapters 5 and 6, summarize these implications.

Hypothesis (Scrutiny). *Ceteris paribus, ministerial proposals are more likely to be subjected to scrutiny by a coalition partner the greater the divergence in preference between the coalition partners on the issues addressed in the bill.*

Figure 2.3 immediately illustrates this hypothesis. As the policy divergence between the partners increases, we move from the ministerial autonomy equilibrium to the squabbling equilibrium to the maximal position-taking equilibrium. As we do so, the likelihood that the radical bill will be scrutinized by the partner increases from 0 to $\frac{(1+\beta)X}{L+X}$ to 1; that is, the likelihood of scrutiny (weakly) increases as policy divergence becomes more pronounced. Similarly, as the position-taking incentives confronting the minister increase, scrutiny (weakly) increases as we move from the squabbling equilibrium to the maximal position-taking equilibrium.[16]

Hypothesis (Change). *Ceteris paribus, ministerial proposals are more likely to be amended by a coalition partner the greater the divergence in preference between the coalition partners on the issues addressed in the bill.*

In the ministerial autonomy equilibrium, ministerial proposals are not subjected to scrutiny, and are therefore not changed. In the squabbling equilibrium, proposals are amended when the minister's proposal is subjected to scrutiny, and the minister is found to have abused her discretion in introducing the radical proposal. The probability of this outcome is given by $(1-p)\pi\mu$. In the maximal position-taking equilibrium, the minister always makes the radical proposal, the partner always scrutinizes this proposal, and it is amended when the moderate policy is feasible. The probability of this outcome is $1-p$. In short, as we move from the ministerial autonomy to the squabbling to the maximal position-taking equilibrium—that is, as we move in a northeasterly direction in the figure, indicating greater preference divergence between the partners—ministerial proposals are increasingly likely to be amended by the coalition partner.[17]

Both hypotheses accord well with intuition concerning the dynamics of coalition government in an environment in which parties confront incentives to "take a position" to send signals to their constituents. When coalition partners largely share the same preferences on an issue, the "agency problem" in coalition government disappears. Ministers are not subjected to scrutiny, and are able to pursue their preferences because in doing so, they are sufficiently close to the preferences of *all* coalition partners. But when preference divergence increases, coalition dynamics change, and the agency problem induced by the need to delegate, coupled with the demands of electoral competition, moves to the fore. Parties face strong incentives to make use of the high-profile act of introducing legislation to "signal" their policy commitments to their constituents. Coalition partners—recognizing the dangers posed by ministerial drift in these circumstances—engage in vigorous scrutiny of ministerial proposals and (where this is feasible) insist on changes that move legislative proposals closer to the coalition bargain.

[16] Formally, $\frac{dPr(Scrutiny)}{dX} \geq 0$ and $\frac{dPr(Scrutiny)}{d\beta} \geq 0$.

[17] There is one nuance to this comparative static. Within the squabbling equilibrium, the likelihood of amendment is given by $(1-p)\pi\mu = \frac{cp(1+\beta)X}{(X-c)(X+L)}$. This probability increases with β but *decreases* with X. Thus, as X increases, the likelihood of amendment generally increases from 0 up to $1-p$, with a temporary decrease in the middle range. We ignore this nuance here because the overall trend—taking both X and β separately and in conjunction—is clearly positive, and because it is impossible to investigate this local feature empirically, given available measures.

2.5 CONCLUSION

The central message of our argument is simple. Multiparty governments face constant, competing pressures. Successful coalition policymaking requires cooperation and compromise, and all parties who agree to join a coalition have some interest in successful governance. At the same time, each party must concern itself with its political survival, and coalition compromises that deviate too far from the policies favored by a party's constituents can pose a threat. As a consequence, parties must balance the need to compromise and cooperate with their partners against the need to signal to supporters that the party is an effective advocate for the policies they favor.

Coupled with the delegation of authority to draft policies to cabinet ministers, the need to engage in "policy-signaling" creates the risk that ministers will make use of their privileged position to draft and introduce legislation that undermines compromise agreements that are in the collective interest of the cabinet. In short, coalition governments are confronted with a challenge in policymaking that is largely absent under single-party governments: The need to prevent subterfuge by their coalition partners through the ministries they control. To do so, parties participating in a coalition must develop effective mechanisms that allow them to "police the bargain" they have struck with their partners. Indeed, as Müller and Strøm (2000: 18) note, understanding how coalition governments do so is one of the central challenges confronting the study of multiparty governance:

> Such slippage, or agency loss,... begs the question of how coalition parties might try to cooperate to limit the power of individual ministers to impose undesirable policy outcomes on their coalition partners.

Importantly, any mechanism that coalition parties settle on to "limit the power of individual ministers" must make it possible to solve two related problems, which we refer to as "scrutiny" and "modification." The first refers to the informational hurdle confronting coalition partners. The central reason for the advantaged position ministers occupy in the policymaking process, and which provides them with the ability to undermine coalition compromises, is that they enjoy privileged access to information. Their position provides them with insight on available policy alternatives, their feasibility, as well as the technical "know-how" of writing statutory language that implements a particular policy choice. To effectively police legislative proposals emerging from ministries controlled by their coalition partners, parties must have access to similar information. They need to be able to understand the proposal as drafted and its likely policy consequences. More importantly, they need to evaluate the justifications offered by the minister for particular choices embodied in the bill as well as the feasibility of alternative proposals. Finally, if they decide that the bill as drafted does not conform to coalition compromise agreements, they need to know, from a purely technical "drafting" perspective, how the bill can be changed to a more palatable alternative. In short, a successful monitoring institution must make it possible to engage in effective scrutiny to level the informational playing field between the partners.

But that is not sufficient. To counteract ministerial drift, it must also be possible for coalition partners to translate effective scrutiny into policy change. That is, they must have access to a forum that allows them to amend ministerial proposals. In the next chapter, we turn specifically to an analysis of institutional mechanisms that, separately or in conjunction, have both features. In particular, we explore the conditions under which the *legislative process* can allow parties to effectively "keep tabs" on their partners.

2.A APPENDIX

This appendix provides the proof for the three equilibria. The model is a version of a canonical signaling game, depicted in the game tree shown in Figure 2A.1.

It is immediately obvious from the figure that the minister has a dominant strategy to introduce the radical bill in the constrained environment, and that the partner has a dominant strategy not to scrutinize the moderate bill if introduced.

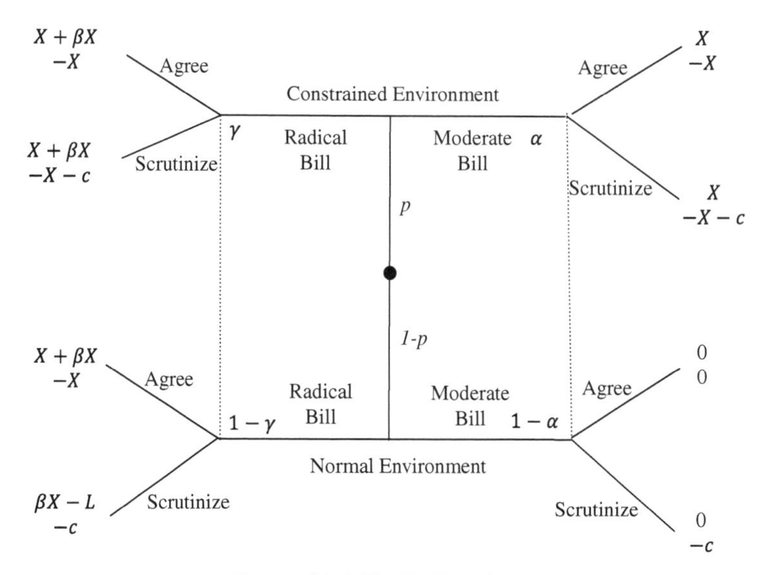

FIGURE 2A.1 The Coalition Game

Note: In the constrained environment, only the radical bill can be implemented.

As a result, the only relevant (pure) strategies for the minister we must consider are $(R|N; R|C)$ and $(M|N; R|C)$. Similarly, for the partner, the only relevant strategies are $(S|R; A|M)$ and $(A|R; A|M)$.

Proposition 4 (No Separation). *There can be no separating equilibrium in which the minister plays strategy* $(M|N; R|C)$.

Proof. If the minister adopts this strategy, the partner learns the nature of the policymaking environment completely (i.e., $\gamma = 1$ and $\alpha = 0$). If this is the case, the partner's optimal strategy is never to scrutinize. But if the partner simply accepts all proposals, the minister will prefer to make the radical proposal in the normal environment. □

We therefore need to consider only two possible pure strategy equilibria and a mixed strategy equilibrium.

Proposition 5 (Ministerial Autonomy). *For* $X \leq \frac{c}{1-p}$, *the strategy profile* $s^* = (R|N; R|C), (A|R; A|M)$ *constitutes a PBE of the game. In this equilibrium, the partner's belief that the environment is constrained when the minister introduces the radical bill is given by* $\gamma = p$. *The minister always introduces the radical proposal and the partner always accepts the minister's proposal without scrutinizing it.*

Proof. If the minister always makes the radical proposal, the partner's updated beliefs are given by $\gamma = \alpha = p$. Given these beliefs, the partner's utilities are given by $EU_{Partner}(Accept) = -X$ and $EU_{Partner}(Scrutinize) = -p(X + c) - (1 - p)c$. The partner is willing to accept the minister's proposal if $X \leq \frac{c}{1-p}$. Given that the partner accepts the radical proposal, it is immediate that the minister will make it. □

Proposition 6 (Maximal Position-Taking). *For* $X \geq \max\left[\frac{c}{1-p}; \frac{L}{\beta}\right]$, *the strategy profile* $s^* = (R|N; R|C), (S|R; A|M)$ *constitutes a PBE of the game. In this equilibrium, the partner's belief that the environment is constrained when the minister introduces the radical bill is given by* $\gamma = p$. *The minister always introduces the radical proposal and the partner always scrutinizes. In the normal environment, the proposal is amended and the moderate proposal is implemented.*

Proof. If the minister always makes the radical proposal, the partner's updated beliefs are given by $\gamma = \alpha = p$. Given these beliefs, the partner's utilities are given by $EU_{Partner}(Accept) = -X$ and $EU_{Partner}(Scrutinize) = -p(X + c) - (1 - p)c$. The partner prefers to scrutinize the minister's proposal if $X \geq \frac{c}{1-p}$. Given that the partner scrutinizes the radical proposal, the minister's payoffs from the two proposals are given by $EU_{Minister}(Radical) = \beta X - L$ and $EU_{Minister}(Moderate) = 0$. The minister prefers the radical proposal if $X \geq \frac{L}{\beta}$. □

Proposition 7 (Coalition Squabbles). *For $\frac{c}{1-p} < X < \frac{L}{\beta}$, the following strategy profile constitutes a PBE of the game: The minister always introduces the radical bill in the constrained environment. In the normal environment, she introduces the radical proposal with probability $\pi = \frac{cp}{(1-p)(X-c)}$. The partner never scrutinizes the moderate bill. She scrutinizes the radical bill with probability $\mu = \frac{(1+\beta)X}{L+X}$. In this equilibrium, the partner's belief that the environment is constrained when the minister introduces the radical bill is given by $\gamma = \frac{p}{p+(1-p)\pi}$.*

Proof. Let π denote the probability with which the minister introduces the radical bill in the normal environment, and let μ denote the probability with which the partner scrutinizes the radical proposal. If the minister makes the radical proposal, the partner's updated beliefs are given by $\gamma = \frac{p}{p+(1-p)\pi}$ and $\alpha = 0$. If the moderate bill is proposed, it is immediate that the partner will agree. If the radical bill is proposed, the partner's utilities are given by $EU_{Partner}(Accept) = -X$ and $EU_{Partner}(Scrutinize) = \frac{-p}{p+(1-p)\pi}(X+c) - \left(1 - \frac{p}{p+(1-p)\pi}\right)c$. The partner is indifferent between accepting and scrutinizing if and only if $\pi = \frac{cp}{(1-p)(X-c)}$. Given the partner's strategy, the minister's expected payoffs from the two proposals are given by $EU_{Minister}(Radical) = (1-\mu)(X+\beta X) + \mu(\beta X - L)$ and $EU_{Minister}(Moderate) = 0$. The minister will be indifferent between these proposals if and only if $\mu = \frac{X(1+\beta)}{X+L}$. The mixed strategy probabilities μ and π are proper probabilities for $\frac{c}{1-p} < X < \frac{L}{\beta}$. □

3

Parliaments as Policing Institutions

Coupled with ministerial discretion in the crafting of policy initiatives, policy differences and the pressures of electoral competition generate tensions for coalition governments. To the extent that coalitions want to pursue policies that balance the interests of the partners, they must be able to monitor and modify legislative proposals to limit the potential damage of "ministerial drift." While some scholars have pointed to monitoring institutions that operate at the cabinet level (Müller and Strøm, 2000; Thies, 2001), we highlight the significance of *legislative* institutions. Indeed, we believe that such institutions often have advantages over those at the cabinet level.

It is important to emphasize at the outset that the argument we make is conditional: The degree to which the legislative process can be helpful for resolving intra-coalition tensions and facilitating coalition governance depends on the precise structure of parliamentary institutions, specifically:

- on the level of policy-relevant expertise that legislative committee systems provide to parties that do not control the government ministry in question, and
- on the ease with which these parties can change policy initiatives they oppose.

Thinking about legislative institutions in terms of the ability of parties to acquire information and to amend ministerial proposals leads us to a classification of legislatures that maps closely onto traditional distinctions between weak and strong legislatures (e.g., see Lijphart, 1984).

It is also important to emphasize that we are not claiming that strong legislative institutions are *necessary* to resolve the tensions inherent in multiparty governments, or that they always serve as substitutes for cabinet-level institutions in doing so. Indeed, strong legislatures can lead to significant complementarities with cabinet-level institutions—a point which plays an important role in our empirical analysis. For example, legislative committee systems that allow parties to gather information and to formulate policy alternatives may make cabinet-level institutions for resolving coalition conflict more effective. Similarly, cabinet-level mechanisms that provide parties with opportunities to "shadow" their partners can enhance the impact of the legislative process on policymaking.

Testing the argument we have developed requires data on the legislative treatment of government legislation under coalition government across parliaments that vary in the strength of their internal institutions. These considerations lead us to focus on five legislatures over a period of about twenty years, beginning (depending on the country) in the early to mid-1980s and ending in the early 2000s. The five legislative chambers are the Danish Folketing, the Dutch Tweede Kamer, the German Bundestag, the French Assemblée Nationale, and the Irish Dáil. In all five countries, coalition government was the norm during the 1980s and 1990s. We discuss the rationale for our time frame, as well as the specific governments in power during this period, in the next chapter.

These five legislatures also exhibit considerable variation in their internal structure. In this chapter, we consider the legislative process as an institution that can allow parties to confront and deal with the tensions of multiparty government. We begin with a general analysis of features that enhance the ability to "keep tabs" on hostile ministers. We then provide an in-depth description of the legislative process in our five parliaments. We conclude with a more general analysis of legislative strength across European democracies that places our five counties in context.

3.1 CABINET INSTITUTIONS AS SOLUTIONS TO COALITION DELEGATION PROBLEMS

The primary emphasis of the existing literature on delegation problems within coalitions has been on institutions that make it possible to "check" coalition partners *before* policy proposals are introduced in the legislature. For example, Müller and Strøm (2000) point out that some coalition agreements include provisions for the creation of "cabinet committees" that jointly review controversial legislative proposals in a specific policy area. Other cabinet-level mechanisms for policing the coalition bargain include committees consisting of cabinet ministers and the parliamentary leaders of the governing parties, or "inner cabinets" composed of a subset of ministers. In contrast to cabinet committees, these fora are typically not confined to a specific policy area (see Anderweg and Timmermans, 2008).

Perhaps the most prominent (pre-legislative) policing mechanism is housed within the ministry itself. As Thies (2001) notes, in many parliamentary democracies, cabinet ministers are assisted by "junior ministers" (JMs). Typically, these JMs are simultaneously members of parliament, and their official role is to assist the minister in overseeing the department and in managing relations between the minister and parliamentary parties. Quite often, JMs are also being "groomed" for ministerial duties down the line. As Thies argues persuasively, in coalition governments, JMs can serve another, less advertised function. When coalition parties are particularly concerned about the possible "slippage" introduced by ministerial control, they may insist on pairing their partner's minister with a "shadow" JM of their own. An important reason for doing so is that by enjoying similar access to specialized knowledge within the ministry, a shadow JM is in a good position to counteract the informational advantage enjoyed by ministers. Even if JMs cannot "stand up" to the minister in a direct confrontation, they can provide their party with information that makes it possible to evaluate ministerial proposals and to offer alternatives. Thies' work provides considerable evidence that coalition parties use JMs to "keep tabs" on their partners. Systematic analysis of allocations of JMs in the Netherlands, Italy, and Japan strongly suggests that parties are particularly likely to assign JMs to "hostile" ministers who have jurisdiction over salient policy areas. In the next chapter, we provide additional evidence for Thies' argument by demonstrating that the likelihood that a partner will appoint a JM to shadow a partner's minister increases as the issues under the jurisdiction of the minister divide the coalition.

3.2 LEGISLATIVE INSTITUTIONS AS SOLUTIONS TO COALITION DELEGATION PROBLEMS

While cabinet-level institutions can play an important role in coalition governance, it is difficult for parties to rely solely on them to control ministerial discretion. As Thies (2001) points out, because JM positions, like ministerial posts, are generally distributed in proportion to party size, small parties in a cabinet typically do not have a sufficient number of JMs to permit shadowing all "hostile" ministers. Similar limitations apply to other cabinet-level institutions, such as cabinet committees or inner cabinets. The very workload and need for specialization in the cabinet that makes delegation necessary in the first place makes it difficult to use these institutions as "routine" checking mechanisms (Laver and Shepsle, 1994, 1996). They may be instituted for particular purposes and specific legislative initiatives (especially if they are salient and controversial), but parties cannot rely on them as a solution to the on-going, day-to-day need to monitor the various proposals of a large number of ministries. As a result, cabinet-level institutions—at least taken on their own—are likely to be insufficient for effective policing.

Given these constraints, institutions at the *legislative* level can provide an important substitute for, and complement to, cabinet-level institutions. In most democracies, major policy changes must be adopted by the legislature. As a policy initiative (a government bill) winds its way through parliament, it can be subjected to intensive scrutiny, affording coalition partners an opportunity to review, and potentially amend ministerial initiatives. Moreover, legislative institutions have another advantage compared to monitoring institutions at the cabinet level. Given the policy-signaling incentives confronting ministers, ministers and parties have strong incentives to resist amendment of proposals prior to bill introduction, as doing so reduces the opportunities for claiming credit. Because legislative scrutiny and correction takes place *after* bill introduction, it does not threaten ministerial credit-claiming, and may therefore encounter less ministerial resistance. We return to this point in more detail in the conclusion.

The extent to which government parties can take advantage of the legislative arena to "keep tabs on their partners" depends crucially on parliamentary procedures and institutions. Counteracting ministerial drift requires: (*a*) information about the policy details of proposed bills and feasible alternatives to it, and (*b*) an opportunity to press for change. In consequence, the easier it is for parties to use the legislative process to acquire relevant information about draft proposals, to develop alternative policies, and to initiate amendments that must be debated and voted on even if they are unpalatable to the drafting minister, the more effectively will they be able to use the legislative process as a mechanism to "rein in" hostile ministers.

The single most important institution in this context is the *legislative committee system*. Other institutions are important as well—particularly legislative procedures and rules that affect opportunities for floor debate and amendment—but the efficacy of these other institutions is likely to be premised on the existence of a strong committee system, which provides opportunities for specialization, scrutiny, and deliberation that can lead to substantive change of bills. As Lees and Shaw (1979: 4) assert, the parliamentary committee is a prime example of "the small, face-to-face group...where the vital decisional and deliberative interactions occur within organizations."[1] More recently, Mattson and Strøm (1995: 250) contend that "[c]ommittees are primarily vehicles of specialization" that are "critical to the deliberative powers of parliaments." That is, the division of legislative labor into committee subgroups with specific organizational tasks can endow parliamentary bodies with influence over policymaking.

As comparative legislative scholars have demonstrated in myriad detailed studies of national legislatures, the precise structure of committee systems varies considerably across parliamentary democracies.[2] Not all structures will provide opportunities to constrain the influence of cabinet ministers. Two features of committee systems, and of legislative institutions more generally, are especially critical:

[1] Their statement about committees echos an earlier point about committees made by Verba (1961: 19) that "it is to the face-to-face group that one must look if one is to find the locus of decision-making in political systems." See also Madron (1969).

[2] These (primarily descriptive) studies of legislatures comprise a sizable literature, and thus we cannot hope to fully review all of them here. For some of the most prominent early works, see Polsby (1975), Loewenberg and Patterson (1979), Mezey (1979), and for more recent work Norton (1998). For an excellent summary, and critique, of the comparative legislatures literature, see Mezey (1993) and Gamm and Huber (2002).

1. *Information acquisition*: The extent to which committee systems enable parties to gather sufficient technical information about the policy issues under consideration.
2. *Amendment capability*: The ease with which committee systems and other legislative rules and procedures enable (informed) parties to make meaningful changes to the proposals of government ministers.

With these features as fault lines, we can readily group our five legislatures into two broad categories: *strong* and *weak* legislatures. We classify two of the five democracies—Fifth Republic France and Ireland—as having weak legislatures, and we classify the other three—Denmark, Germany, and the Netherlands—as having strong legislatures. Most scholars, of course, would not view this classification as surprising or controversial. Previous legislative research has similarly distinguished between institutions that enhance or diminish the ability of legislators to develop policy expertise (e.g., see Lijphart, 1984; Strøm, 1984; Powell, 2000). Statistical analysis of the characteristics of a broader set of European parliaments at the end of this chapter validates our classification.

What has not yet been established—in large part due to an absence of systematic, cross-national data on the legislative treatment of government bills—is whether these differences actually matter for policymaking. In the chapters that follow, we use a unique data set that tracks the legislative history of approximately 1,300 government bills to examine whether the differences in legislative institutions systematically affect the ability of coalition partners to scrutinize and amend government policy initiatives.

3.2.1 Strong Legislative Institutions

The key criterion for characterizing legislative institutions as either "strong" or "weak" is the extent to which they enable parties to gain informational expertise and—once they are informed—to make meaningful changes to ministerial policy proposals. This, in turn, depends on how the features of legislative institutions (committee systems in particular) affect the ability of coalition partners to oversee and modify the actions of "hostile" cabinet ministers. A useful starting point is LaPalombara's observation that "it is axiomatic that if the national legislature is to be a significant political factor, then it must have specialized committees of limited membership and considerable scope of power" (LaPalombara, 1974: 121). That is, *specialization* of committees is critical to the ability of parties to gather sufficient information to engage in effective policymaking. Many prominent theories of legislative organization highlight this need for information acquisition, and the consequent reduction of uncertainty in the effects of legislation, as the driving force behind the development of specialized committee systems (e.g., Gilligan and Krehbiel, 1989; Krehbiel, 1991). Our argument extends this logic to explore its implications for *intra*-coalition politics.

Several structural characteristics of committees affect the ability of legislators to specialize. LaPalombara notes the importance of the *size* of the committee membership; smaller committees lower the decision costs of bargaining, reduce opportunities for free-riding, and increase the influence of individual members. As a result, smaller committees increase legislator incentives to specialize (Francis, 1982; Mattson and Strøm, 1995; Buchanan and Tullock, 1962). Perhaps more importantly, committee systems encourage the development of specialized expertise if they are comprised of numerous *permanent* committees since legislators who expect to serve longer tenures on a committee have greater incentives to invest time and resources in information acquisition (Strøm, 1984, 1990*b*). Finally, for the ability to scrutinize ministerial proposals, the *focus* of specialization matters. Committees that correspond to the jurisdiction of the departments headed by government ministers give rise to legislative expertise that maps onto the policy proposals that are developed within a ministry (Mezey and Olson, 1991; Strøm, 1984, 1990*b*). As Mattson and Strøm (1995: 270) note, they also "[facilitate] influence through expert knowledge and [enable] individual committee members to build personal networks" with civil servants and members of outside interest groups. In contrast, committee systems that favor ad hoc committees, or in which the jurisdictions of committees do not correspond to those of cabinet ministers, will make it more difficult to develop the policy expertise that makes effective scrutiny possible.

Strong committee systems also enjoy powers (either by convention or through the formal legislative rules of procedure) that enhance the availability of information and permit parties to make meaningful changes to ministerial proposals. For example, strong committees typically have ready access to ministers, civil servants, outside experts, and have the right to subpoena policy documents. They generally control the timetable of committee deliberations, thus ensuring adequate time to engage in intensive scrutiny. Strong committees also have meaningful power to initiate changes. At a minimum, they allow party groups to craft amendments, and to propose them to the committee or the plenary for a vote, even if the minister introducing the bill finds the amendments unpalatable.

The power to act independently of the minister is particularly crucial. Strong committees cannot be prevented by ministers from proposing changes to a bill, deliberation and debate on amendments cannot be restricted by the minister, and amendments deemed unacceptable by the minister cannot be simply dropped from the agenda, preventing the committee, or the plenary, from taking a vote.[3]

[3] All democratic legislatures, as far as we are aware, have a "germaneness" rule concerning amendments, which requires that the nature and scope of the amendment be related to the subject matter under consideration in the section of the bill under consideration and related to the fundamental purpose of the bill as a whole. We distinguish procedural restrictions of this kind, which are normally imposed by legislative speakers or presidents acting in a non-partisan capacity, at least in Western Europe, from restrictions that can be imposed at the behest of ministers simply because they disagree with the substance of the amendment (Jenny and Müller, 1995).

Three of the legislatures in our study—the Danish Folketing, the Dutch Tweede Kamer, and the German Bundestag—feature procedures and committee systems that fit this general characterization. We therefore classify them as "strong" legislative bodies.

The Danish Folketing

The legislative committee system in Denmark was dramatically reformed in the early 1970s. Since then, the Folketing has had roughly twenty specialized, permanent committees. Among Western European democracies, only the Dutch Tweede Kamer has consistently had a larger number of committees.[4] For the time period of our study, there were more committees than ministries in both countries so that some ministries were monitored by more than one parliamentary committee. On average, Danish committees are comprised of fewer than twenty members, and correspond almost exactly to government ministries in their jurisdictional responsibilities. In short, the Folketing features a committee system "permitting far-reaching diversification and a high degree of specialization" (Mattson and Strøm, 1995: 267).

The Danish committees also possess significant powers to gather information and to develop specific policy expertise. As Damgaard (1992: 40) explains:

> The committees may discuss any matter within their jurisdiction whether it is related to formal proposals being considered or not. They may ask for information from the responsible minister, and they may request the presence of the minister in the committee to give such information. Thus committee members have plenty of opportunity to interfere with the legislative and administrative activities of ministers who are responsible for the work performed by their civil servants.

Danish committees also possess a high degree of control over their agenda. Government ministers cannot discharge bills from committees, or reassign them from one committee to another. They cannot set limits on how long committees deliberate (Döring, 1995).

Danish committee members also have considerable powers to initiate changes to ministerial draft bills. While they cannot rewrite government bills during their deliberations, members are unfettered in crafting substantive amendments to ministerial policy initiatives. Once these amendments are brought to the floor, they must be debated and voted on regardless of the preferences of the proposing minister. All together, then, the rules and procedures of the Folketing and the nature of the committee system provide legislators with meaningful opportunities to scrutinize and to propose modifications to ministerial policy initiatives.[5]

[4] As in most parliaments, there are slight variations in the number of committees across legislative periods.

[5] One feature that may appear to separate Denmark from the other two strong legislatures in this study is that committee deliberations *follow* a plenary debate on the general principles of the bill.

The Dutch Tweede Kamer

Only the Tweede Kamer—the lower house of the Dutch parliament, the Staten-Generaal—has surpassed the Folketing in the number of specialized standing committees. Over the period of our study, there were more than twenty-five permanent committees, with an average membership of fewer than twenty-five deputies. The policy jurisdictions of these committees correspond very closely to the jurisdictions of government ministries—indeed, the committees outnumber the ministries. This specialized committee system was created in 1953, when "it was felt that the ever more detailed and technical proposals from the government required a level of specialization from MPs that could not be guaranteed by randomly composed committees" (Anderweg and Irwin, 2005: 134).

Like the Danish system, the Dutch committee system affords party groups the opportunity to use committee deliberations to acquire relevant technical information about government bills. Cabinet ministers in the Netherlands cannot discharge bills from committees, reassign them from one committee to another, nor can they set limits on the length of committee deliberation. For these reasons, the committee systems in Denmark and the Netherlands are regarded as particularly independent in controlling their proceedings (Mattson and Strøm, 1995: 300). Another feature of the parliamentary process in the Netherlands that accentuates the ability of committees to scrutinize legislation is that government bills never expire: once a bill is introduced, it remains in the legislative process until it is either passed, rejected, or withdrawn by the government, and can thus have a lifespan of several legislative terms.[6] This implies that committees face no hard constraint that equates the failure to conclude committee deliberations with a decision to reject the bill.

After a bill is referred to a committee (a step usually taken almost immediately after the introduction of the bill in the legislature), the committee begins its deliberations. These typically consist of a review of government documents, consultations with outside interest groups, civil servants, or the minister himself, as well as a back-and-forth shuffle of documents from party groups on the committee and the proposing minister. Policy concerns are aired, technical questions asked, and potential amendments discussed. This exchange between committees and the relevant government department provides party groups with a substantial amount

In some countries, such as Ireland, the United Kingdom, and Spain, this sequence may constrain the ability of committees to make significant changes to a bill by pre-committing parties and their members to specific policy alternatives. As Mattson and Strøm (1995: 284) point out, however, initial debate at the plenary stage in the Folketing does not strictly constrain committees in the same way. Döring (1995: 234) also concluded that the preceding plenary debate in Denmark does not actually bind its legislative committees.

[6] As Anderweg and Irwin (2005: 137) point out, the record for a bill remaining alive in the Dutch legislature is twenty-six years. In our sample of legislation, discussed in more detail in the next chapter, approximately 15 percent of government bills in the Netherlands span more than one legislative term.

of information that can be used to propose changes. As Anderweg and Bakema (1994: 66) conclude:

> Despite its initiating role, the cabinet is by no means predominant in legislative affairs. The process of legislation is characterized by an intricate system of checks and balances, allowing MPs to interfere at several points in the process. One such point is the "preparatory enquiry" of bills by a parliamentary committee. In committee meetings the bill is discussed by the responsible minister and a small number (about twenty) of technically informed MPs. Minister and MPs interact in writing as well, through the exchange of various legislative reports. . . . [Our] impression is that, even in this early stage of legislation, substantive deals and concessions are being made both by the MPs and by the minister.

In the process of acquiring information, party groups serving on the committees also craft amendments. While Dutch committees cannot rewrite a minister's bill behind closed doors, once amendments are introduced on the floor of the Tweede Kamer, ministers cannot curtail debate or voting on amendments short of withdrawing the bill from consideration—a drastic and potentially costly step. As a result, party groups are in a strong position to advance modifications even if the minister opposes them. Anderweg and Bakema (1994: 66) go on to describe this stage of the legislative process:

> At this point, there is not very much a minister can do to avert an unwanted parliamentary amendment to his bill except informally squeezing the MPs belonging to his party. As a last resort he can declare the proposed amendment unacceptable. By using this traditional formula the minister indicates that the acceptance of the amendment by a majority of MPs will either cause him to withdraw the bill or to resign. In practice it is quite common for Second Chamber MPs to change government bills by means of parliamentary amendments. Each year hundreds of amendments are proposed, of which about one-third are actually enacted into law.

In summary, the Tweede Kamer features procedures and a committee system that embody the characteristics of a strong legislature. Deputies who serve on committees have the ability to specialize along lines that correspond to the policy jurisdictions of the government ministries they oversee, they have substantial powers to acquire information to evaluate ministerial proposals and to formulate policy alternatives, and they have the means to bring these alternatives to a public vote even against the wishes of the proposing minister.

The German Bundestag

As in Denmark and the Netherlands, the lower house of the German parliament, the Bundestag, provides coalition partners tools to monitor and modify legislative proposals by government ministers. Indeed, the Bundestag is arguably one of the most thoroughly examined popularly elected houses in Western Europe precisely because of its significant role in policymaking (e.g., see Loewenberg, 1967). As two prominent scholars of the German legislature assert, "(a)n elaborate committee structure, with most influential parliamentarians of all parties acting as chairmen of the important committees, assures to the Bundestag a degree of autonomous influence in policy-making which is not found in the classical parliamentary system based on the Westminster model" (Paterson and Southern, 1991: 123). Over the period of our study, the German committee system consisted of roughly twenty committees, with an average membership of twenty-five deputies. The committees have jurisdictions that correspond almost exactly to the jurisdictions of government ministers.

Their procedural prerogatives place German committees in a strong position to acquire detailed policy information. Committees set their own agenda. Ministers cannot discharge bills, nor can they impose limits on the length of committee deliberations. Committees have access to experts from the civil service, outside interest groups, and the like. As Paterson and Southern (1991: 120) report, "[The] real meeting ground of ministers, civil servants and members of parliament is in the committee." As in the Dutch and Danish cases, these meetings allow coalition partners to develop the necessary technical expertise to evaluate, and to formulate alternatives to, ministerial initiatives.

In addition to the ability to develop expertise, German committees have extensive authority to amend government bills—authority that even exceeds that of the Folketing and the Tweede Kamer. Specifically, Bundestag committees possess the power to amend bills "behind closed doors": The lead committee rewrites the original ministerial bill during its deliberations, and it is the amended committee version that becomes the agenda on the floor for subsequent stages in the parliamentary process. A new round of parliamentary amendments would be required to restore the minister's original version of the bill. In short, the committees of the Bundestag are among the most powerful legislative institutions in contemporary parliamentary systems. They enable legislative party groups to subject ministerial proposals to serious scrutiny, to develop policy alternatives, and to make substantive changes to government bills.

3.2.2 Weak Legislative Institutions

In stark contrast, "weak" legislatures provide parties that do not control the relevant ministry little opportunity to scrutinize bills and to make meaningful substantive changes to their content. The two democracies we place into this category are Ireland and the French Fifth Republic.

The Irish Dáil

We begin with the Irish Dáil, the lower house of Ireland's parliament, the Oireachtas. The overwhelming scholarly consensus is that the Dáil is an "exceptionally weak" (Gallagher, 2005: 211) and "emasculated" (Ward, 1994: 298) parliament, a "woefully inadequate institution" (Dinan, 1986: 71) that is no more than "a glorified rubber stamp" (Dinan, 1986: 76), and provides legislators with virtually no independent policymaking capacity. Chubb (1982: 205) sums up this view most forcefully, stating that the Dáil is "a puny parliament peopled by members who have a modest view of their functions and a poor capacity to carry them out."[7]

One of the principal explanations for the powerlessness of the Irish parliament lies in the structure of its committee system. For the period of our study, the Irish Dáil featured no specialized committees. With the exception of the United Kingdom (the archetype of the Westminster (or majoritarian) system), Ireland was the only country in Western Europe over this period to have this characteristic (Mattson and Strøm, 1995). As Mitchell (2003: 434) describes, "there are no permanent Standing Committees. Committees . . . are established anew at the beginning of each Parliament and their number and functions vary. Thus, there is no sense in which Irish committees could establish 'property rights' over jurisdictions." Instead, committees were established only on an ad hoc basis and did not correspond in their (temporary) jurisdictions to those of government ministries. As a result, almost all legislation in Ireland over this period was examined either by an ad hoc committee or—more typically—by the "Committee of the Whole House" (i.e., all the members of the Dáil "convening in committee"). These structural attributes discourage the development of policy expertise needed to monitor ministerial activity, and provide little opportunity for parties not in control of a ministry to acquire the technical information and expertise to scrutinize bills introduced by hostile ministers.

These structural weaknesses are reinforced by the committees' lack of procedural prerogatives and by the nature of the legislative process in the Dáil. In contrast to strong legislatures, committee deliberations are preceded by a floor debate on the broad principles of the bill. This debate is typically followed by a vote that is viewed as binding at the committee stage, meaning that any amendments proposed by committees cannot conflict with the principles of the bill (Gallagher, 2005: 220, 224).[8] According to a recent report, this makes Ireland "[along] with Spain and the UK . . . one of only three European legislatures that restrict the committee stage in this manner" (Hughes, Clancy, Harris and Beetham, 2006). Second, a committee (which may simply be the "Committee of the Whole House") has no control over the length of its deliberations. Not even the plenary

[7] The inadequacy of the Dáil in policymaking appears not to be lost on its deputies, as evidenced by a policy document by the Fine Gael party in the 1980s (Fine Gael, 1980: 3), which claimed that, "In practice [the Dáil] plays practically no effective part in either making the laws or even the expert criticism of them" [Chubb (1982: 214)].

[8] Recall that in Denmark, committee deliberations are also preceded by a floor debate. However, no vote is taken, and the debate is not considered binding on the members of the committee.

can control the timetable of deliberations once a bill and proposed amendments reach the floor (Döring, 1995). Instead, the minister proposing the bill sets the agenda for deliberation and debate, and can rush bills through the process with very few impediments. Most importantly, ministers have the authority to force an end to debate before all amendments have been discussed on the floor. If a minister invokes this "guillotine" procedure, all outstanding amendments that have not been endorsed by the minister are considered defeated.[9] As a result, ministers are in a strong position to oppose amendments they find unpalatable. In short, the legislative process in the Dáil during the time period of our study was not designed to afford coalition parties much opportunity to scrutinize bills, to develop alternative policies, or to press for meaningful change. Parties were severely constrained in their ability to use this forum to monitor and to counteract ministerial drift, and to "police the coalition bargain."

In more recent years (following the period of our study), the Irish committee system has undergone a transformation that appears to have resulted in the emergence of stronger committees. In part, this change may have been motivated by the rise of consistent multiparty government. In 1997, the Co-ordinating Group of Secretaries-General recommended the establishment of permanent committees consisting of no more than eleven members. Although the entering coalition in 1997 ignored the report (MacCarthaigh, 2005: 155–6), in 2002, thirteen small specialized committees with jurisdictions corresponding to those of ministries were set up, and now have the task of examining government bills. Murphy (2006: 448) asserts that, "[it] is now possible to refer to a functioning committee system in Dáil Éireann, and even one where specific committees have come to assume a greater degree of influence in the wider policy process." At the same time, there is good reason to believe that these changes have far from established the kind of effective legislative committee system we encountered in our three "strong" legislatures. For example, government ministers serve on these committees, and have a vote, thus reducing the ability of committees to confront them (Gallagher, 2005: 220).

The French Assemblée Nationale

The other weak legislature in our study is the lower house of the French parliament. Like the Dáil, the Assemblée Nationale suffers from a number of structural and procedural barriers to effective legislative monitoring. Because of these barriers, "[the] National Assembly under the Fifth Republic is . . . often regarded as one of the weakest legislatures in any modern democracy" (Huber, 1996: 2). The legislative committee system is one such impediment. While the French Assembly has a permanent committee system, the committees are few, large,

[9] MacCarthaigh (2005: 100) reports that, through the rigorous use of the guillotine, twelve bills were rushed to passage in the Dáil in a single week before the 2004 summer recess.

and limited in their specialization. The 1958 constitution fixes the number of committees at six—by far the lowest number of all Western European parliaments with a permanent committee system. Since the number of cabinet ministries is substantially larger than six (over our time frame, there were approximately twenty ministries per cabinet), this implies that the jurisdictional correspondence of committees to ministries is necessarily quite low. Parliamentary committees have expansive jurisdictions and cannot specialize in ways that parallel the organization of executive portfolios. Moreover, the size of the committees is large, with some committees consisting of up to 145 members (Mattson and Strøm, 1995: 261), more than the size of some full parliaments.[10]

Interestingly, this committee structure differs dramatically from that of the Fourth Republic, as Wright (1989: 137–8) has noted:

> During the Fourth Republic there were nineteen permanent highly specialized committees, each composed of forty-four prominent members (although, in practice, they were often controlled by a much smaller group) and each zealously monitoring the activities of a particular ministry... Ministerial bills were often savaged beyond recognition at the committee stage... [In the Fifth Republic] parliamentary committees are much less specialized and more unwieldy than the smaller committees of the previous régime, and are far less capable of detailed interference in governmental legislation.

The elimination of strong committees, of course, was part of President Charles de Gaulle's effort in drafting the 1958 constitution to strengthen the powers of the executive and weaken those of the legislature (Williams, 1968; Huber, 1996). In the French semi-presidential system, this change has implications beyond presidential–legislative relations for the ability of parliament to serve as a forum for managing conflict among coalition partners.

In addition to these structural deficiencies, the French parliament faces a number of procedural characteristics that make it difficult for legislators to assert themselves vis-à-vis cabinet ministers. The procedural rights available to ministers—anchored in the constitution—include the right to declare a bill to be a matter of urgency, as well as the "package vote," or *vote bloqué*. If a minister invokes the urgency procedure, the bill is accelerated through the Assembly and can only be changed by amendments the minister deems acceptable. The package vote allows ministers to insist on an up-or-down vote on the ministerial draft bill with only those amendments the minister has proposed or accepted. That is, as in the Irish case, ministers have the ability to preclude amendments they oppose from being debated and voted on the floor. As Thiébault (1994: 140–1)

[10] In the late 1980s (the earliest part of our sample of legislation from France), four of the committees—the Defense, Finance, Foreign Affairs, and Legal and Administrative Matters committees—had sixty-one members, and the other two—the Cultural, Social, and Family Affairs committee and the Production and Trade committee—had up to 121 members (Wright, 1989).

explains, "Government ministers make frequent use of the so-called blocked or package vote (Article 44) to restrain the government's own supporters from voting for amendments. All in all, government ministers have a number of procedural weapons for pushing their policy proposals through parliament" (see also Huber, 1992). In short, the structural features of the French committee system and the procedural advantages of government ministers make it extremely difficult for coalition partners to scrutinize policy initiatives as part of the legislative process, or to press for meaningful changes to ministerial draft bills.

3.3 POLICING STRENGTH IN EUROPEAN PARLIAMENTS

Our survey of these five legislatures suggests a number of features that are likely to affect the ability of coalition partners to police government ministers. Although the discussion is helpful in identifying these features, it is also limited in several respects. First, it does not allow us to assess, at least not very precisely, the relative importance of these features to the overall "policing strength" of legislatures. Second, it does not give us a very good sense of how the strength of these five legislatures compares to that of other parliaments. To address these issues, we consider information from sixteen West European parliaments on eight structural and procedural variables that represent key aspects of policing strength. We classify these variables onto an underlying dimension of legislative strength and create a ranking of European parliaments in terms of their policing powers.

The first four factors relate to structural features of legislative committees and the place committees occupy in the sequence of legislative decision-making. They are:

1. *The Number of Legislative Committees*: A larger number of committees, along with the specialization in committee focus this allows, is likely to enhance the ability of legislators to oversee the work of ministers.
2. *Correspondence to Ministerial Jurisdictions*: Committees that specialize along the jurisdictional boundaries of ministries are more likely to generate specialization relevant to the draft bills produced by ministries.
3. *The Size of Committees*: Large committees inhibit the ability to effectively scrutinize because they become unwieldy, and discourage specialization by committee members.
4. *Binding Plenary Debate before Committee Stage*: Binding plenary debate before the committee stage constrains deliberation and proposals for change.

The next two factors capture specific committee powers that enhance the ability to scrutinize and amend legislation:

5. *Right to Compel Witnesses and Documents*: Committees that can subpoena documents and witnesses (which may include ministers and senior civil servants) are in a better position to scrutinize legislation than those that cannot.
6. *Rewrite Authority*: Committees that have the right to rewrite draft bills are in a more powerful position to amend ministerial drafts than those that cannot (and must therefore rely on sponsoring amendments on the floor).

The last two factors concern the ability of ministers to resist legislative scrutiny and amendment of draft bills:

7. *Urgency Procedure*: If a minister can declare a piece of legislation "urgent" and thereby restrict the timetable for legislative consideration of a bill, effective legislative scrutiny becomes more difficult.
8. *Guillotine Procedure*: If a minister has the right to reject amendments that are deemed unacceptable and force an up-or-down vote on a bill, the ability of committees to counteract ministerial drift is compromised.

Table 3.1 lists these factors for sixteen European legislatures. Our primary data sources are a study by Mattson and Strøm (1995) on committee powers and a study by Harfst and Schnapp (2003) on instruments of parliamentary control of the executive. The first column lists the number of permanent committees in the lower chamber, which varies from 0 (in Ireland and the United Kingdom) to 28 (in the Netherlands).[11] The second column captures the correspondence between committees and ministerial jurisdictions. Harfst and Schnapp (2003) develop a useful continuous measure of this concept, namely the difference between the number of committees and the number of ministries.[12] For our set of countries, this measure ranges from −20 in France (meaning that there are 20 more

[11] We use the Harfst and Schnapp (2003) statistics for this variable, except for in the cases of Ireland and the United Kingdom. For the United Kingdom, Harfst and Schnapp (2003) decide to code "select committees" as equivalent to permanent committees. However, these are not equivalent for our purposes. The ten select committees in the United Kingdom are merely oversight committees that are supposed to inspect government implementation of enacted legislation, or perform functions such as auditing government expenditures and publicizing instances of waste or financial mismanagement (see Mattson and Strøm, 1995: 260–67). The select committees in Ireland, as we have already discussed, did not fully come into being until after 2002, which is outside the time frame of our study (and even after 2002, their legislative review functions are questionable). Thus, we code Ireland and the United Kingdom as having no permanent committees, which corresponds with the coding of Mattson and Strøm (1995).

[12] The difference between the number of permanent committees and ministries does not directly imply that (some of) these committees have the same jurisdiction as ministries. Nevertheless, there are two reasons to adopt this measure. The first is theoretical: If there is an excess of permanent committees to ministries, it becomes easier for committees to specialize on the work of particular ministries; if there is a deficit, committees would necessarily have to deal with legislation coming out of different jurisdictions. The second reason is empirical: Classifying the correspondence of ministries to committees in a binary fashion is not always easy (see, e.g., the unclear codings in the Mattson and Strøm (1995) study). Moreover, the continuous measure correlates highly with the binary measure of

TABLE 3.1 Policing Variables for Sixteen European Parliaments

Country	Number of Permanent Committees	Surplus of Permanent Committees to Ministries	Committee Size	Binding Plenary Debate Before Committee Stage	Authority to Compel	Rewrite Authority	Urgency	Guillotine
Austria	24	8	21	No	Witnesses, documents	No	No	No
Belgium	10	−9	22	No	Documents	Yes	No	No
Denmark	23	2	17	No	Witnesses	No	No	No
Finland	12	−5	17	No	Documents	Yes	No	No
France	6	−20	97	No	Witnesses, documents	No	Yes	Yes
Germany	21	4	28	No	Neither	Yes	No	No
Greece	10	−13	40	No	Neither	No	Yes	No
Ireland	0	−16	166*	Yes	Neither	No	Yes	Yes
Italy	16	−11	43	No	Neither	Yes	No	No
Luxembourg	22	11	11	No	Documents	No	No	No
Netherlands	28	14	22	No	Neither	No	No	No
Norway	12	−6	14	No	Neither	Yes	No	No
Portugal	12	−4	24	No	Witnesses	No	No	No
Spain	19	1	41	Yes	Witnesses, documents	Yes	No	No
Sweden	16	−5	17	No	Documents	Yes	No	No
United Kingdom	0	−22	650*	Yes	Neither	No	Yes	Yes

*Committee of the Whole House.

ministries than legislative committees) to +14 in the Netherlands. The average size of committees that review government bills ranges from 11 legislators in Luxembourg to 650 in the United Kingdom, where the "committee" reviewing government bills is the Committee of the Whole House (i.e., the plenary formally convened as a committee). Binding plenary debates are found in Ireland, Spain, and the United Kingdom.

The next two columns list the powers of legislative committees. In addition to Germany, six other legislatures in Western Europe give committees the power to rewrite the original draft bill submitted by a minister. Approximately half the committees in our sample have the authority to compel witnesses and/or documents.[13] Finally, the table lists two procedural rules that dampen the policing power of legislators. Ministers can invoke an urgency procedure and the guillotine in France, Ireland, and the United Kingdom, and Greek ministers can declare urgency, but they cannot stave off unwelcome amendments.

To classify European parliaments according to their ability to police government ministers, we perform a factor analysis of these variables—specifically, a principal components analysis.[14] Factor analysis is a common approach for reducing a larger set of variables to a smaller set of unobserved latent variables, or factors, and to detecting structure in the relationships between variables. In many (if not most) applications in political science, scholars have employed factor analysis in a rather ad hoc fashion—including variables not related to the theoretical concept(s) of interest, positing no a priori hypotheses about how the variables should relate to one another or to the common factors, incorporating no substantively meaningful constraints on the dimensionality of the variable structure (i.e., the number of factors), and offering only loose interpretations of what the factors "mean" after the exploratory analysis is complete.

Our approach differs in several important ways. First, although there may be several conceptual dimensions of "parliamentary strength," we are interested in only one—the power of legislators to "police" government ministers in the process of legislative review. We have theoretical reasons to believe that the eight features described earlier are relevant to the policing strength dimension in that they enhance the ability of legislators to gather policy-relevant information and amend bills. Because we view these variables as relating to a single underlying concept, we have decided, a priori, to retain only one extracted factor (a decision that the factor analysis will allow us to validate). Second, we specify hypotheses about the relationship of the eight variables to one another and to the policing

correspondence provided by Harfst and Schnapp (2003) in the same data set while providing more fine-grained information.

[13] Our measure of this variable takes a value of "0" where committees do not have this authority, a value of "1" when committees can compel witnesses or demand documents, and a value of "2" when they can do both.

[14] We also performed a principal factors analysis and obtained virtually identical results.

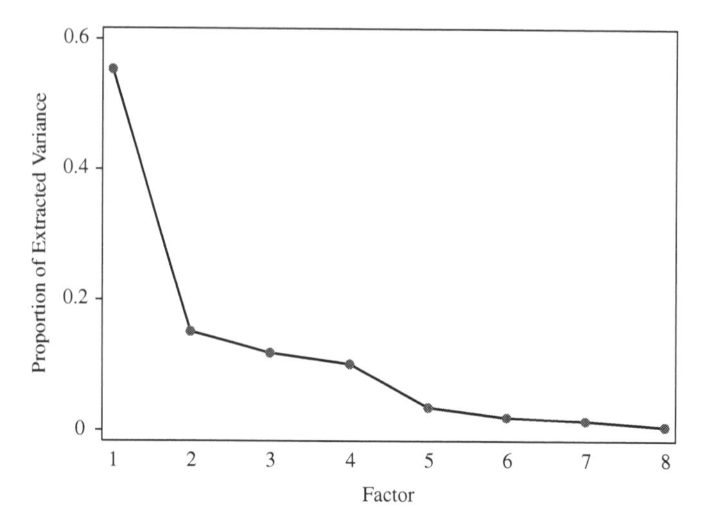

FIGURE 3.1 Scree Plot of Eigenvalues from Factor Analysis

strength dimension. We believe it is possible to construct a valid measure of parliamentary policing strength *if and only if* these eight features are correlated in the manner implied by our theoretical argument. We expect that legislatures with strong policing powers have a relatively large number of specialized committees, small in size, which correspond to government ministries, that they have the authority to rewrite bills and to demand outside information, and are not bound by previous debates of the plenary body. Further, we expect that ministers in such legislatures do not have tools at their disposal to curtail deliberation or to curb the passage of amendments. In contrast, we expect that legislatures with weak policing powers have a small number of specialized committees that are unwieldy in size, have little jurisdictional correspondence to ministries, have no authority to demand supplementary information or rewrite government bills, and are restricted to making incremental amendments to bills previously agreed to at the plenary stage. We also expect that ministers operating in weak legislatures have tools such as the urgency procedure and the guillotine that allow them to run roughshod over legislators opposing their policies.

Before examining the correlations between variables and the underlying factor (i.e., the factor loadings), we plot the proportion of extracted variance associated with each of the factors we could potentially retain (which is equal to 8, the number of variables in the model). Figure 3.1 displays this plot.[15] As theory led us

[15] This is a variation on the well-known scree plot, first proposed by Cattell (1966). A scree plot normally graphs the *eigenvalues* from a factor analysis against the potential factors. The eigenvalues simply reflect the proportion of the total variability in the data (equal to 8 in our case) that is explained by each of the successively extracted factors. We believe that the proportion of extracted variance for

TABLE 3.2 Factor Analysis of Legislative Policing Strength

Variables	Factor Loadings	Score Coefficients
Number of Permanent Committees	−0.886	−0.200
Surplus of Permanent Committees to Ministries	−0.839	−0.189
Committee Size	0.820	0.185
Binding Plenary Debate Before Committee Stage	0.666	0.150
Authority to Compel	−0.231	−0.052
Rewrite Authority	−0.354	−0.080
Urgency	0.900	0.203
Guillotine	0.914	0.206

to expect, a single underlying factor explains most of the variation in the variables (almost 60 percent). The figure shows a very steep drop-off in the explained variance with the extraction of the second factor, which accounts for a mere 15 percent of the total variance, after which it levels off.[16] In short, these results provide confirmatory evidence that our eight variables are strongly associated with a *single* underlying dimension.

Whether this underlying dimension can be interpreted as policing strength depends on whether the factor loadings conform to the patterns we have hypothesized. We present the loadings for our eight variables in Table 3.2. The most important point to take away is that the signs of the loadings (which reflect the correlation of the variables with one another and the underlying dimension) are just as we expect. Parliaments will tend towards one side of the dimension when the number of permanent committees is high, the number of committees versus ministries is high, the size of committees is small, committees have the authority to rewrite government bills, committees can demand documents and compel witnesses, committees are not bound by a prior plenary stage, and ministers do not have powers to curtail debate and curb amendments. Parliaments will tend toward the other side of the dimension when the number of permanent committees is low, the number of committees versus ministries is low, the size of committees is large, committees have no authority to rewrite government bills, committees can neither demand documents nor compel witnesses to testify, committees are restricted a prior decision by the plenary, and ministers have powers at their disposal to curtail debate and curb amendments.

Second, most of the variables are highly related to the underlying dimension. The presence or absence of restrictive procedures for ministers, the number and size of committees, and the correspondence of committees to ministries are

a factor (which is equal to the ratio of its eigenvalue to the total variability) is a more intuitive quantity, and so this is what we display in the graph.

[16] The suggestion by Cattell (1966) is to retain only those factors to the left of the point where "leveling off" begins. This inductive criterion would lead to the same result as our a priori theoretical decision to retain only one factor.

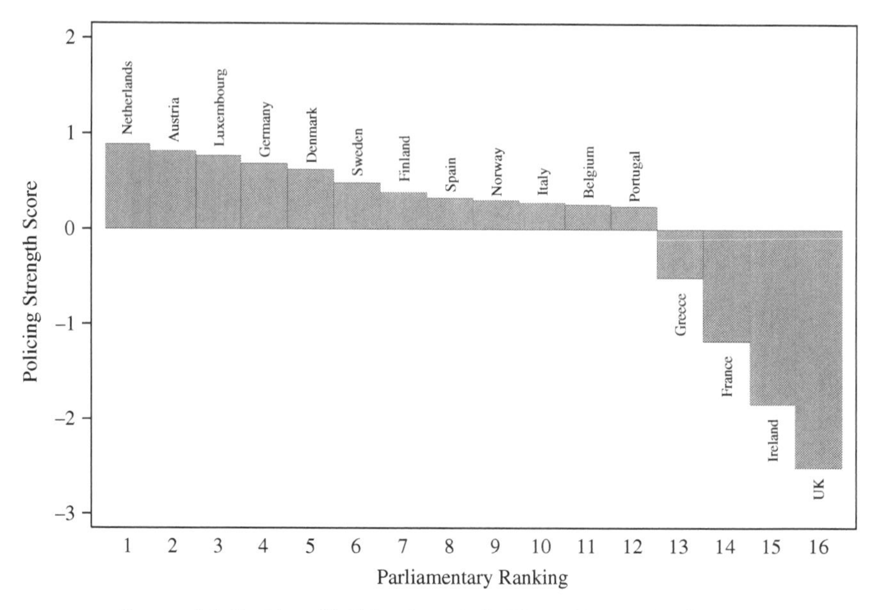

FIGURE 3.2 Ranking of Policing Strength for Sixteen European Parliaments

the most important features differentiating parliaments from one another. Also important is whether committees are restricted by prior plenary debates. Less important are committee powers to compel witnesses to testify or demand outside documents, as well as their ability to rewrite the draft bill submitted by a minister. The fact that the authority to directly rewrite bills is less important should perhaps not be surprising. Although the ability to rewrite bills can be useful, the critical feature in changing bills may be the ability to force a vote on amendments that ministers oppose. As long as ministers do not have the ability to curtail amendments, the ability to offer an amendment and force a vote should be sufficient for effective legislative scrutiny. In summary, the results lend strong support to our expectations about the relationship between the structural and procedural features we have identified and the policing strength of parliaments.

These results provide a solid foundation for constructing a meaningful index of parliamentary policing strength. Using the score coefficients from Table 3.2, we predict the factor scores for our sixteen European parliaments, which we present in Figure 3.2.[17] The index reveals stark differences between European legislatures. It is clear that four democracies—Greece, France, Ireland, and the United Kingdom—have legislatures that are poorly equipped to monitor

[17] The scale of the factor scores in Table 3.2 is such that large negative values indicate strong policing powers, while large positive values indicate weak policing powers. To ease interpretation, we reverse the scale so that higher scores in the figure reflect more policing strength and smaller scores reflect less policing strength.

the actions of government ministries. This will come as no surprise to most comparative scholars, who consistently rank these countries as "majoritarian" democracies with largely ineffectual parliaments (see, e.g., Gallagher *et al.*, 2005: 63–4). At the other end of the scale are the parliaments of the Netherlands, Austria, Luxembourg, Germany, and Denmark. These legislatures rank highest in the number of permanent committees and the degree of committee–ministry correspondence, which (given the factor analysis results) largely accounts for their high rankings overall.[18] Most important for our present purposes, the figure supports our claim that Denmark, Germany, and the Netherlands are good examples of democracies with strong legislative institutions, while Ireland and France have parliaments that are extremely weak in their capacity to police government ministers.

3.4 EMPIRICAL IMPLICATIONS

The distinction between strong and weak legislative institutions has clear implications for coalition governance. Strong legislatures provide coalition partners with an opportunity to develop policy expertise and to gather information, allowing them to effectively assess the content of ministerial draft bills and to formulate workable alternative policies if ministerial proposals are found to violate some implicit or explicit coalition compromise. Strong legislatures also provide opportunities for parties to propose changes that cannot be rejected out of hand by the minister. The consequence is that the legislative arena allows parties to monitor the policymaking activities of their coalition partners. Parliament becomes not simply a place in which opposition and government parties interact and debate policy, but also a site for resolving the *intra*-coalition tensions to which multiparty governments are subject.

In contrast, weak legislatures severely restrict the opportunity for parties to rely on the parliamentary review process for scrutinizing and modifying bills. Legislators in such systems will be limited in their ability to assess the implications of bills. And even if this informational problem could be resolved, the power of ministers to curtail debate and to reject amendments makes it significantly more difficult to force changes to a bill that a minister finds unpalatable. As a result, in

[18] Scholars might be somewhat surprised to see that Italy does not receive a higher score, since it is often portrayed as having one of Europe's stronger parliaments (Gallagher *et al.*, 2005: 65). The reason for this view is that Italian committees have the power to initiate, and approve, legislation (usually of a minor nature) without having to refer it to the full parliament. However, we do not believe that the power of committees to enact legislation is a key component in monitoring and counteracting the actions of government ministers. On features that are more relevant to this task, such as committee–ministry correspondence and committee size, the Italian parliament ranks among the lowest in Europe.

weak systems the legislative process is generally not a useful forum for dealing with the tensions of multiparty government. Instead, parties will be forced to rely on other mechanisms to rein in their partners.[19]

This broad characterization guides our empirical investigation. Recall the central testable implications of the theoretical model presented in Chapter 2. The model *assumed* that coalition partners have access to institutional mechanisms that allow them (at some cost) to scrutinize and change ministerial proposals. The expectation we derived is that—in the face of policy-signaling incentives for ministers—coalition partners will engage in more rigorous scrutiny and more extensive change of ministerial proposals as the policy divisions within the coalition increase. Applying this insight to the legislative context implies a conditional expectation: In *strong* legislatures, the process of parliamentary review of legislation provides a mechanism that makes scrutiny and change possible. We therefore expect to find evidence that coalition parties are taking advantage of the opportunities afforded by the institutional features of the review process to scrutinize and to modify bills that originate in ministries controlled by their partners, and that they do so with greater determination on bills that internally divide the coalition. In contrast, weak legislatures do not meet the assumption of the theory presented in Chapter 2. The legislative process is not an effective forum for "keeping tabs" on hostile ministers. As a result, we expect to see little evidence that parties are able to successfully use the review process to monitor and to change their partners' policy initiatives, and scrutiny and change of legislation should not be related in a systematic manner to the policy divisions within the coalition. If there is support for both expectations, the conclusion is obvious: Given an appropriate institutional framework, parliaments can play an important role in making coalition governance successful.

The last point is important. Effective legislative oversight requires two components. First, parties must be able to use the review process to acquire *information* about draft bills and feasible alternative policies. Second, they must be able to translate such information into policy, that is, they must be able to force *change* to ministerial draft bills. As a result, there are four logically possible scenarios of how the legislative process is used by coalition governments.

1. Parties use the legislative process to scrutinize bills and to force change.
2. Parties use the legislative process to scrutinize bills but are unable to use it to force change.
3. Parties do not use the legislative process to scrutinize bills but they use it to force change.
4. Parties do not use the legislative process to scrutinize bills or to force change.

[19] An obvious and important question in this context concerns the issue of institutional choice: How are legislative institutions created and maintained, and why would parties in weak systems not simply adopt a strong committee system? We return to this issue below.

In order to conclude that parliaments serve as a mechanism for "keeping tabs on partners," we require evidence that the legislative process is used for *both* scrutiny and change (Scenario 1). The other combinations are not sufficient because they are potentially compatible with other explanations. Scenario 2, for example, is consistent with an account in which parties gather information for uses other than policymaking. For example, parties might be seeking policy information to advertise to constituents or to improve their ability to defend or criticize proposals in public, thus placing them in a better competitive position at the next parliamentary elections. The legislative process still serves an important function in this case, but not in reining in ministerial drift. Scenario 3 also provides no clear indication that the legislative process is central to containing ministers. Instead, it is consistent with a dynamic in which parties rely on extra-parliamentary processes to screen proposals (e.g., interest groups, JMs), and then press for appropriate changes in the legislative process—something that may simply be a function of the fact that parliaments are the only bodies that are legally empowered to pass legislation. Once again, parliament matters in this scenario because it is the forum in which change takes place, but it is not central to keeping tabs on coalition partners. Parliament simply plays the role of formalizing policy changes originating elsewhere. Finally, Scenario 4 suggests that the legislative process hardly matters at all for policymaking—it neither promotes information-gathering nor does it generate change to ministerial policy proposals. Thus, the empirical investigation we present in the next three chapters focuses on attempts by parties to employ the legislative process to gather information *and* to force changes to proposed legislation.

3.5 CONCLUSION

Where legislative institutions are strong, parliaments can play a far more important role in parliamentary systems in periods of coalition government than is generally appreciated. This conclusion matters because it challenges the conventional view that legislatures generally play "a rather marginal role in the policy-making process" (Huber and Shipan, 2002: 28). This broad characterization does not imply that scholars have not recognized the potential importance of legislative institutions. But when scholars have emphasized that "parliaments matter," the focus has generally been on the legislature as an arena that can allow *opposition parties* to affect the content of policy. Indeed, in much of this work, the strength of legislative committees has been used as a proxy indicator for opposition influence (e.g., see Strøm, 1990*b*; Powell, 2000). The evidence presented in the chapters to come opens up a new perspective. Parliamentary scrutiny can play a critical role in allowing *coalition* parties to deal with the agency problems that emerge among the partners in multiparty government. As a result, parliament provides an institutional forum that is important in allowing parties with divergent preferences to govern jointly—it is an institution that is critical to the *internal* politics of coalition governments.

Legislative institutions are only one type of "checking mechanism" that multiparty governments can employ. Parties can create institutional safeguards against ministerial drift at the cabinet level, or even within ministries (e.g., see Müller and Strøm, 2000; Thies, 2001). Empirically, however, the study of these institutions often faces an important methodological hurdle: The process of checking ministers and coalition parties through these mechanisms is largely unobservable, as it takes place behind closed doors. As a result, systematic, micro-level studies of the impact of cabinet committees or the work of junior ministers are difficult to conduct, and must often rely on indirect indicators that are divorced from specific policy proposals. For example, Thies' ground-breaking work on junior ministers focuses on the assignment of JMs. Assignments are directly observable, but they provide only indirect evidence concerning the impact of these "shadows" in the policy-making process.[20] One appealing feature of an empirical focus on legislative scrutiny is that it allows us to analyze the treatment of specific policy proposals in detail—that is, to see coalition politics "at work."

This raises a second, substantive point. The theory we have laid out concerning the origins of the "delegation problem" in coalition governments focuses heavily on the "policy-signaling" incentives that parties face. Ministers (in the service of their party) use their influence over legislative proposals in an attempt to convince constituents that the party is working hard for their concerns. Other coalition parties in turn must constrain such policy-signaling from biasing coalition policy in ways that their own constituents will find unacceptable. Importantly, both sets of parties are likely to benefit if this "tug of war" is carried out at least somewhat publicly; the publicity of having introduced a bill, and legislative activity on this bill (including amendment activity), enable parties to signal their efforts on behalf of their constituents (Huber, 1996). In contrast, other checking institutions—cabinet-level institutions and junior ministers—work largely behind the scenes. These mechanisms make policy-signaling more difficult. Ironically, parties might therefore prefer the legislative process as an arena in which to settle differences within the coalition. Naturally, such displays involve a trade-off: Public displays of disagreement may also have negative consequences if a coalition is perceived to be dysfunctional and ineffective.

What does all of this imply for institutional design and choice? The institutions that allow parties to engage in monitoring of their coalition partners are *endogenous*. The assignment of junior ministers, the creation of cabinet committees,

[20] As we will discuss in Chapters 5 and 6, an analysis of the legislative treatment of particular pieces of legislation enables us to trace the influence of junior ministers in the legislative process—an exciting and interesting supplement to Thies' approach.

and even the legislative committee system are not imposed structures that parties have to accept. Instead, governments and parliamentary majorities typically have considerable leeway to *choose* institutions that allow them to engage in such monitoring. To the extent that the agency problems we have outlined present a challenge, political environments that make coalition governance a necessity are likely to induce parties to engage in efforts to create monitoring institutions to keep an eye on their partners.

The recent Irish experience offers a telling example. The committee system in the Dáil had traditionally been quite weak. Beginning in the late 1980s, coalition government became a more prevalent feature of Irish politics. Partly in response, legislative institutions were strengthened. Similarly, since the change in New Zealand's electoral system to a mixed-member proportional representation system in 1996, governments in New Zealand have, predictably, been composed of multiple rather than single parties. As coalition government became the norm, parliamentary institutions were strengthened and parliament now boasts a considerably stronger committee system. Both developments are clearly in line with the spirit of our argument: When strong legislative committees could be useful in policing the coalition bargain, incentives to create such a system emerged, and institutions were adapted.

If parties—or more accurately, the politicians who compose them—can choose institutions that permit monitoring of coalition partners, why do we observe weak legislatures in countries that are characterized by coalition government, such as France and Ireland during the period of our study? Legislative institutions are not, of course, chosen *solely* on the basis of their usefulness in resolving intra-cabinet tensions. Institutions are "sticky," and the process of institutional choice is subject to competing incentives among participating actors. The two weak committee systems in our study provide useful illustrations: In the French case, weak committees limit the ability of parties to effectively monitor coalition partners in the Assemblée Nationale, but the presence of a weak committee system also strengthens the position of an independently elected president vis-á-vis parliament—and it was precisely for this reason that this institutional structure was chosen. Similarly, even when the incentives of the relevant actors align, legislative institutions are difficult to change overnight. Institutions are imbued with historical significance and legitimacy, and they interact in significant ways with the expectations and beliefs of those who act within them. As a result, they are subject to a degree of inertia that can prevent, or at least slow down, the adaptation of institutions to changing circumstances. Committees in the Irish Dáil eventually gained strength, but only after a sustained period of coalition governance. Nevertheless, one of the implications of our study is that strong legislative committees provide significant benefits to parties and politicians in an environment dominated by coalition governance, and we would therefore expect a general trend toward the adoption of such institutions in these contexts. We return to a discussion of these broader implications in the final chapter.

4

Coalition Governments and Legislative Activity in Five Parliamentary Democracies

If government parties use strong legislative institutions to "police" the coalition bargain, policy proposals dealing with issues that divide partners should receive a greater amount of scrutiny, and be amended more extensively, than proposals that are not divisive. Evaluating this argument requires detailed analysis of the legislative treatment of ministerial policy proposals. In this chapter, we describe original data on approximately 1,300 government bills introduced by twenty-eight coalition governments in the five parliamentary democracies in our study. These bills deal with five distinct types of policy issues and involve a number of government ministries. We discuss how we assess the degree to which these bills were scrutinized and amended in the legislative process. We also develop our measure of policy divisiveness and describe how it varies across issues and governments. In addition, we discuss a prominent argument in the coalition politics literature that emphasizes the potential influence of junior ministers, and we provide new empirical evidence on the importance of this cabinet-level institution in enabling coalition partners to manage their internal tensions.

4.1 THE SAMPLE OF GOVERNMENT LEGISLATION

To understand how multiparty governments manage the problems of delegation, and to evaluate whether legislative institutions shape their ability to do so, we must be able to compare the behavior of coalition partners on legislation that divides them to their behavior on legislation that does not. This poses a first hurdle: Most research on the impact of party ideology on coalition politics (e.g., research on the formation and termination of coalitions) has focused on one-dimensional, left–right scales to place parties. While this approach is sensible for questions in which the general or aggregate ideological disposition of a party is critical, a left–right placement obviously is insufficient for the problem at hand because it does not allow us to investigate how *variation* in ideological divisions *across* specific issues within the *same* coalition shapes policymaking.

Fortunately, two well-crafted studies allow us to overcome this difficulty. In 1989, Laver and Hunt (1992) conducted expert surveys that asked country specialists to place political parties on ideological scales in several distinct policy areas. The experts were also asked to indicate the salience of each policy area for parties. The resulting scores were averaged across experts, providing a placement for each party. In 2003, the survey was extended by Benoit and Laver (2006). These two sets of surveys provide precisely the information we require: estimates of party policy positions across different issue areas.[1]

There are, however, issues one must confront in making use of these data. First, it is obvious that political parties move in ideological space over time. Thus, we might feel confident that the two surveys provide good estimates of party positions *around the time of the survey*. But as we move away from the date of the survey, the positional information is likely to be less and less reliable as an indicator of party positions. As a result, a decision about the time span over which we are willing to extend the data is necessary. The trade-off is clear: The more tightly restricted the time frame around the surveys, the more accurate the ideological scores are likely to be. But the wider the time frame, the greater the number of different coalitions we can include and the greater the number of legislative proposals we can analyze.

There is no clear answer to this trade-off. The midpoint between the two surveys is 1996, seven years from each survey. Extending the information in each survey back or forward by approximately seven years—a little less than two electoral periods in most democracies—appears to be a reasonable (and fairly conservative) solution. In most cases, we therefore use the Laver and Hunt survey for the years 1982–95. Similarly, for most cases, we use the Benoit and Laver survey for the time period 1996–2002.[2] The time frame of our study thus begins in 1982 and ends in 2002.

[1] As Müller and Strøm (2000: 9) note, the Laver and Hunt study is "the most suitable exemplar of expert judgments." The survey, and the follow-up conducted by Benoit and Laver, is comprehensive and methodologically rigorous. The Chapel Hill Expert Survey, which provides placements for parties in 1999, 2002, 2006, and 2007 is similarly rigorous, but focuses almost exclusively on issues related to European integration, and does not cover the range of domestic policy issues that are critical for our purposes (Hooghe *et al.*, 2010). The main alternative to expert surveys, the content analysis of party manifestos conducted by the Comparative Manifestos Project (CMP), has several problems that scholars have increasingly come to view as troublesome. These include a lack of consensus over how to generate policy positions from data that were originally intended to measure issue saliency (Janda *et al.*, 1995), the "ambiguous methodological status of the coding scheme" used to place manifesto quasi-sentences into policy categories (Laver and Hunt, 1992: 31), and a substantial amount of inter-coder unreliability (Volkens, 2001). Also problematic for our purposes is that CMP researchers typically excluded parties that they viewed as "non-coalitionable," including, for example, all far-left parties and far-right religious parties in the Netherlands.

[2] Specifically, we use the Laver and Hunt (1992) data for Denmark (1984–94), France (1986–8, 1993–5), Germany (1983–94), Ireland (1982–97), and the Netherlands (1982–94). We use the Benoit and Laver (2006) data for Denmark (1994–2001), France (1997–2002), Germany

A second critical issue is to decide which legislative proposals should be included and how to classify them into the issue areas covered by the expert surveys. To construct our sample, we began with the full set of proposals introduced by governments over the twenty-year period of the study.[3] From this set, we eliminated proposals that are either outside the scope of our theory or concerned with policy areas for which we have no positional information.

First, we do not include proposals to amend the constitution. Constitutional amendments are generally subject to super-majority requirements that require support *beyond* the parties included in the coalition. Additionally, there are often non-legislative hurdles that must be crossed before constitutional amendments can be enacted.[4] As a result, such proposals involve political considerations that go beyond the internal politics of a coalition.

We also exclude legislation that requires special (usually restrictive) legislative procedures. For example, in considering legislation that ratifies international treaties, agreements within the EU, and EU directives, parliaments are generally restricted to approving or rejecting proposals in an up-or-down vote. Legislators

(1994–2002), Ireland (1997–2002), and the Netherlands (1994–2002). Our rules for deciding which of the two surveys to apply to a given time period were to use the Laver and Hunt survey for all governments forming and ending before 1996 (the midpoint between the two surveys), the Benoit and Laver survey for all governments forming and ending after 1996, and the Benoit and Laver study for all governments whose time in office spanned the pre-1996 and post-1996 periods (e.g., the 1994–8 Kohl government in Germany). The exception to the latter rule was the Bruton government (1994–7) in Ireland—the Benoit and Laver (2006) survey does not include positional information for the Democratic Left, a government party, and so we chose to use the Laver and Hunt (1992) survey (which does include this party) in that case.

[3] In four of our five democracies, this is a straightforward exercise because government legislation is identified as such. In Germany, we followed a slightly different procedure. German governments are required to provide the upper house (the Bundesrat, which represents the state governments) an opportunity to comment on proposed government legislation before it can be introduced in the Bundestag. To work around this requirement, German governments occasionally introduce a government bill through its parliamentary factions in the Bundestag (instead of identifying it as a government bill). For Germany, we therefore also treat any bill introduced jointly by the government factions as government legislation, which is immediately validated by the fact that a cabinet minister will usually submit an *identical* government bill to the Bundesrat for comment. We do not include legislation introduced by only one of the coalition parties as it is less clear that such bills represent joint proposals.

[4] For example, in Denmark and the Netherlands, a constitutional amendment must be passed in identical form by two successive parliaments before it can be enacted. In the case of the Netherlands, the parliament passing the amendment initially must be dissolved immediately upon its passage, and the successive parliament reviewing the amendment must approve it by a two-thirds majority in each chamber. In Denmark, after passage by a simple majority vote in successive parliaments, an amendment must be approved in a popular referendum. In France and Ireland as well, a constitutional amendment passed by parliament must subsequently be approved by the electorate. (In France, however, the President of the Republic may bypass a popular referendum and instead present a proposed amendment to parliament alone for approval, but in that case, the parliament must pass it by a three-fifths majority of the votes cast.)

are not able to fine-tune those proposals as they can "ordinary" (domestic) legislation.

For similar reasons, we exclude budget bills (and any bills directly related to appropriations, such as budgetary adjustment or supplementary budget bills). Unlike most other pieces of legislation, budgets must be submitted to parliament within a relatively fixed time frame, and the process of legislative review is usually accelerated, routinized, and subject to various restrictions. For example, a common restriction is that amendments proposed in parliament must be revenue-neutral (Hallerberg *et al.*, 2009).[5] These special procedures circumscribe the legislative process in a way that makes such bills incomparable to "ordinary" legislation. Finally, budgets, which allocate public money across ministries, differ from ordinary legislation in that they typically are omnibus bills that are the product of coordination across government departments (although the coordination effort is usually led by the Minister of Finance). As a result, budget bills typically do not feature the level of delegation to a single minister that characterizes the principal–agent problem with which we are concerned.

The final step in the construction of our sample is to link up government-sponsored legislation with the ideological data on party positions. To do so, we considered each remaining piece of legislation to determine whether the primary issue area addressed by the bill matched one of the issue dimensions included in both expert surveys. While these categories are expansive, we were nonetheless forced to discard a significant amount of legislation that did not match any of the common issue dimensions (which implies that we lack measures of the ideological positions of parties with respect to these proposals). For example, we excluded bills dealing with matters such as criminal justice, public transport, sports and recreation, and arts and culture, to name a few. Although several of these issues may not be particularly salient for most governments, they do account for a non-trivial amount of legislation.

Fortunately, the surveys encompass the most important policies that coalition governments deal with on a regular basis. Country experts were asked to rate the saliency of each issue dimension for the political parties in their country, and to place the parties on a continuum according to their views on the issue. Beginning with the full set of government bills not already excluded by the criteria above,

[5] Of our set of countries, the Netherlands provides perhaps the best example of the routinization of the budget review process. All annual budget appropriation bills are presented simultaneously on the third Tuesday of September (*Prinsjesdag*, or Prince's Day), when the Minister of Finance opens a briefcase containing the national budget estimates and his budget memorandum. The day afterwards, all ministers must meet with legislators in a plenary session of the *Tweede Kamer* to debate the general political principles of the budget. Then, in October, the Finance minister must meet with legislators in a plenary session to debate the financial aspects of the budget. In November and December, all other cabinet ministers must defend their individual budget chapters in parliament. By the end of December, the *Tweede Kamer* must conclude its review and vote on all parts of the budget package.

and discarding bills that did not clearly match one of the dimensions, we were able to classify bills into *five* policy dimensions. This procedure yielded a sample of 1,296 bills: 549 from Denmark, 239 from Germany, 321 from the Netherlands, 70 from France, and 117 from Ireland.[6]

4.1.1 Issue Dimensions

The first of our five issue dimensions concerns *tax and welfare* issues. Experts were asked to place parties on a scale according to whether they favor raising taxes in order to increase public services or cutting public services in order to lower taxes. Common types of legislation we classify into this category are (on the tax side) bills that changed personal income tax rates, tax allowances and exemptions, the value-added tax, corporation taxes, salary taxes, capital-gains taxes, or property taxes, and (on the welfare side) bills that changed health benefits, child benefits, or benefits for economically vulnerable groups such as low-income individuals, the unemployed, pensioners, the elderly, widows and orphans, and the disabled. Not surprisingly, a large number of bills fall into this dimension. As shown in Figure 4.1, tax and welfare issues account for approximately two-thirds of the legislation in our sample. Across countries, a smaller proportion of bills in France and Ireland fall within this category, while in Denmark, almost three out of every four bills deal with either tax or welfare issues—likely a reflection of the greater size and scope of the Danish welfare state.

The second issue dimension deals with *industrial affairs* and *market regulation*. In the Laver and Hunt (1992) study, experts located parties in terms of whether they promote or oppose state ownership of business and industry. The Benoit and Laver (2006) follow-up study asked experts (in the advanced industrial democracies) to locate parties in terms of whether they favor high levels of state regulation and control of the market or deregulation of markets at every opportunity. We interpret both questions as tapping into the same theme, which concerns the degree to which parties favor state intervention in the private sector.[7] The types of legislation we classify into this issue category include bills regulating production or supply levels of goods and services, bills dealing with

[6] Two reasons account for the higher number of bills from the three strong legislatures than the two weak ones. France and Ireland experienced episodes of single-party government during the period of our study, thus reducing the amount of time spent in office by coalitions. Second, governments in both countries tend to introduce fewer (but more comprehensive) pieces of legislation. This is especially the case in Ireland, where governments only introduce about 40–50 bills per year. This compares to roughly 135 bills per year in the Netherlands for example, and 171 bills per year in Denmark (Anderweg and Nijzink, 1995: 171).

[7] For all countries in our sample except the Netherlands, party position scores on the Benoit and Laver (2006) market regulation dimension were imputed by Benoit and Baturo (N.d.). We imputed the missing party saliency scores on this dimension.

the minimum wage or wage agreements in the private sector, bills regulating relations between employers and unions, bills privatizing state-owned companies, bills granting subsidies to certain business sectors, and bills deregulating markets. As Figures 4.1–4.6 show, economic legislation of this type was quite common, constituting approximately 15 percent of the bills in our sample. Industry and market legislation represents the second largest category in four of the countries, but is edged out in Denmark by environmental legislation. In France and Ireland, where governments engaged in sizable privatization campaigns beginning in the mid-1980s, the amount of legislation on this dimension almost rivals that dealing with tax and welfare policy.

The third issue dimension captures *social policy*. Experts placed parties according to whether they favor or oppose liberal policies on matters such as abortion, homosexuality, and euthanasia. The types of bills we classified on this dimension were bills regulating family planning, bills regulating abortion procedures, bills regulating medically assisted suicide, bills dealing with medical experimentation on human embryos, and bills dealing with gay rights, including those involving civil unions, registered domestic partnerships, and same-sex marriage and adoption. Overall, these proposals account for only one in thirty bills in our sample, although many of the societal changes they engendered were obviously quite significant. It is also worth noting that legislation on social issues began to increase markedly in the mid-1990s. For example, in the Netherlands, approximately 60 percent of all legislation on social issues was introduced by the (socially liberal)

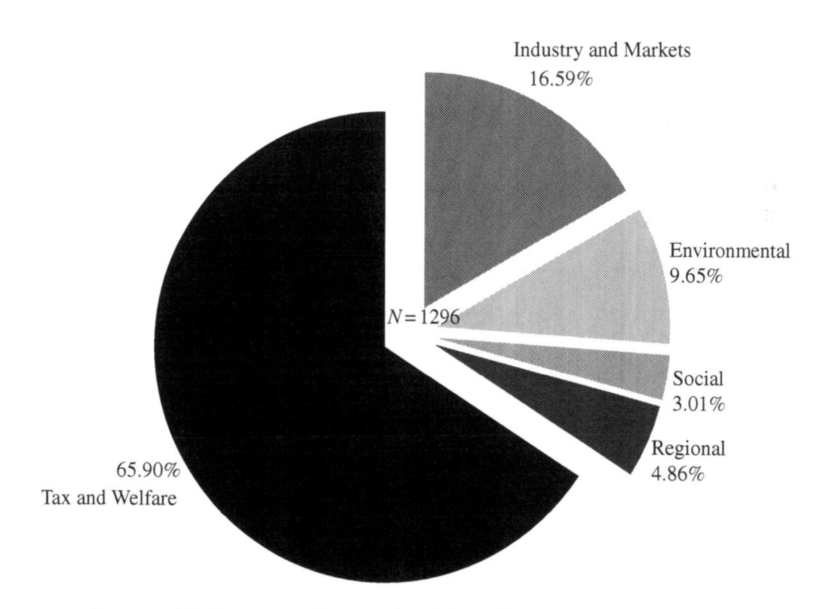

FIGURE 4.1 Frequency of Proposed Legislation by Issue Area, All Countries

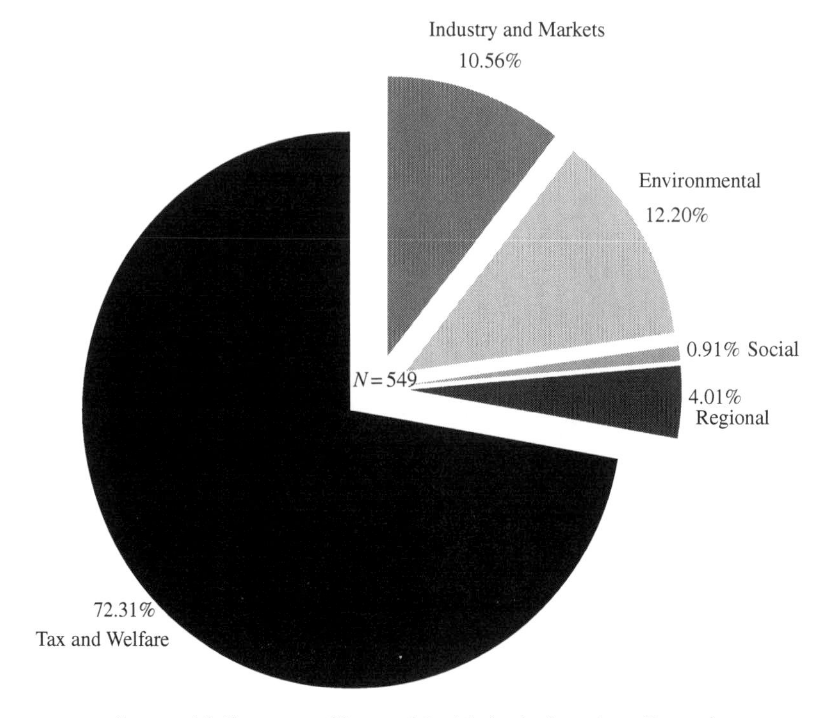

FIGURE 4.2 Frequency of Proposed Legislation by Issue Area, Denmark

"Purple Coalition" in the period after 1994, which legalized same-sex marriage and adoption and decriminalized euthanasia in a matter of a few years.

The fourth issue dimension in our study involves *regional policy*. Experts placed parties according to whether they promote or oppose devolution of administration and decision-making to regional governments. The types of bills that deal with this matter include those that restructure regional or municipal institutions, those that take away powers from the regional or municipal levels and give them to the national government, and (most commonly over our time frame) those that devolve powers from the national government to governments at the local level. For our set of countries, legislation dealing with issues of decentralization generally increased in the 1990s. And for all countries except Germany—a federal system in which state and national powers are specified in the Basic Law—regional policy accounts for approximately 5–10 percent of all legislation in the sample.

The final issue dimension concerns *environmental policy*. Experts located parties in this policy area according to whether they support protection of the environment, even at the cost of economic growth, or whether they support economic growth, even at the cost of damage to the environment. The types of bills we classified as environmental legislation include all bills dealing with air, soil, or water

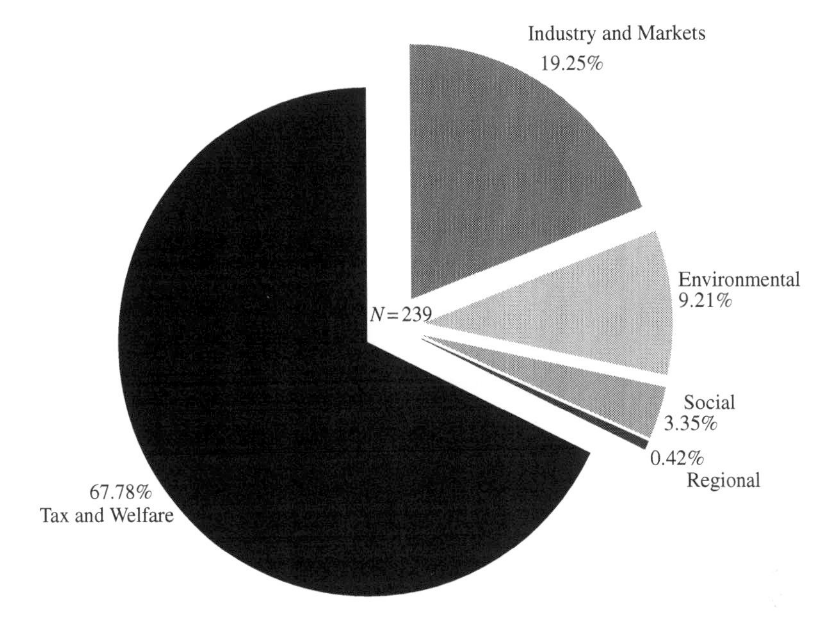

FIGURE 4.3 Frequency of Proposed Legislation by Issue Area, Germany

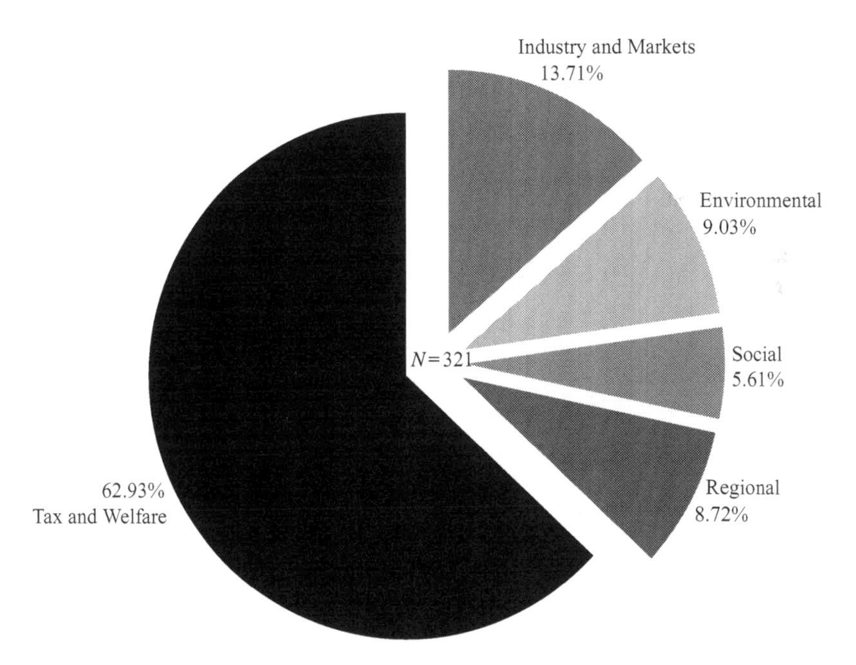

FIGURE 4.4 Frequency of Proposed Legislation by Issue Area, the Netherlands

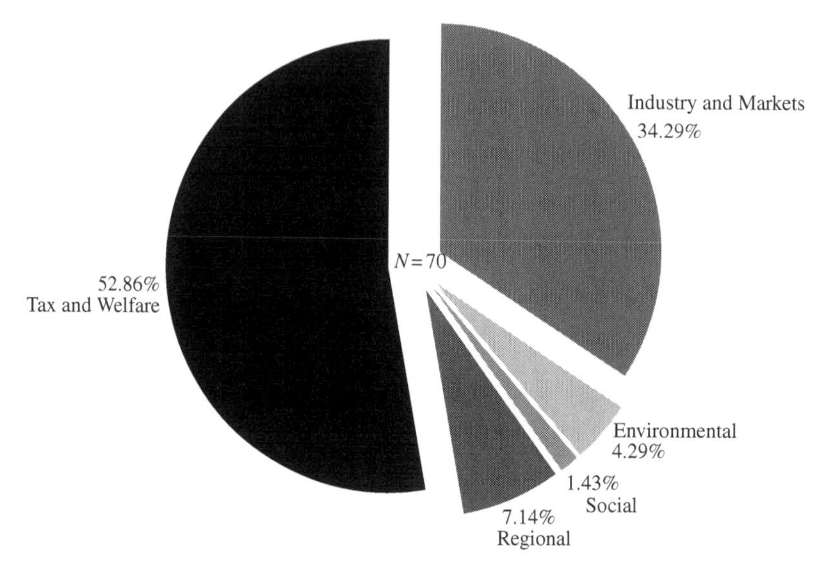

FIGURE 4.5 Frequency of Proposed Legislation by Issue Area, France

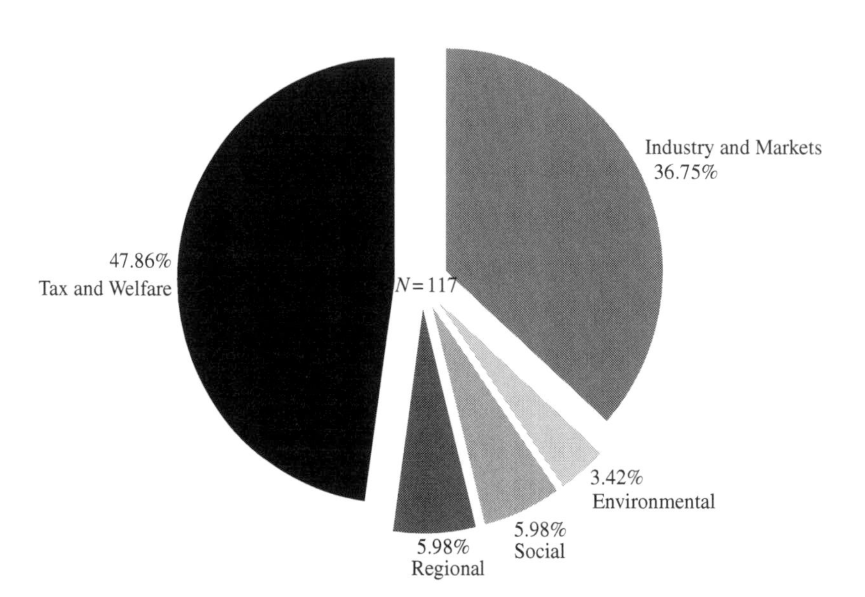

FIGURE 4.6 Frequency of Proposed Legislation by Issue Area, Ireland

pollution, for example, those that seek to regulate emissions standards, industrial waste, the use of pesticides, and the production of chlorofluorocarbons. There was a significant amount of environmental legislation introduced—approximately 10 percent of the sample overall—and as one might suspect, governments began introducing more of this legislation as the years went on. Danish governments proposed more environmental bills than any other governments in our sample, both in sheer number and as a proportion of all legislation. Ireland and France, in contrast, devoted little legislation to this policy area.

4.1.2 Proposing Ministries

The five issue dimensions are broad and cover a number of specific policy areas. As a result, various ministries drafted proposals within each dimension. For example, Figure 4.7 shows that while much tax and welfare legislation emerges from the finance ministry—which is almost solely responsible for changes to tax

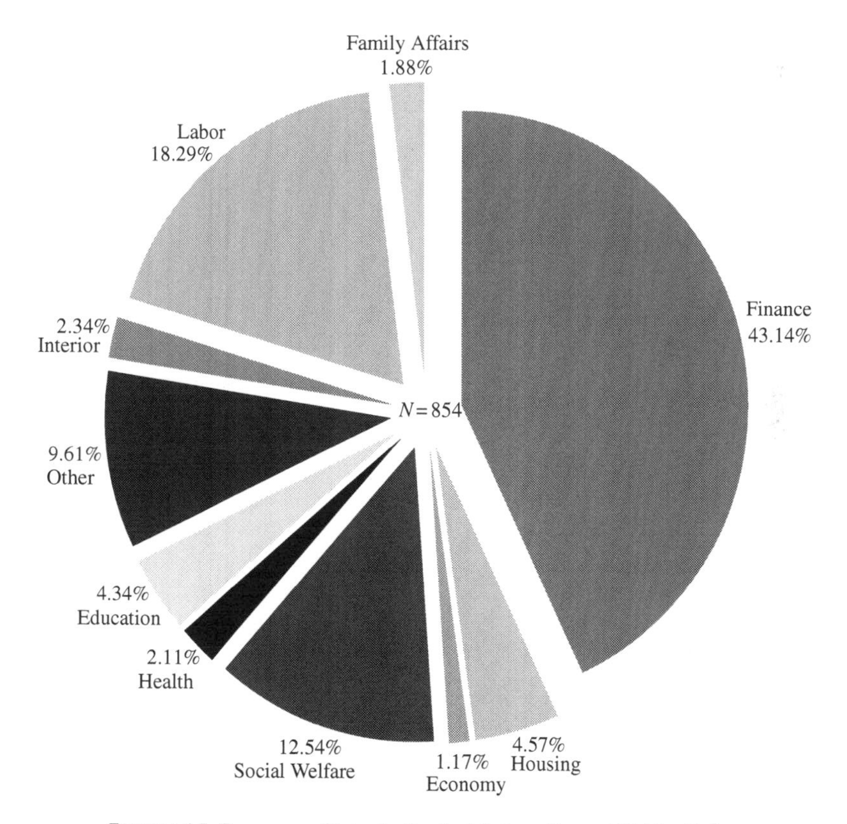

FIGURE 4.7 Frequency of Introduction by Ministry, Tax and Welfare Policy

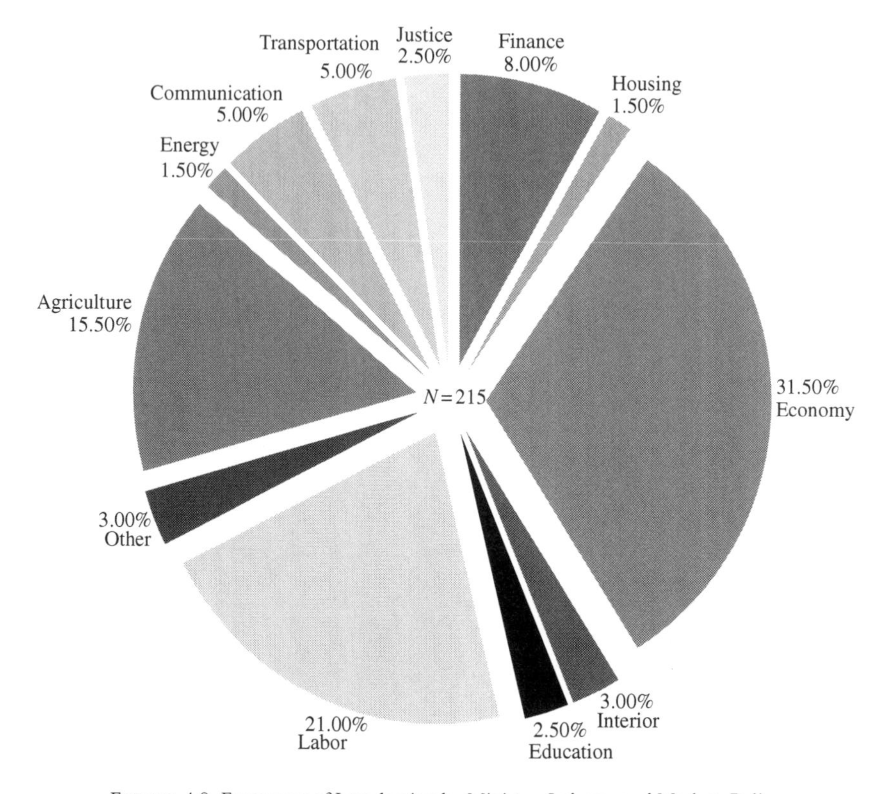

FIGURE 4.8 Frequency of Introduction by Ministry, Industry and Markets Policy

law—there are a number of other ministers who contribute to this area (often because they are responsible for drafting social welfare legislation).[8] For example, labor ministers are normally accountable for legislation dealing with unemployment benefits, disability insurance, and pensions (except where the legislation involves pensions for civil servants, which sometimes falls under the purview of the interior minister). Meanwhile, social welfare ministers are usually responsible for legislation dealing with benefits for families or the elderly. Education ministers are in charge of state subsidies for students, and housing ministers typically deal with rental subsidies.

In Figure 4.8, we see a similar situation for industry and markets policy. The bulk of bills in this dimension come from the labor minister and the economic affairs (or industry) minister, and involve issues of industrial relations and wage policy. Most other legislation revolves around market (de)regulation and

[8] In Denmark, there is not only a Ministry of Finance (*Finansministeriet*) but a separate Ministry of Taxation (*Skatteministeriet*), which is primarily responsible for the drafting of tax legislation. For the purpose of this figure, we consider both as part of the Finance Ministry.

privatization, and normally falls under the competence of the economic affairs minister. To the extent such matters are sector-specific, other ministers may have primary drafting responsibility. For example, a few bills involve the deregulation of telecom companies (the province of communications ministers), or the privatization of state-controlled airlines (usually under the control of transportation ministers), or regulations of financial markets and banks (the responsibility of finance ministers). Thus, even though this issue area is not quite as broad as tax and welfare, the responsibility for policymaking is dispersed across more departments.

In the remaining policy areas, responsibility for proposing legislation is generally shared among fewer ministers. For social policy (Figure 4.9), justice ministers were responsible for about 50 percent of legislation. These ministers drafted legislation dealing with the legalization of registered domestic partnerships and civil unions, same-sex marriage and adoption, as well as legislation relaxing restrictions on (and punishments for) medically assisted suicide. Also responsible

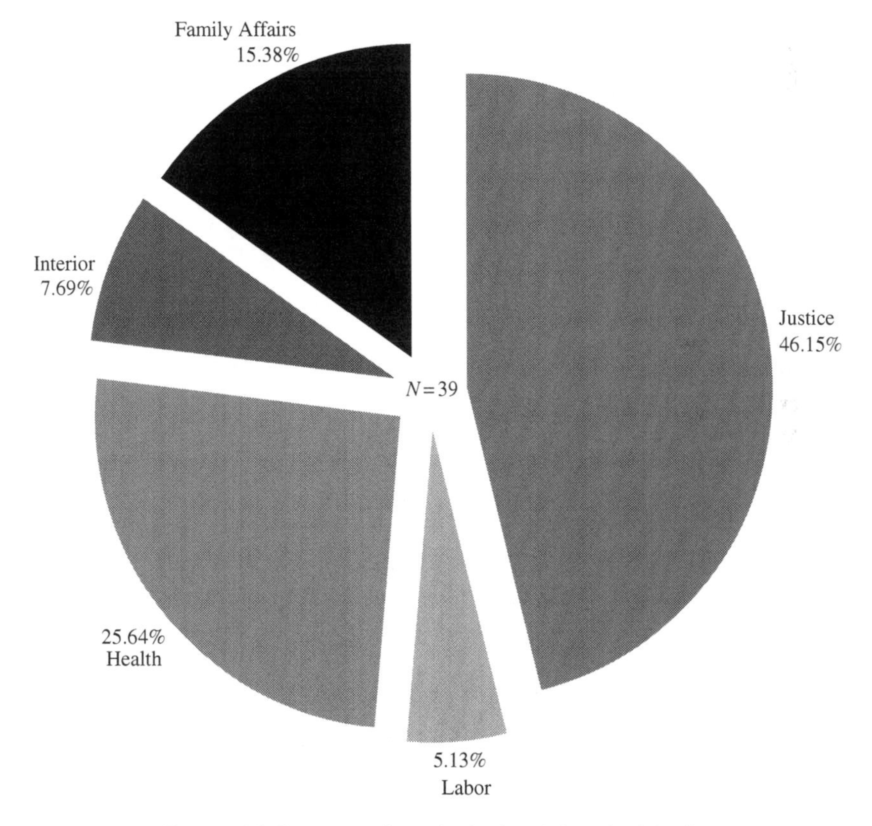

FIGURE 4.9 Frequency of Introduction by Ministry, Social Policy

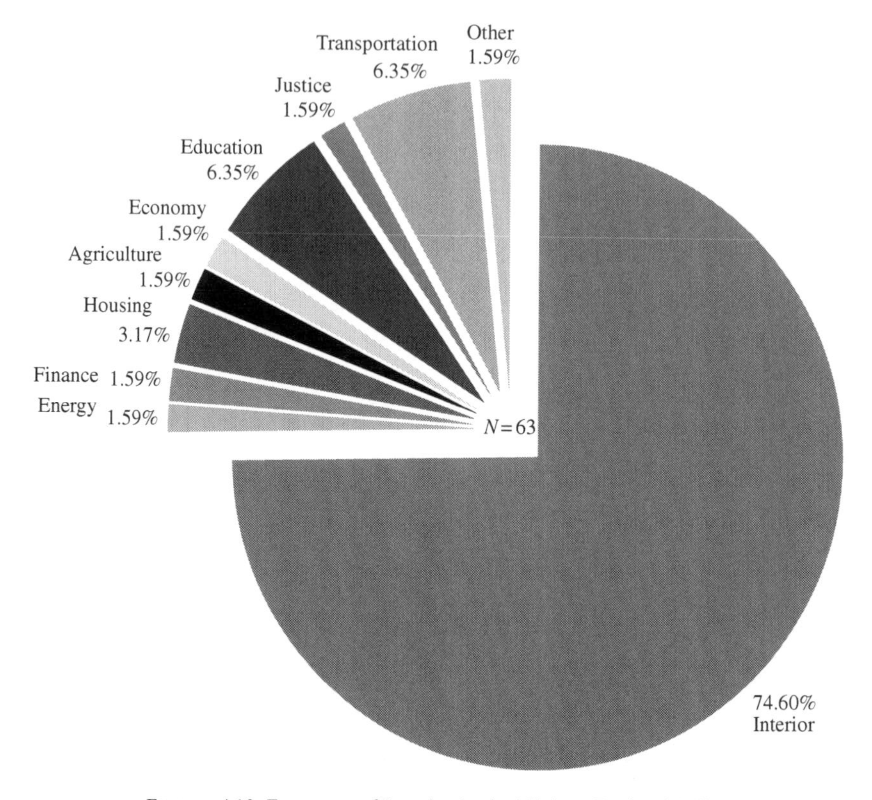

FIGURE 4.10 Frequency of Introduction by Ministry, Regional Policy

for drafting policy in the latter issue area were health ministers, who introduced almost all bills dealing with abortion policy, and policies regulating research involving human embryos.

Figure 4.10 shows that interior ministers were primarily responsible for legislation dealing with regional and municipal policy. Most of the remaining workload was split among eight other ministries, with education and transportation taking the lead. Their legislation was aimed primarily at devolving powers over schools and public transport (respectively) to local authorities.

Finally, in Figure 4.11, we see that environment ministers, not surprisingly, were responsible for the bulk of legislation on environmental policy. Finance ministers were significantly involved in this area as well, primarily because pollution taxes became an increasingly prominent policy instrument over the later years of our study. In general, the types of tax bills introduced by finance ministers were designed to encourage enterprises to clean up industrial waste and to provide individuals incentives to curb automobile emissions (e.g., by offering tax breaks for the purchase of fuel-efficient vehicles).

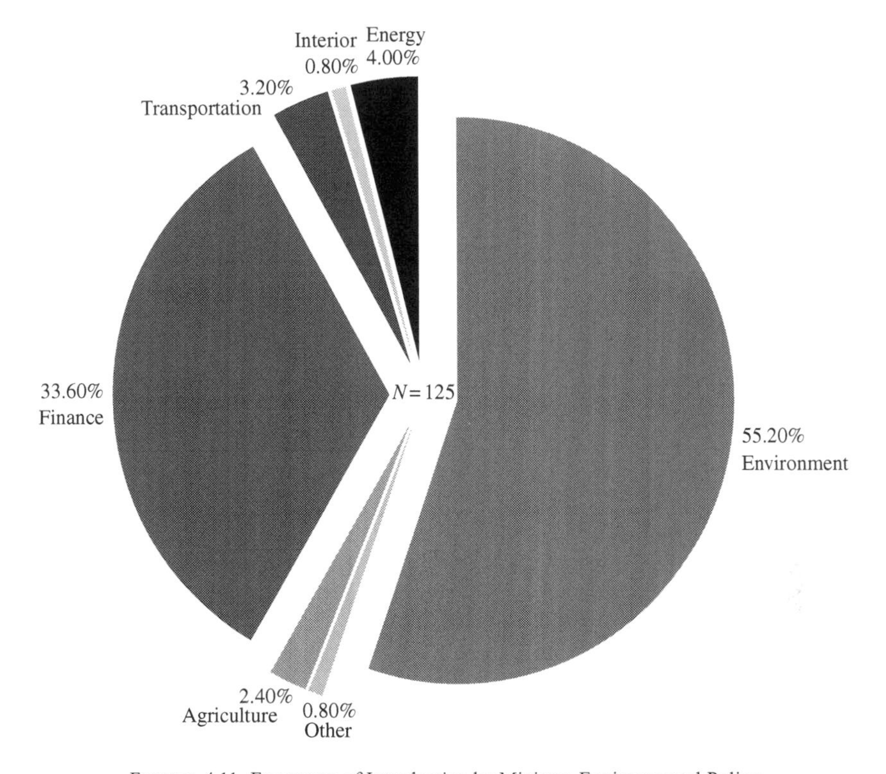

FIGURE 4.11 Frequency of Introduction by Ministry, Environmental Policy

4.2 MEASURING SCRUTINY AND AMENDMENT

Testing the hypotheses from the previous two chapters requires measures of the degree to which coalition parties take advantage of the opportunities presented by the legislative process to *scrutinize* and to *amend* bills drafted by "hostile" ministers. Both concepts involve potentially tricky questions of measurement.

4.2.1 Assessing Scrutiny

Measuring the level of legislative scrutiny of a minister's proposals is not an easy task, given that much of what goes on in a typical parliament occurs "behind closed doors." Most deliberation on government policy happens within parliamentary committees, not on the legislative floor. Unfortunately, committee meetings are often closed to the public (e.g., as in Germany), or committees do not systematically record and publish detailed information on their activities, including scrutiny of legislation through hearings, consultations with outside experts, exchanges with civil servants, and requests for policy documents.

We therefore focus on a proxy for these monitoring activities. In general, bills that are scrutinized more carefully will tend to require more *time* in the legislative process than bills that are not subjected to close scrutiny.[9] As an example, consider the "Law for the Deregulation of Price Rebates," introduced by the Christian-Democratic/FDP coalition in the Bundestag on February 1, 1994. The law—consisting of just two paragraphs—had a seemingly simple purpose: to eliminate the traditional prohibition on price rebates in consumer retail that prohibited stores from holding "sales" or providing discounts on bulk purchases. The coalition partners diverged significantly in their enthusiasm for this measure, which would have potentially far-reaching and profound economic consequences. The Bundestag scrutinized the draft bill closely. The proposal (BT 12/6722) was referred to four separate committees (the Economic Affairs Committee, the Finance Committee, the Committee on Tourism, and the Rules Committee). Each committee held at least one meeting on the bill. The Economic Affairs committee, which had been assigned the lead in reviewing the proposal, held four separate committee meetings in May, as well as a public hearing in April. During the public hearing, dozens of interest groups testified. The committee issued a report, which led to further written questions posed to the Economics minister by members of the committee. Those questions were answered by the minister in the middle of May. At the end of May, the lead committee issued its final committee report, along with substantial revisions to the bill, and the bill was passed in a roll call vote in the Bundestag on June 16, 1994, roughly four-and-a-half months after its initial introduction.

As this example suggests, the various activities that constitute parliamentary scrutiny of a bill—scheduling committee hearings and expert testimony, requesting documents, posing written questions, issuing reports—take a significant amount of time to complete. Thus, we believe that the amount of time the bill spends in the legislative process can serve as a useful proxy measure for the degree of scrutiny to which a bill is subjected. The dependent variable we use in our empirical analysis to measure scrutiny, therefore, is the length of time a minister's policy proposal spends in parliament, coded as the number of days between bill introduction and the disposal of the bill in the lower chamber.[10]

[9] Of course, we might also expect that factors other than scrutiny could lengthen the time a bill spends in the legislative process. Most importantly, opponents of a bill might simply stall or delay a bill, even if there is no scrutiny taking place. We cannot reject this possibility out of hand. However, our empirical results cast serious doubt on this alternative interpretation later in the book.

[10] A bill may be disposed of in one of three ways: it can be approved, rejected, or withdrawn. A bill might also expire before any of these actions are taken. In most legislatures, bills expire either at the end of a legislature's term (such as in Germany, France, Ireland) or at the end of a legislative sitting (such as in Denmark, where bills lapse if they are not resolved by the time the Folketing goes into summer recess). In the Netherlands, bills never expire. In our empirical analysis in Chapters 5 and 6,

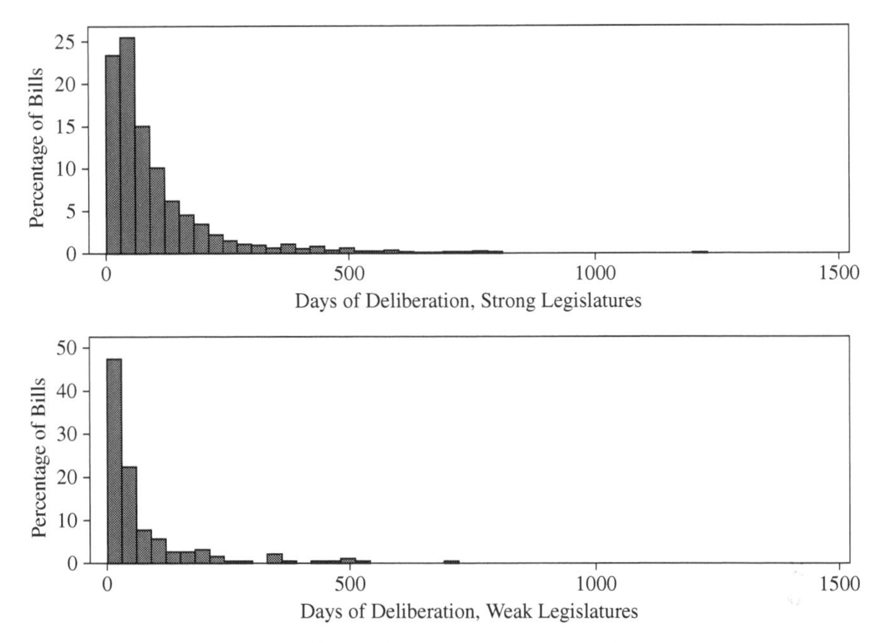

FIGURE 4.12 Length of Legislative Deliberation, Strong and Weak Legislatures

Figure 4.12 displays a histogram of the length of legislative review. The top panel shows the three countries with strong legislative institutions and the bottom panel the two with weak legislative institutions. The width of each bar in the graph is thirty days, and the height represents the percentage of bills in the sample that were reviewed for that length of time. For example, slightly fewer than 25 percent of the bills in strong systems spend less than a month in the legislative process. Another 25 percent spend between one and two months in the legislature (the modal category for bills in these systems). Almost 40 percent of bills in strong systems spend more than three months under review. Meanwhile, in weak legislatures, almost half the bills spend less than a month in the legislative process. Another quarter spend between one and two months under review. Finally, 20 percent or so are reviewed for more than three months. In short, a preliminary

in which we will use survival models (or duration models) to examine the length of legislative review, we treat expired bills as "censored" observations. That is, our models incorporate the assumption that these bills would have spent more time in the legislative process, and would have eventually been resolved, had they not expired prematurely. We also treat bills as censored if they are under review in the legislature when a change in government composition takes place. If such a change occurs, the fate of bills in the process after that point is no longer relevant for testing our theory since the principal–agent relationship in which we are interested ceases to exist. Only 6.7 percent of the bills in our sample are treated as censored.

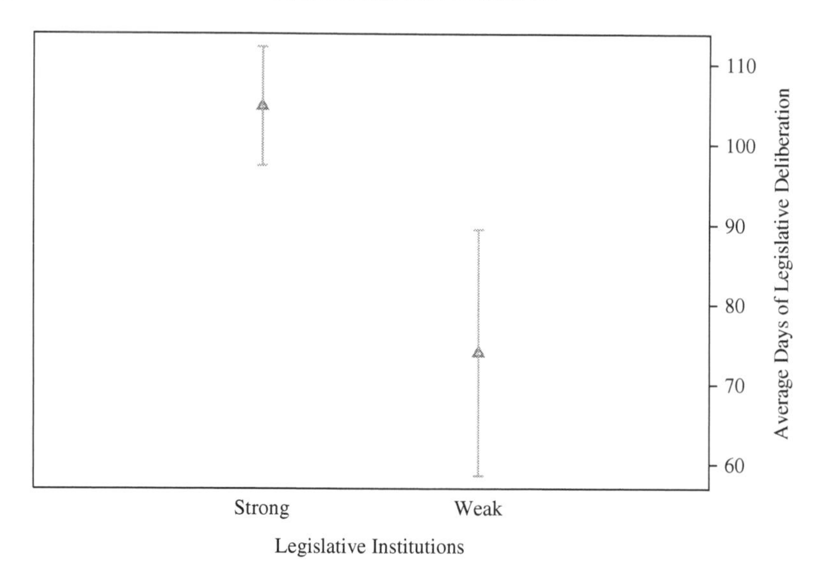

FIGURE 4.13 Average Length of Legislative Deliberation, Strong and Weak Legislatures

look at the descriptive statistics suggests a relationship between the length of legislative scrutiny and the strength of parliamentary institutions.

Figure 4.13 plots the average length of deliberation in strong legislatures and weak legislatures (along with 95 percent confidence intervals). In strong legislatures, bills have an average lifespan of 105 days, while in weak legislatures, bills have an average lifespan of seventy-five days. In other words, the average period of review for bills is approximately 50 percent longer in countries with strong legislative institutions. This is a substantively as well as a statistically significant difference ($p < 0.001$).

Of course, these statistics tell us only that bills are reviewed for a longer period of time in strong legislatures than weak ones—they do not necessarily imply that there is a systematic increase in the level of coalition "policing" in strong legislatures. It is possible that all bills in strong legislatures undergo a good deal of scrutiny, regardless of the incentives of ministers to renege on the coalition bargain, and that bills in weak legislatures (even though they receive less scrutiny on average) are scrutinized more closely if they deal with issues that divide the coalition than if they do not.

4.2.2 Assessing Amendment

Scrutiny of ministerial proposals is only one part of effective "policing" of the coalition bargain. Coalition partners must also be able to *modify* ministerial proposals that stray too far from acceptable compromise positions using legislative amendment procedures. To evaluate whether greater coalition policy differences lead to more policing in strong legislatures than weak ones, we also need a measure of the *changes* made to legislation. To develop such a measure, we must compare the final version of each bill as resolved in the legislature to the version of the bill as drafted by the proposing minister. Through this comparison, we can then construct a summary measure of bill change.

Ideally, such a measure would have two features. First, it would be possible to code reliably and consistently across countries. Second, it would allow us to assess the substantive policy impact of changes made to a draft bill. For obvious reasons, creating such a measure poses a thorny problem. Given the technical nature of most modern legislation, grasping the policy significance of changes to a draft bill by classifying the substantive content and language of such changes requires extensive expertise in the policy areas dealt with by the bill. Indeed, this issue is at the heart of the delegation problem we analyze—a high level of expertise across multiple policy areas is extremely hard to come by, even for seasoned legislators and cabinet ministers. The situation is even worse for political scientists, and any measure based on our perceptions of substantive policy impact is therefore bound to be highly unreliable, especially when applied to a large number of bills across a variety of policy areas in several different languages.

We therefore focus on developing a more objective measure of change. Legislative bills are normally divided into several articles, which are themselves often sub-divided. Each of these articles and sub-articles typically addresses a different substantive aspect of the bill. As a result, articles and sub-articles can justifiably be treated as logical "policy subunits." As our measure of the degree of change of a bill, we therefore use the aggregate number of (sub-)articles altered (or deleted) in the draft version of a government bill plus the number of (sub-)articles added.[11] In doing so, we ignore clearly minor changes, such as the correction of misspellings, the renumbering of articles made necessary by deletions or additions to the bill, etc. We believe this measure successfully allows us to tap into the substantive impact of the changes made to a bill.

We illustrate the logic of our measure with a particular example. In late 2001, the Irish government, composed of Fianna Fáil and the Progressive Democrats, introduced a bill entitled "Housing (Miscellaneous Provisions) (No. 2) Bill," intended to promote the availability of affordable housing. Among other things, the bill raised the ceiling on public debt for the provision of social housing, and provided the Housing Finance Authority and local housing authorities with greater flexibility in encouraging the provision of affordable housing. Figure 4.14

[11] This variable is therefore bounded from below by zero (a case in which the draft bill is not changed at all in the legislative process), and unbounded from above. This latter quality allows us to distinguish between a draft bill in which every article is amended from a draft bill in which every article is amended and extra articles attached, which we would view as a more significant degree of change.

BILLE NA dTITHE (FORÁLACHA ILGHNÉITHEACHA) (UIMH. 2), 2001

HOUSING (MISCELLANEOUS PROVISIONS) (NO. 2) BILL, 2001

5 **BILL**

entitled

AN ACT TO PROVIDE FOR THE MAKING AVAILABLE, AND RESALE, OF AFFORDABLE HOUSES, TO PROVIDE FOR THE PURCHASE OF THE INTEREST OF A
10 HOUSING AUTHORITY IN A HOUSE WHICH IS SUBJECT TO A SHARED OWNERSHIP LEASE AND THE SALE OF SUCH A HOUSE, TO PROVIDE FOR THE MAKING OF GRANTS IN RESPECT OF NEW HOUSES AND TO APPROVED BODIES, TO PROVIDE FOR THE GIV-
15 ING OF CERTAIN INFORMATION BY MORTGAGE LENDERS TO THE MINISTER, TO EXTEND THE POWERS AND INCREASE THE BORROWING LIMIT OF THE HOUSING FINANCE AGENCY, TO AMEND AND EXTEND THE HOUSING ACTS, 1966 TO 1998, THE
20 HOUSING FINANCE AGENCY ACT, 1981, AND THE BUILDING SOCIETIES ACT, 1989, AND TO PROVIDE FOR RELATED MATTERS.

BE IT ENACTED BY THE OIREACHTAS AS FOLLOWS:

PART 1

25 PRELIMINARY AND GENERAL

Short title and commencement.

1.—(1) This Act may be cited as the Housing (Miscellaneous Provisions) Act, 2001.

(2) The Housing Acts, 1966 to 1998, and this Act, other than *sections 17* and *18* and *Schedules 2* and *3*, may be cited together as
30 the Housing Acts, 1966 to 2001, and shall be read together as one Act.

(3) This Act, other than *section 12*, shall come into operation on such day or days as the Minister may appoint by order or orders either generally or with reference to any particular purpose or pro-
35 vision and different days may be so appointed for different purposes or different provisions or for the repeal of different enactments effected by *section 4*.

FIGURE 4.14 Irish Housing Bill, 2001

Interpretation.

2.—(1) In this Act, except where the context otherwise requires—

"Act of 1992" means Housing (Miscellaneous Provisions) Act, 1992;

"house" includes any building or part of a building used or suitable for use as a dwelling and any outoffice, yard, garden or other land appurtenant thereto or usually enjoyed therewith and "housing" shall be read accordingly; 5

"housing authority" has the meaning assigned to it by section 23 (as amended by *section 16*) of the Act of 1992;

"Minister" means the Minister for the Environment and Local Government; 10

"prescribed" means prescribed by regulations made by the Minister under this Act;

"Principal Act" means the Housing Act, 1966.

(2) In this Act—

(*a*) a reference to a Part, section or Schedule is to a Part or section of, or Schedule to, this Act, unless it is indicated that a reference to some other enactment is intended, 15

(*b*) a reference to a subsection or paragraph is to the subsection or paragraph of the provision in which the reference occurs, unless it is indicated that a reference to some other provision is intended, and 20

(*c*) a reference to any other enactment shall, unless the context otherwise requires, be read as a reference to that enactment as amended by or under any other enactment, including this Act. 25

Regulations.

3.—(1) The Minister may make regulations—

(*a*) prescribing any matter referred to in this Act as prescribed or to be prescribed or in relation to any matter referred to in this Act as the subject of regulations, or

(*b*) for the purposes of, and for the purposes of giving full effect to, this Act. 30

(2) Regulations made under this Act may—

(*a*) include any incidental, supplemental and consequential provisions that appear to the Minister to be necessary or expedient, or 35

(*b*) apply either generally or to a specified class or classes of persons or to any other matter that the Minister may consider to be appropriate and include different provisions in relation to different classes of persons.

(3) Every regulation made by the Minister under this Act shall be laid before each House of the Oireachtas as soon as practicable after it is made and, if a resolution annulling the regulation is passed by either House within the next 21 days on which that House has sat after the regulation is laid before it, the regulation shall be annulled 40

FIGURE 4.14 (*cont.*)

reproduces the first two pages of this bill as introduced by Minister Bobby Molloy of the Progressive Democrats on December 12, 2001.[12]

The text is divided into clearly identifiable sections. In this case, the most general section is labeled "Part" (e.g., "Part 1" on the first page), the next level of section is identified by bold numbers (e.g., "**1.**" on the first page), the next level by numbers in parentheses (e.g., "(1)" on the first page), and the lowest level by letters in parentheses (as seen on the second page).

Because the bill is divided into different levels of sections, there are, of course, a number of different ways in which we could approach the creation of a summary measure, even if we restrict ourselves to counting "sections." Which level is the appropriate level for the count? At the "Part" level, the pages reproduced here have only one section; at the level of "bold" sections, there are three. At the level of parenthetical numbers, there are eight. Finally, at the level of parenthetical letters, there are twelve sections. While there is no immediately apparent answer to this question, a closer look at the substantive content of the different sections suggests an approach.

Each of the eight numbered sections (i.e., division at the third level—the parenthetical numbers) describes a separate aspect of the policy. Consider the following list, which provides a short summary of the purpose addressed by each numbered section.

- Section **1.**-(1) defines the legal name of the Act.
- Section **1.**-(2) defines how this Act relates to other existing statutes.
- Section **1.**-(3) regulates the effective date of the Act.
- Section **2.**-(1) defines the objects to which the Act applies, and which governmental agents are endowed with authority under the Act.
- Section **2.**-(2) regulates how the language in the Act is to be interpreted.
- Section **3.**-(1) provides the Minister with authority to make regulations under the Act.
- Section **3.**-(2) regulates the nature and scope of the regulations that the Minister may make.
- Section **3.**-(3) provides for oversight of the Minister's regulations by parliament.

Dividing the bill at this level breaks it into sections that address logically separate features of the policy—that is, we could easily imagine changing each of these features in isolation from the others. For example, section **3.**-(2) might be changed in such a way as to restrict the minister from treating separate "classes of persons" differently, rather than allowing him to do so. Similarly, we could

[12] The total length of the bill was fourteen pages; the entire bill is available at http://www.oireachtas.ie/viewdoc.asp?fn=/documents/bills28/bills/2001/6401/b6401d.pdf.

imagine a change to section **1.**-(3) that provides a specific date on which the act will come into effect, rather than leaving that decision in the hands of the minister.

We could, of course, "go down" one more level beyond this division to the sections indicated by parenthetical letters. However, to do so, we would be separating parts of the bill that might reasonably be construed as part and parcel of the same aspect of the bill. For example, to subdivide section **2.**-(2) into the three blocks indicated by letters would separate what appears to be a logically coherent unit, namely instructions to institutions or individuals about the appropriate interpretation of language in the Act. In short, a substantive reading of the bill suggests that using the parenthetically numbered units as the sections that are counted captures our main concern, which is being able to distinguish logically separate aspects of a particular draft bill.

Naturally, the structure of bills differs somewhat across legislatures but, in general, this example is representative of the layout of the bills in the five countries. Bills are consistently divided into identifiable parts, and a substantive reading of the bills suggest that the sub-articles of major articles are logically separate units. It is the number of these logically separate subunits that are changed in the legislature that we code as the value of the dependent variable for a bill.

In Figure 4.15, we present a histogram of the extent of changes made to bills across the two types of legislatures. As we shall discuss below, the total number of

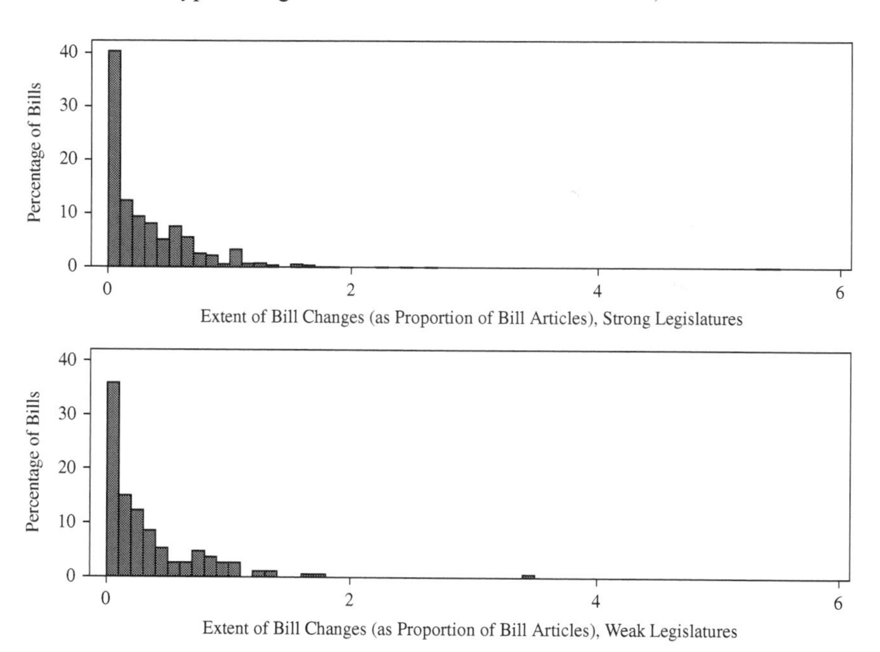

FIGURE 4.15 Extent of Legislative Change, Strong and Weak Legislatures

articles in bills across the two systems differs greatly (bills in Ireland and France are substantially larger than those in Denmark, Germany, and the Netherlands). For presentational purposes, we therefore divide the number of changes made to a bill by the total number of sub-articles in the bill. Thus, the quantity on the horizontal axis is the proportion of the sub-articles in draft bills that were changed in the legislature (which can be greater than 1 in cases where sub-articles were added to the bills). The width of any given bar in the graph corresponds to a 10 percent change in a bill, and its height represents the percentage of bills in the sample that are changed to that degree. As a comparison of the two sub-graphs shows, there does not appear to be a substantial difference in the extensiveness of legislative changes to government bills across the two systems. For roughly 40 percent of bills in both systems, fewer than 1 in ten sub-articles are altered in the legislative process. Further, cases in which 50 percent or more of a bill is changed constitute about a quarter of the sample in both systems.

Figure 4.16 shows this point even more clearly. The figure presents the average proportion of sub-articles that are changed in bills for strong and weak legislatures. There is little difference (substantively or statistically) across the two types of legislatures. In both cases, an average of about 30 percent of the sub-articles in a bill are amended.

Naturally, this does not imply that there is no difference in the level of policing across the two legislative environments. Bills in weak legislatures may be changed in roughly the same degree as bills in strong legislatures, but if our argument is correct, the *kinds* of bills that are changed will be different. In

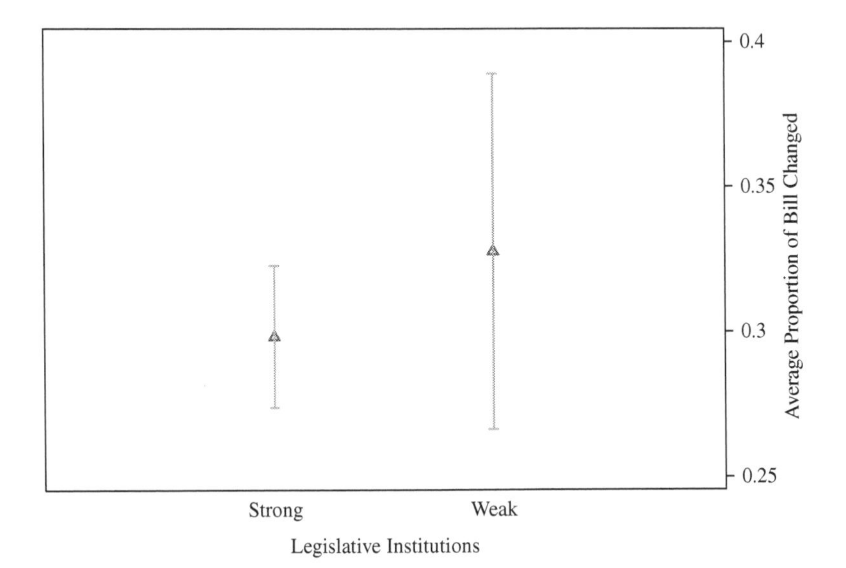

FIGURE 4.16 Average Proportion of Bill Changes, Strong and Weak Legislatures

strong legislatures, coalition partners should be able to use procedures to change bills dealing with issues that divide them from the proposing minister, while in weak legislatures, there should be no systematic, positive relationship between amendments to legislation and the policy divisions within the coalition.

4.3 MEASURING DIVISIVENESS

The central explanatory factor in our theoretical argument is the level of policy divergence within a coalition: Those policy proposals that divide the coalition pose the greatest risk for ministerial drift and, as a result, the greatest need for policing of the coalition bargain. These are also the bills for which we are most likely to observe modification (in strong legislatures) as coalition partners "pull back" the proposals coming out of hostile ministries. A key task is therefore to develop an index of the *aggregate level of policy disagreement* between the proposing minister and the coalition partners' legislative party groups for each of the bills in our sample.

This index, which we call *government issue divisiveness*, is built from three components. The first component is a measure of the *policy distance* between coalition partners and the proposing minister on the relevant issue dimension. The second is a measure of the *importance* coalition partners attach to the issue dimension. We include this because, for a given distance between the proposal and their preferred policy, the (dis)utility legislators receive from a proposal should increase in the priority they place on the policy area. The third component is a measure of coalition partner *size*, which is likely to be relevant to the *de facto* divisions between a proposal and the coalition compromise. To see why, consider that most "spoils" of coalition governance are divided in rough proportion to the relative sizes of the coalition partners, including ministries and junior minister posts. A similar principle is likely to apply to the kinds of compromise policies that coalitions agree to explicitly or implicitly: Mutually acceptable compromises (holding salience of the issue constant) are likely to fall closer to the position of the *larger* coalition partner. This implies that when a large partner holds the drafting ministry, ministerial "drift" poses a lower risk than when a small partner holds the ministry: The large partner is less likely to deviate significantly from the compromise, because the compromise is already closer to its preferred policy. In short, for the same absolute policy difference between partners and the same salience, the *effective* divisions with respect to the problem of controlling ministerial drift will likely be *larger* when small parties hold the relevant ministry than when large parties do.

As our source of information on party policy preferences, we draw upon the Laver and Hunt (1992) and Benoit and Laver (2006) expert studies discussed earlier in the chapter. Country experts contributing to the study were asked to assess, on a twenty-point scale, the saliency of several types of issues for the political parties in their country, and to place the parties along a twenty-point continuum according to their views on each of the issues.[13] Using this information, we construct our measure in several steps. First, we use the twenty-point position scores (for the five policy dimensions in our sample of legislation) to calculate the *absolute policy distance* in the relevant issue area between each partner party in the coalition and the party that controls the ministry responsible for drafting the bill. Then, we weight each partner-to-minister distance by the *relative saliency* placed on the issue dimension by the partner.[14] Next, we weight each saliency-weighted partner-to-minister distance by the legislative seat share of the partner as a proportion of the legislative seats controlled by all parties in the government. To create the final aggregate measure, we sum the seat-weighted, saliency-weighted distance measures across coalition partners.

In Table 4.1, we present the descriptive statistics for this variable, as well as for the other explanatory variables that will be used in our analysis in Chapters 5 and 6.[15] As the summary statistics show, the government issue divisiveness index lies on roughly a ten-point scale, ranging from a minimum of around 0 to a maximum of 9.6. Although, on average, government issue divisiveness is only 1.8 on this scale (both in strong and weak legislatures), it varies substantially across governments and issues. Before presenting the details of this variation, we first provide the list of coalition governments in our sample in Table 4.2.[16] While *all* governments in Denmark, Germany, and the Netherlands during the time frame of our study were composed of multiple parties, there were brief periods of single-party government in France (Socialist governments between 1988 and 1993) and Ireland (a Fianna Fáil government between 1987 and 1989).

To give a better sense of how the government divisiveness differs across countries, governments, and issues, we provide issue divisiveness scores in Figures 4.17–4.21.[17] Figure 4.17 presents divisiveness scores for the eight Danish

[13] The experts were asked to locate the positions of party leaders and party voters. We use their estimates for party leaders in our analysis.

[14] We calculate the relative saliency of an issue dimension for a given party by dividing the party's twenty-point saliency score for that dimension by the party's average saliency score on all five dimensions. Thus, the relative saliency score for any party will be centered at 1.0. Issue dimensions that are relatively more salient for a party will have a score greater than 1.0, while issues that are relatively less salient will have a score less than 1.0.

[15] We omit from the table descriptive statistics for country and issue dimension indicators, which will also be included as variables.

[16] The primary source for these tables is the collection of country-specific chapters in the Müller and Strøm (2000) volume.

[17] Recall from our earlier discussion that multiple ministers in a government may propose bills dealing with the same issue (e.g., bills dealing with benefits to the poor may come from a social welfare minister, a housing minister, a health minister, etc.). If the proposing ministers are from different parties, the divisiveness index may vary across bills in the same issue area. For presentational purposes, Figures 4.17–4.21 display the *average* divisiveness for bills on each of the five issue dimensions.

TABLE 4.1 Summary of Explanatory Variables, Strong and Weak Legislatures

Strong legislatures				
Explanatory variable	*Mean*	*Std. Dev.*	*Min.*	*Max.*
Government Issue Divisiveness	1.78	1.74	0.11	7.28
Shadow JM	0.29	0.45	0	1
Non-Pivotal Opposition Issue Divisiveness	7.14	2.38	0.93	12.93
Pivotal Opposition Issue Divisiveness	2.19	2.95	0	10.47
Minority Government	0.44	0.5	0	1
Number of Committee Referrals	1.85	2.02	0	15
Number of Subarticles in Draft Bill	24.06	50.46	1	727
Expiration of Bill before Plenary Vote*	0.07	0.26	0	1
Length of Legislative Review*	105.42	127.76	1	1226
(N = 1109)				
Weak legislatures				
Explanatory variable				
Government Issue Divisiveness	1.79	2.5	0.02	9.56
Shadow JM	0.44	0.5	0	1
Non-Pivotal Opposition Issue Divisiveness	5.36	3.05	0.55	12.87
Pivotal Opposition Issue Divisiveness	0.08	0.56	0	4.89
Minority Government	0.18	0.38	0	1
Number of Committee Referrals	0.68	0.6	0	3
Number of Subarticles in Draft Bill	83.56	118.31	1	1027
Expiration of Bill before Plenary Vote*	0.03	0.18	0	1
Length of Legislative Review*	74.66	109.9	1	720
(N = 187)				

*Used only in the analysis of legislative amendments.

governments in our sample. A couple of patterns are immediately apparent. One is that the four center-left Rasmussen governments (1993–2001) were, on average, less divided than the four preceding center-right Schlüter goverments. A second is that, in the center-right governments, the more divisive legislation tended to deal with either regional and municipal reforms or environmental legislation. For environmental issues, the divisiveness scores reflect the fact that, in the first two governments, the Christian People's Party (KrF) held the environment ministry, which passed to the Radical Left (RV) in the third government. For both these parties, the environment was an important issue—for the leftist RV, it was the most important issue, and for the (agrarian-based) KrF, it was second only to social issues. Their ecology-friendly stance (especially for the RV) clearly separated them from their rightist partners, the Conservatives (KF) and the Liberals (V). Once these latter two parties were left to govern on their own (in the fifth Schlüter government), environmental legislation was no longer a notable source

TABLE 4.2 Coalition Governments in Five Parliamentary Democracies

	Date in	Date out	Party composition
Denmark			
Prime Minister			
Schlüter II	1/10/1984	9/8/1987	KF-V-CD-KrF
Schlüter III	9/10/1987	5/10/1988	KF-V-CD-KrF
Schlüter IV	6/3/1988	12/12/1990	KF-V-RV
Schlüter V	12/18/1990	1/15/1993	KF-V
P.N. Rasmussen I	1/25/1993	9/21/1994	SD-RV-CD-KrF
P.N. Rasmussen II	9/27/1994	12/30/1996	SD-RV-CD
P.N. Rasmussen III	12/30/1996	3/11/1998	SD-RV
P.N. Rasmussen IV	3/11/1998	11/20/2001	SD-RV
France			
Prime Minister			
Chirac II	3/20/1986	5/10/1988	RPR-UDF
Balladur I	3/29/1993	5/10/1995	RPR-UDF
Juppé I	5/17/1995	6/2/1997	RPR-UDF
Jospin I	6/2/1997	4/21/2002	PS-PC-RCV
Germany			
Chancellor			
Kohl II	3/29/1983	3/10/1987	CDU/CSU-FDP
Kohl III	3/11/1987	10/29/1990	CDU/CSU-FDP
Kohl V	1/17/1991	11/14/1994	CDU/CSU-FDP
Kohl VI	11/15/1994	10/26/1998	CDU/CSU-FDP
Schröder I	10/27/1998	9/22/2002	SPD-Greens
Ireland			
Taoiseach			
FitzGerald II	12/14/1982	2/17/1987	FG-Labour
Haughey IV	7/12/1989	2/11/1992	FF-PD
Reynolds I	2/11/1992	11/25/1992	FF-PD
Reynolds II	1/12/1993	11/17/1994	FF-Labour
Bruton	12/15/1994	6/6/1997	FG-Labour-DL
Ahern I	6/26/1997	4/25/2002	FF-PD
The Netherlands			
Prime Minister			
Lubbers I	11/4/1982	5/21/1986	CDA-VVD
Lubbers II	7/14/1986	5/2/1989	CDA-VVD
Lubbers III	11/7/1989	5/3/1994	CDA-PvdA
Kok I	8/22/1994	5/5/1998	PvdA-D66-VVD
Kok II	8/3/1998	5/15/2002	PvdA-D66-VVD

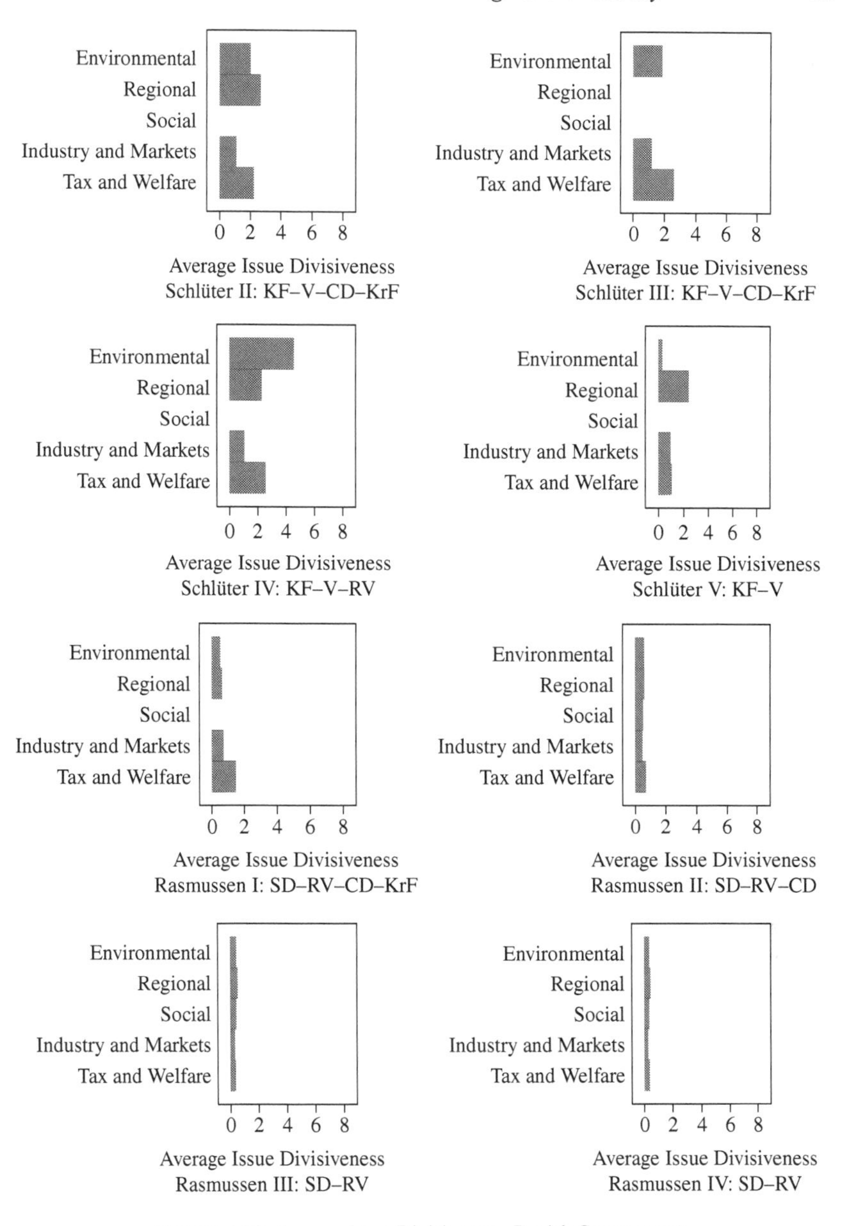

FIGURE 4.17 Average Issue Divisiveness: Danish Governments

of division. On issues dealing with regional and municipal policy, however, the two right-wing parties were substantially divided throughout their partnership. These differences were reflective of the fact that, while this issue was of average importance for both parties, the Liberals supported decentralization significantly more than the Conservatives.

In Figure 4.18, we show how issue divisiveness varied across the five governments in Germany. The four Kohl governments, which were all partnerships between the Christian Democrats (CDU/CSU) and Liberals (FDP) were fairly united on economic issues (though slightly more so on tax and welfare policy than on industry and markets policy), but were divided on social issues.

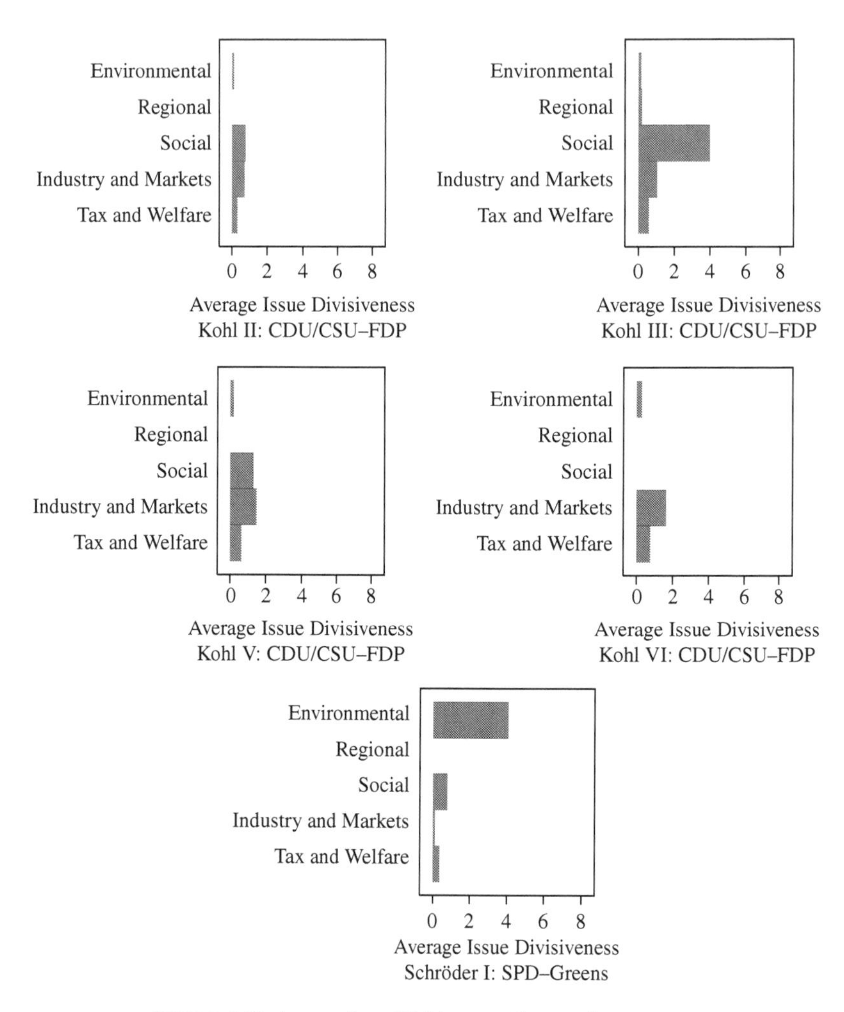

FIGURE 4.18 Average Issue Divisiveness: German Governments

The CDU/CSU held traditional religious positions on these issues, whereas the FDP held libertarian positions focused on the rights of individuals. The divisions between these parties were most evident in Kohl III, when the FDP was in control of the justice ministry. Because the CDU/CSU was the dominant party in this coalition, and the two parties differed markedly on social issues falling under the jurisdiction of the justice minister, the measure appropriately indicates a high degree of tension. For example, the justice minister in this government was responsible for drafting a bill banning cloning and gene manipulation as well as certain in vitro procedures and surrogacy; this was a bill for which the minister's views probably differed significantly from a mutually acceptable coalition compromise. In contrast, in the Kohl II and Kohl V governments, the CDU/CSU had control of the ministries proposing social policy legislation (in this case, the family affairs ministry), and we see lower divisiveness within the coalition on these issues. Similarly, in the Schröder government of the SPD and Greens, we note that the only issue of serious contention was the environment. The Greens held the environment ministry (which introduced environmental protection legislation) and the SPD held the finance ministry (which introduced bills imposing pollution taxes). The environmental issue was, far and away, the most important issue for the Greens, and one of greater than average importance for the SPD, and it was one that substantially separated the two parties.

In the Netherlands, shown in Figure 4.19, legislation was more divisive than in Denmark and Germany. Dutch governments consisted of one "grand coalition" between the Christian Democrats (CDA) and the Labor Party (PvdA)—which were significantly at odds over both economic policy and social policy—and two coalitions (the "purple coalitions" from 1994 to 2002) consisting of parties that were extremely divided on economic policy—the Liberal VVD on the right, the Labor Party (PvdA) on the left, and the small D66 in the middle. However, the parties in the purple coalition were quite comfortable with one another on social issues, such as same-sex partner rights and euthanasia, and indeed passed many reforms in these areas during their tenure. Finally, the two early Dutch governments consisted of Christian Democrats and Liberals that, like their German analogs, were fairly united on economic legislation but significantly divided on social policy.

Turning to the weak legislatures, we see similar differences in divisiveness across issues and types of governments. In France, Figure 4.20 shows that the conservative Gaullist (RPR) and Liberal (UDF) coalitions exhibited divisiveness scores much like those of the KF and V coalitions in Denmark. They had no significant divisions on any issues, but held somewhat different views on regional policy (with the UDF favoring greater decentralization). Meanwhile, in the Jospin government of the Socialists (PS), the Communists (PC) and Greens (RCV), environmental issues were most divisive, separating the ecology-focused RCV (which controlled the environment ministry) from the more moderate Socialist Party and the industrial, labor-based Communist Party. This is similar to the

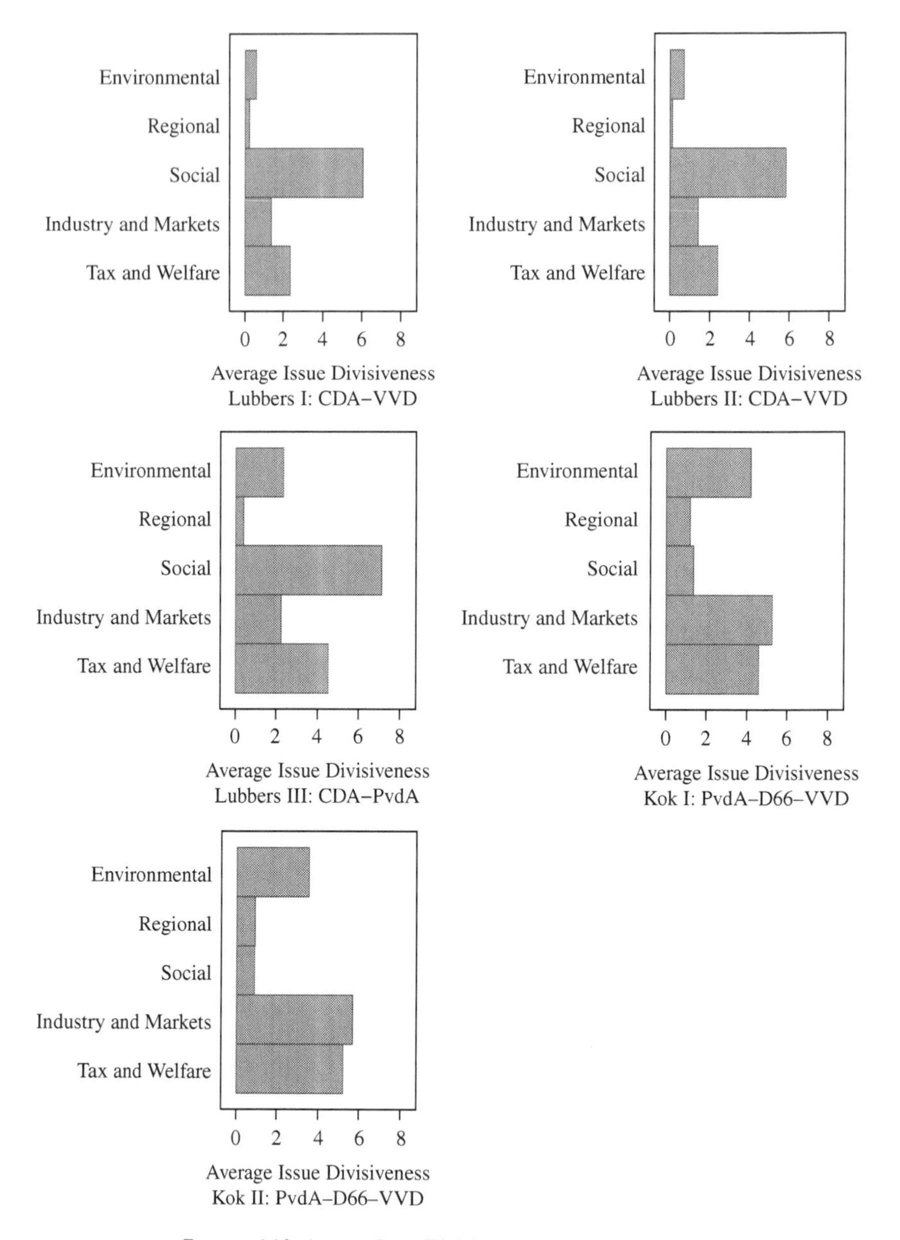

FIGURE 4.19 Average Issue Divisiveness: Dutch Governments

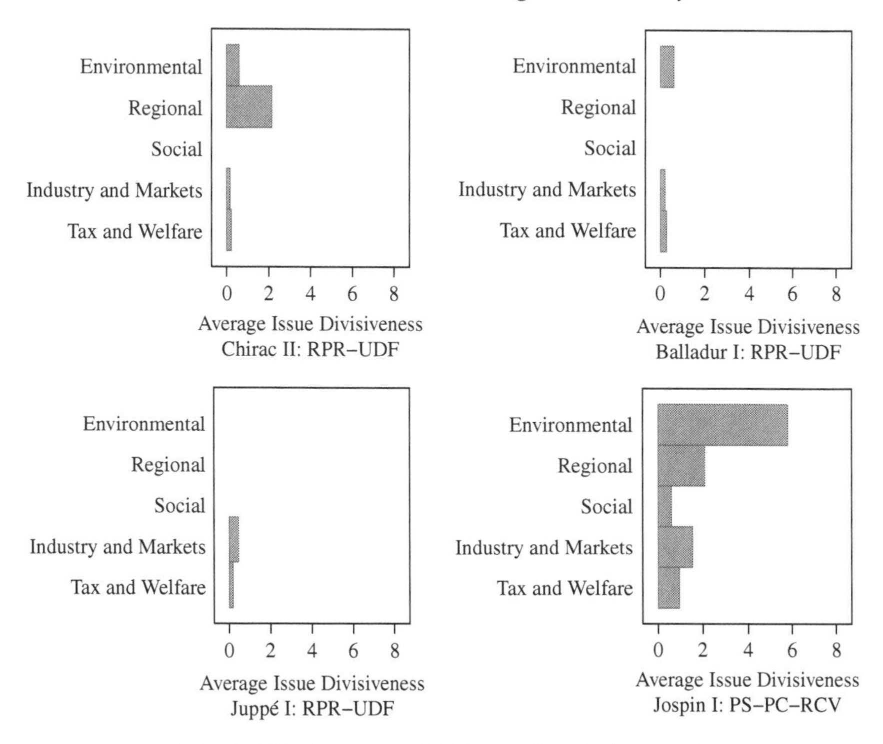

FIGURE 4.20 Average Issue Divisiveness: French Governments

Schröder government in Germany, with the notable exception that there were greater divisions on the French left on economic issues than in Germany (especially on industry and markets policy), owing primarily to the presence of the Communists in government.

Finally, in Ireland (Figure 4.21) the three conservative coalitions between the Christian Democratic Fianna Fáil (FF) and the (liberal) Progressive Democrats (PD) were relatively close ideological fits, with little divisiveness on economic legislation, or on any other issue for that matter. One reason is that the parties were not far apart in absolute terms on most issues; another is that the dominant FF controlled most of the portfolios, which implies that the incentives to renege on the coalition bargain (which is likely to fall close to the FF position) were generally small, which the divisiveness measure captures. In contrast, the Reynolds II government, in which Fianna Fáil joined Labour, was quite divided on both economic and social issues (a clear parallel to the grand coalition between the CDA and PvdA in the Netherlands). Finally, two Irish coalitions were formed by the center-right Fine Gael (FG) and Labour (Fitzgerald II and Bruton). The Bruton government also contained the left-wing Worker's Party/Democratic Left. Both coalitions were divided on economic issues (similar to the Dutch grand coalition

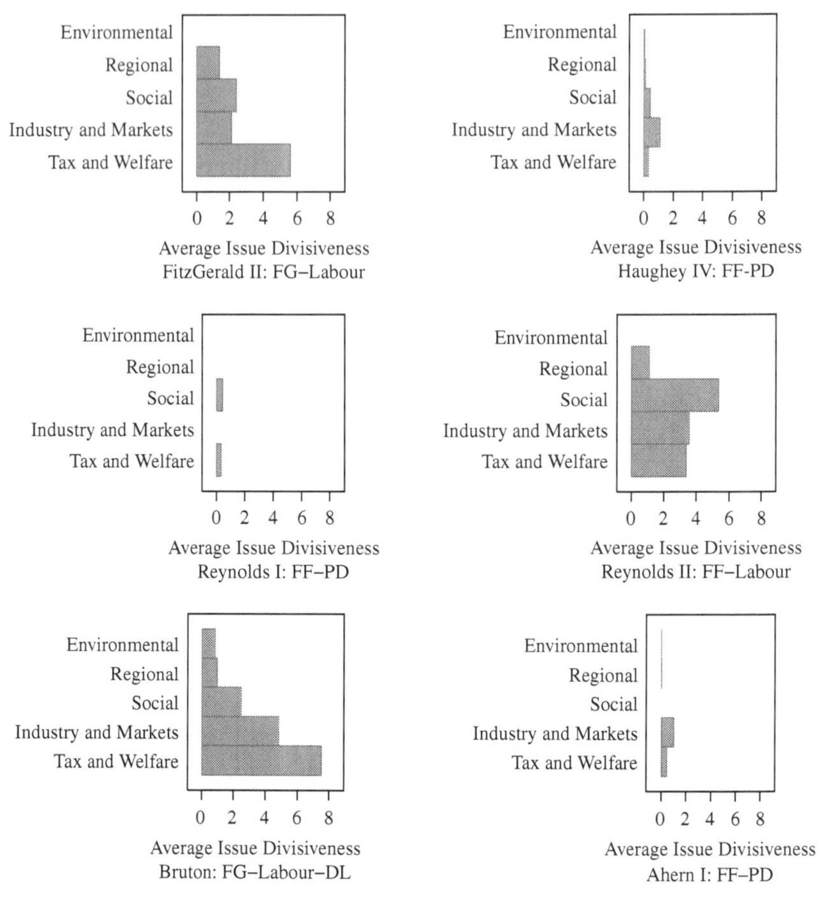

FIGURE 4.21 Average Issue Divisiveness: Irish Governments

and the FF–Labour coalition), but less so on social issues—largely a result of the absence of a Christian Democratic party in government.

4.4 COALITION DIVISIONS AND JUNIOR MINISTERS

Cabinet-level institutions, just like legislative institutions, can enable coalition partners to monitor hostile ministers. As Thies (2001) and several contributors to the Müller and Strøm (2000) volume have pointed out, appointing junior ministers to a hostile ministry is one of the most common cabinet-level mechanisms employed by government parties to gather policy information and "keep tabs" on their partners. For example, Thies (2001: 585) argues that shadow JMs "have ample incentive to report (at least to their own parties) any behavior within the ministry that deviated from the agreed-upon policy platform of the coalition, or any information that might help the cabinet to deal with forthcoming ministerial proposals." As Table 4.1 shows, shadow JMs have ample opportunity to get involved in the policy-making process.[18] Approximately 30 percent of bills in strong legislatures come from ministries with a shadow JM. When we exclude Denmark, where the post of junior minister does not exist, that number rises to 60 percent. Similarly, a large proportion of legislation in weak systems originates in ministries where shadow JMs are present.

One implication of Thies' argument is that parties should systematically seek to appoint JMs to shadow ministers whose preferences diverge from their own. In other words, if coalition parties assign junior ministers to keep an eye on their partners, the likelihood of a shadow JM being placed in a department will be a function of the divisiveness of the policy area under the ministry's jurisdiction: the more divisive the issue area, the higher the likelihood that a shadow JM will be assigned. Unfortunately, Thies did not have sufficient data to investigate this hypothesis empirically. However, our data allow us to do so. The findings not only provide unambiguous support for Thies' argument; they also validate our decision to incorporate the presence of shadow JMs in our analysis of legislative policing in Chapters 5 and 6, as well as our decision to consider possible interactive effects between these cabinet-level institutions and those in the legislature.

In our set of countries (excluding Denmark), there are 164 ministries (i.e., across all governments in Germany, the Netherlands, France, and Ireland) to which shadow JMs could have been appointed. A simple way to test the expectation that emerges from Thies' argument is to run a logistic regression predicting the placement of a shadow JM in a given ministry as a function of the average issue divisiveness of the bills introduced by that ministry.[19] We present our results in Table 4.3, for all countries jointly, and then for strong and weak legislatures. The findings are clear: Government ministries that introduce legislation dealing with internally divisive issues are more likely to be "shadowed" by their coalition partners. Moreover, this effect is consistent across the two types of legislatures. Regardless of whether partners have access to legislative mechanisms that can help to rein in ministers, they make use of JMs for the same purpose.

[18] Our measure of shadow JM is dichotomous, taking a value of "1" for a bill that comes from a ministry where a coalition party other than the minister's party controls a junior minister position, and "0" otherwise.

[19] We also include country indicators in the regression to account for the possibility that the tendency to appoint shadow JMs, after accounting for issue divisiveness, may vary across systems. Ireland is the excluded category in Columns 2 and 4, and Germany is excluded in Column 3. As the results show, in the strong legislative systems, the Netherlands is more likely to make use of shadow JMs than Germany. This accords with the results in Thies (2001).

TABLE 4.3 Government Issue Divisiveness and Appointment of Shadow JMs

Explanatory variable	All legislatures	Strong	Weak
Average Issue Divisiveness	0.343***	0.327**	0.353***
	(0.097)	(0.160)	(0.123)
The Netherlands	1.780***	1.728***	
	(0.514)	(0.579)	
Germany	0.077		
	(0.476)		
France	0.745		0.761
	(0.546)		(0.561)
Intercept	−1.434***	−1.336***	−1.457***
	(0.394)	(0.394)	(0.435)

Logit coefficients with standard errors in parentheses. $N = 164$ (all legislatures), $N = 86$ (strong legislatures), $N = 78$ (weak legislatures). Significance levels: $*$, 10%; $**$, 5%; $***$, 1%.

We illustrate the substantive impact of divisiveness on JM appointment in Figure 4.22. Because the effects are similar across weak and strong legislatures, the figure is based on the pooled model. The vertical axis represents the probability that a shadow JM will be appointed to a ministry, the horizontal axis represents the average issue divisiveness for bills coming out of a ministry. The solid line is

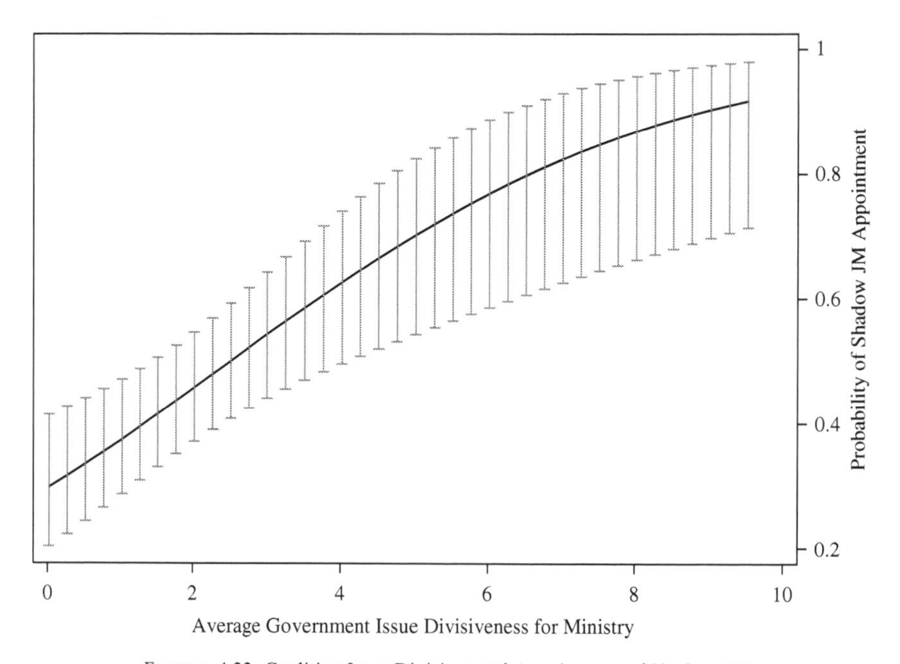

FIGURE 4.22 Coalition Issue Divisions and Appointment of Shadow JMs

the mean predicted probability of appointment (bounded by 95 percent confidence intervals). The figure shows that the probability of a shadow JM appointment increases quite steeply as issue divisiveness increases. When divisiveness is relatively low, there is only about a 30 percent chance that coalition partners will appoint a shadow JM. In contrast, when internal divisiveness is relatively high, the probability of a shadow JM appointment jumps to around 80 percent. This provides compelling support for the idea that coalition partners make use of positions at the cabinet level in a way that will allow them to rein in potentially hostile ministers.

It is worth pushing this analysis a bit further. As Thies (2001: 590) also points out, the relative sizes of the parties in a coalition directly affects their ability to use junior ministers as shadows. This is the case because junior minister positions—like ministerial positions—are usually allocated in proportion to the seats contributed by each party to the coalition. Large parties—especially those that hold more than 50 percent of a coalition's seats—are therefore relatively unconstrained in their ability to shadow ministries held by their partners: In principle, they have a sufficient number of junior ministers to shadow *all* of the ministries controlled by other parties. Smaller parties, in contrast, are constrained. Because they do not have a sufficient number of JMs to shadow all of their partner's ministries, they must choose how to allocate them. As a result, we would expect that for smaller parties that face such an "allocation constraint," the degree of tension between the party and their partners significantly affects the placement of shadow JMs.

This line of argument readily suggests a more subtle test of Thies' argument. We can split the sample of ministries in our data into two sets: those ministries that are controlled by "large" coalition parties that contribute at least 50 percent of the coalition's seats, and those ministries held by "small" coalition parties that contribute less than 50 percent of the seats. For ministries in the first group, a shadow JM must be appointed by a smaller coalition partner that is constrained in its ability to monitor all hostile ministers. We would therefore expect to see a strong positive relationship between the divisiveness of the issue under the jurisdiction of the ministry, and the presence of a shadow JM. In the second group, a shadow JM is appointed from (a group of) larger coalition partners that are able (collectively) to monitor all ministers belonging to small coalition parties. Because the "appointment constraint" is not present in this case, we would expect to see a weaker (or no) relationship between the divisiveness of the issue under the ministry's jurisdiction and the presence of a shadow JM.

Table 4.4 presents the results of a logistic analysis of the likelihood of observing a shadow JM when the coalition partners to the minister are relatively small (i.e., when the minister's party has more than 50 percent of portfolios) and when they are relatively large. When coalition partners are small, the appointment constraint has bite, and we would expect a strong positive relationship between divisiveness and the presence of a shadow JM. This is indeed what the results show. The

TABLE 4.4 Government Issue Divisiveness and Appointment of Shadow JMs, by Partner Size

Explanatory variable	All partners	Small	Large
Average Issue Divisiveness	0.343***	0.693**	−0.235
	(0.097)	(0.308)	(0.165)
The Netherlands	1.780***	0.010	0.535
	(0.514)	(1.040)	(0.871)
Germany	0.077	0.052	−0.126
	(0.476)	(0.708)	(1.068)
France	0.745	1.507*	−2.627**
	(0.546)	(0.787)	(1.205)
Intercept	−1.434***	−2.213***	2.390**
	(0.394)	(0.618)	(1.182)

Logit coefficients with standard errors in parentheses. $N = 164$ (all partners), $N = 92$ (small partners), $N = 72$ (large partners). Significance levels: *, 10%; **, 5%; ***, 1%.

coefficient on divisiveness is positive and statistically significant. In contrast, when coalition partners are relatively large, we expect little or no relationship since there should be a sufficient number of potential shadow JMs available to monitor all of the smaller party's ministers. This is again what the results suggest. The coefficient on divisiveness is actually negative, though statistically indiscernible from zero.

We present these results graphically in Figure 4.23. For large coalition partners (the left pane of the graph), we see that the probability of appointing a shadow JM is always quite high: the probability they will appoint a shadow JM to watch over a small coalition party's minister is around 80 percent on relatively less divisive bills and around 50 percent on relatively divisive bills. In other words, a large partner is more than likely going to have a shadow junior minister monitoring a smaller partner's minister whatever the extent of their policy disagreement. In contrast, for small coalition partners (the right pane of the graph), who are forced to use their junior minister appointments sparingly, divisions from the party of the minister matter a great deal. If the minister typically deals with issues on which the government is relatively united, coalition partners are unlikely to appoint a shadow JM. The probability of such an appointment is about 20 percent. However, if the minister deals with issues that divide the government, the likelihood that coalition partners will appoint a shadow JM rises to between 70 percent and 80 percent.

In short, these results unambiguously support the argument made by Thies (2001) and strongly suggest that coalition parties make systematic use of junior ministers to confront the principal–agent problem facing them. Especially for smaller coalition parties, doing so presents tough choices: Because they are unable to monitor *all* of the ministers belonging to other parties, they must be strategic in their allocation of JMs. The data reveal that they prefer to assign this valuable

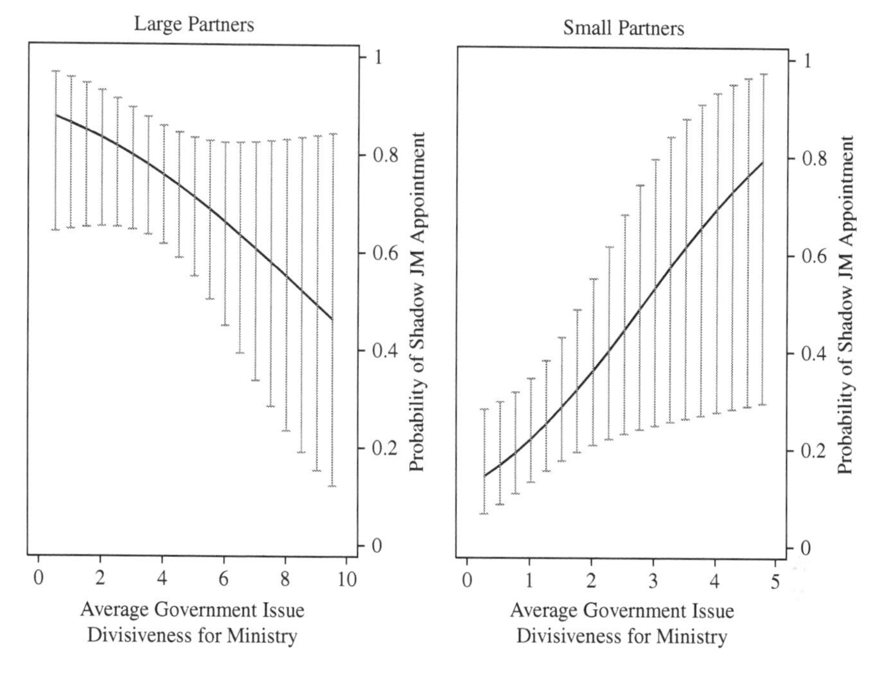

FIGURE 4.23 Coalition Issue Divisions and Appointment of Shadow JMs, by Partner Size

resource to ministries with jurisdiction over those issue areas that most sharply divide them from their coalition partners.

4.5 ADDITIONAL CONSIDERATIONS

In the empirical analysis to come, we take into account a number of additional variables that may be relevant in explaining the changes made to government bills. First, it is possible that the divisions that exist between the party of the proposing minister and its coalition partners also exist between the minister and parties in the opposition (i.e., the minister's party could hold an extreme position with respect to all parties in the legislature on the issues at hand, not just the parties in the coalition). To isolate the effect of intra-coalition policy differences on the legislative treatment of government bills, we must therefore also consider the policy preferences of the opposition. This also allows us to assess the empirical strength of previous comparative research, discussed in Chapter 3, that has highlighted the opportunities legislative institutions provide to opposition parties for exerting influence over policymaking, especially under minority government

(Strøm, 1990*b*; Döring, 1995; Powell, 2000; Müller and Strøm, 2000). If these arguments are correct, we would expect that divisions between opposition parties and the proposing minister may have a different effect on legislative scrutiny and amendment when a minority government is in power.[20] We therefore include a minority government indicator, as well as two variables (developed along the same lines as the government divisiveness variable) that measure the policy distance between parties in the opposition and the minister responsible for initiating the bill.

The first, which we refer to as *pivotal* opposition issue divisiveness, only takes into account the positions of opposition parties that we consider to be the "natural" majority-pivotal support parties for a minority government on the issues at hand. By this, we mean those opposition parties that, simultaneously, are the most likely among all opposition parties to support a minister's policy proposal *and* have the necessary votes, when combined with those of the government parties, to pass the bill. Operationally, we designate the opposition parties most likely to support a bill to be those closest to the minister in terms of their saliency-weighted distances on the issues dealt with by the bill. We calculate the sum of these saliency-weighted distances for every set of opposition parties in the legislature (in periods of minority government), and then, we choose the lowest summed score from the set of opposition parties that collectively have enough seats to give the government a legislative majority. The pivotal opposition divisiveness measure is the summed saliency-weighted, seat-weighted distances between the pivotal opposition parties and the proposing minister. This seems to us to be a reasonable conceptual measure of pivotal opposition parties and also fits with most accounts of how minority governments in our sample achieve legislative majorities—that is, by forging ad hoc (or issue-based) coalitions.[21] Our second variable, which we

[20] All Danish governments in the sample were minority governments except for the four-party Rasmussen I government. There were no minority governments in the Netherlands, Germany, or France. In Ireland, all governments were majority governments except for the Ahern I coalition between Fianna Fàil and the Progressive Democrats. However, this government accounted for a fair share of legislation, approximately 18 percent of legislation in the sample of bills from weak legislatures (see Table 4.1).

[21] For more on the propensity of Danish governments to rely on ad hoc coalitions, see the accounts of Damgaard (1992) and Strøm (1990*b*). Of course, in certain kinds of minority government situations, it might make more conceptual sense to count so-called *formal* support parties, who pledge at the time of government formation to support the minority government on major legislation and votes of (no-) confidence, as the "natural" support parties for a minority government. Such formal support occurs fairly often in Norway and Sweden (e.g., Strøm, 1990*b*). In Ireland, the ad hoc coalitions for the Ahern I government were actually made with independents rather than other parties. Fortunately, we were able to identify information on the ideological leanings of a sufficient number of independents to construct our measure of pivotal opposition divisiveness. Only three independents were necessary to give the government a majority, and all of these are commonly known as being part of Fianna Fáils "gene pool" of independent candidates: Niall Blaney, Mildred Fox, and Jackie Healy-Rae (*Irish Times*, "Fianna Fáil Star Continues to Rise," November 30, 2006; *Irish Times*, "Independents with a Chance

refer to as *non-pivotal* opposition divisiveness, is simply the sum of the saliency-weighted, seat-weighted distances between all non-pivotal opposition parties and the proposing minister on the issues at hand. Under majority government, all opposition parties are treated as non-pivotal since their support is not necessary to the government's majority, and under minority government, all opposition parties apart from the pivotal ones discussed above are treated as non-pivotal.

As we see from Table 4.1, proposed bills generally divide opposition legislators from a minister more so than they divide coalition partners from the minister. In strong legislatures, non-pivotal opposition parties, on average, are four times more divided from a minister than his coalition allies; in weak legislatures, they are three times more divided, on average, than coalition parties. Not surprisingly, pivotal opposition parties are significantly closer to the proposing minister on policy than non-pivotal opposition parties. In Denmark (the source of minority governments in our strong legislative systems), the pivotal opposition parties are only slightly farther away from the minister than his coalition allies, while in Ireland (the source of the one minority government in the weak legislative systems), they are actually closer. This reflects the fact (discussed in our most recent footnote) that the legislators on which this government relied were independents with positions corresponding to those of the dominant government party.

Another control variable we incorporate into the analyses is the number of standing committees to which a bill is referred. In strong legislatures, it is quite common for bills to be referred to more than one legislative committee. As shown in Table 4.1, two committees, on average, are assigned the task of reviewing a government bill. In weak legislatures, bills are commonly sent to only one standing committee and occasionally none. This was often the case in Ireland, where bills were commonly reviewed by the plenary (formally, a "Committee of the Whole House"). We control for multiple committee referral because the greater the number of committees reviewing a bill, the greater the number of legislators from a party who are able to scrutinize a minister's proposal, and the greater the likelihood that unacceptable ministerial drafts can be "caught" and modified.

Our analyses also take account of the amount of material and time legislators have to work with when they review a government bill. We use the number of subarticles in the draft version to account for the possibility that draft bills with many articles are likely to take longer to scrutinize and to have more articles changed than draft bills with few subarticles. As Table 4.1 shows, there is a notable difference in the size of bills across the two types of legislatures. Specifically, legislators in weaker parliaments are usually given larger bills to work with (though also fewer bills altogether). Further, in our analysis of the extensiveness of legislative changes to government bills, we include a measure of the time a bill spends in the legislative process (in days) and an indicator for whether a bill

Admit It Is Much Tougher This Time Round," May 19, 2007). We therefore use Fianna Fáil's position on the issues as a proxy for the positions of these legislators to construct the measure.

expires before the plenary vote.[22] Naturally, we expect to find that bills that have undergone more scrutiny, all else equal, will be changed more extensively than bills that have undergone less scrutiny, and that bills that have received a full review in the legislative process will be changed more extensively than bills that expired prematurely.

Finally, we include "fixed-effects" indicators for countries to account for the possibility that cross-national institutional and contextual differences may have an effect on the level of scrutiny and amendment even after we have taken account of coalition-specific differences such as issue divisions. We also include separate indicators for the particular issue area addressed by a bill to control for the possibility that bills dealing with certain types of issues may tend to be scrutinized and changed more or less extensively, regardless of the policy preferences of coalition partners. This could occur for a variety of reasons. For example, some types of issues are inherently more complex than others, thereby requiring greater informational resources from legislators to initiate changes. Moreover, outside lobby groups or advisory bodies are better organized in some policy areas than in others, and consequently, the information provided by these groups to legislators may make scrutinizing bills more or less difficult or may make proposing feasible changes to government bills more or less likely. We examine these effects in detail in the empirical analysis in Chapters 5 and 6.

4.6 CONCLUSION

The overview of legislative activity presented in this chapter demonstrates that coalition governments address a wide range of issues, and that there is significant variation in the degree to which these issues divide coalition partners. We have also presented some initial evidence that the dangers posed by such divisions have tangible effects. Coalition parties—especially if they are small, and therefore constrained in the number of junior ministers they can appoint—make careful use of their opportunities to "shadow" their coalition partners through "watchdogs" within ministries. But do parties make use of the legislative process to police the coalition bargain? And if so, is their ability to do so influenced in significant ways by the strength of legislative institutions?

[22] The first of these two variables is the dependent variable in the analysis of the length of legislative scrutiny and the second variable serves as an indicator for right-censoring in our survival model. This is discussed in more detail in the next chapter.

5

Strong Legislative Institutions and Multiparty Governance

In this chapter, we turn to an investigation of the legislative process in parliamentary systems with strong legislative institutions—that is, legislatures with procedures and committee systems that enable coalition partners to scrutinze ministers, and to change their proposals if necessary. We begin by reviewing the central hypotheses derived from our theory. We then move to a brief discussion of the statistical techniques we use to evaluate our hypotheses. Finally, we present findings from an analysis of legislation in Denmark, Germany, and the Netherlands.

5.1 POLICING IN STRONG LEGISLATURES

The central argument of Chapter 3 is that legislative institutions—under the right circumstances—can play a crucial role in equipping parties to confront the challenges of multiparty governance. Where parliaments, most importantly the committee systems, are "strong," coalition parties can take advantage of the legislative process to engage in meaningful monitoring of their coalition partners. This is true in at least two senses. First, strong committee systems generate opportunities to engage in *scrutiny*, that is, in gathering information about policy proposals and potential alternatives. Such information is crucial. Parties must know what the consequences of particular proposals are likely to be and—if these consequences are not acceptable—what policy options represent feasible substitutes. Strong legislative committees make it possible to engage in precisely such information gathering by encouraging the development of policy expertise along the jurisdictional lines of cabinet ministries, providing parties with opportunities to hold investigative hearings, meet with outside policy experts, access the information possessed by civil servants in the ministry, and so on.

Of course, the gathering of information—while clearly important—is not the entire story. A second central feature of strong institutions is that they make it possible for parties to *change* ministerial proposals if they are found to stray too far from an acceptable coalition compromise. The power to offer amendments that must be considered on the floor or even—as in the German Bundestag—for the committee version of the bill to become the floor agenda gives parties the opportunity to introduce changes to legislation and to reduce the power of ministers.

Naturally, the need to engage in monitoring and amendment is not constant across all issues. As the model we presented in Chapter 2 demonstrated, the principal–agent problem that arises between cabinet ministers and their coalition partners grows particularly pressing as the divisions within the coalition on the issues under consideration *increase*. It is precisely for highly divisive issues that ministers face incentives to deviate from agreed-upon compromises in ways that advantage their own party at the expense of their partners. Similarly, it is precisely on divisive issues that other parties are most likely to be hurt by ministerial drift. In short, as divisions within the coalition increase, the opportunities and incentives for ministerial drift grow, and consequently, the incentives for coalition partners to detect and counteract such drift intensify.

Thus, the central empirical implication of our argument is clear: As issues become more and more divisive for a coalition, parties should increasingly take advantage of the opportunities for scrutiny and amendment offered by strong committee systems. Legislative scrutiny can take many forms. Empirically, we focus on a proxy variable that can be reliably measured across policy areas, time, and countries: the amount of time a bill spends in the legislative process. As we discussed in Chapter 4, the activities that constitute parliamentary scrutiny (e.g., committee hearings, contact with outside experts and interest groups, etc.) require significant time. As a result, bills that are scrutinized more carefully will tend to spend more time in the legislative process than bills that are not subjected to close scrutiny. Thus, we expect that bills dealing with issues that divide the coalition are likely to experience greater delay in the legislative process than bills that do not divide them. Moreover, it is precisely on such divisive bills that ministers have strong incentives to deviate from coalition compromises. As a result, coalition partners will see the greatest need for amending a proposal to ensure that it reflects a collectively acceptable policy when the issue is divisive. As we also described in Chapter 4, we measure the extent of amendment in a bill by counting the number of (sub-)articles that were changed in the bill over the course of legislative review. In sum, if coalition parties use the legislative process to "keep tabs" on their partners, and to control ministerial drift, we should find support for the following expectation:

Hypothesis (Policing). *Under strong legislative institutions, greater policy divisions between coalition partners and the proposing minister on the issues addressed by a bill lead to greater policing of the minister in the legislative process.*

Recall from Chapter 3 that our concept of "policing" is quite strict. We require evidence that an increase in the level of policy divisions within the coalition leads *both* to greater scrutiny of ministers *and* to more extensive changes in the bills they propose before we are comfortable concluding that coalition partners use legislative institutions to solve the problems of multiparty governance. The hypothesis reflects our view that the legislative process provides an important forum in which parties can confront the tensions of coalition. However, the legislative process is only one possible institutional solution to this dilemma. Parties can make use of other mechanisms, including cabinet-level institutions, to police the coalition bargain. For our purposes, one of these mechanisms is particularly important—the use of *junior ministers*.[1] As Thies (2001) has argued convincingly, coalition partners can make use of junior ministers (JMs) to "shadow" hostile ministers. Moreover, the argument presented in Chapter 2 implies that parties have particularly strong incentives to use JMs in this way in issue areas in which the preferences of the coalition partners diverge significantly. As we demonstrated in Chapter 4, our data provide clear support for this expectation. Shadow JMs are more likely to be appointed to those ministries that introduce bills that are highly divisive for the coalition.

The availability of other institutional solutions to the "coalition dilemma" introduces potential complications into our argument regarding the importance of the legislative process as a policing mechanism. The general theoretical argument presented in Chapter 2—which provides the basis for our empirical expectations—is agnostic with respect to the precise nature of the institutional mechanism that allows coalition partners to engage in scrutiny and change. The argument simply implies that *whatever* the mechanism, it will be used more extensively as policy divisions within the coalition increase. The presence of alternative monitoring institutions therefore modifies our expectations regarding the legislative process. Consider the need to procure information about ministerial proposals and feasible alternatives. A shadow JM placed inside the department responsible for drafting a proposal is in a position to provide her party with detailed information about the drafting process, including information about the anticipated consequences of the proposal and feasible alternatives. That is, where a shadow JM is available, parties need to rely *less* on legislative committees to provide the information required to effectively scrutinize and critique a ministerial

[1] We have also pointed out that there are other important cabinet-level institutions, such as cabinet committees, inner cabinets, and coalition committees that can serve the purpose of monitoring coalition partners (Müller and Strøm, 2000; Strøm *et al.*, 2008). There are two primary reasons for not focusing on these other mechanisms in the current context. First, they are difficult to measure across cabinets and countries, especially because many of them are established informally. More importantly for the current analysis, it is difficult to link these institutions to particular legislative proposals. In contrast, the presence of "shadow" JMs can be reliably measured across time and across countries, and they can be linked to specific legislative proposals via the ministries from which these proposals emanate.

draft. Junior ministers can serve as *substitutes* for strong legislative committees as monitoring devices. Moreover, just as we would expect a coalition partner's legislative party groups to engage in more monitoring as divisions between it and the party of the minister increase, we would expect the monitoring activities of shadow JMs to increase.

This suggests an interactive effect of cabinet-level and parliamentary institutions on legislative scrutiny. As the monitoring activities of the shadow JM increase because of greater divisions, the activities of the partner's legislative party groups should *decrease* (as the JM, who "moves" before the legislative stage, can serve as a substitute for parliamentary scrutiny). Indeed, the presence of a shadow JM may even completely eliminate the need for information-gathering at the legislative stage if the JM can provide her party group with sufficient "inside" knowledge. As a result, the unconditional expectation we expressed in Hypothesis 1 requires a qualification: The impact of coalition policy divisions on legislative scrutiny will be *suppressed*, or even completely eliminated, by the presence of a JM.

While shadow JMs are in a good position to provide relevant policy information, they probably encounter greater difficulty in serving a substitute function in *amending* ministerial proposals. Recall that our argument places primary emphasis on the *position-taking* incentives of political parties in coalition governments. In order to distinguish themselves from their coalition partners, and to convince their support base that the party is vigorously advancing the base's interests, party leaders face constant pressure to find opportunities to engage in "policy-signaling." The introduction of legislative proposals presents an especially important opportunity to do so. Even if a minister recognizes that a particular proposal will need to be amended to accommodate the interests of coalition partners before it is accepted, he faces incentives to introduce the bill in the form favored by constituents rather than preemptively accommodating his partner's concerns. In short, policy-signaling incentives lead to the expectation that we will not observe the same "substitution effects" when we consider the degree to which parties use the legislative process to amend the bills emanating from hostile ministries. Our expectations concerning the interactions between shadow JMs and strong legislative institutions are captured in the following hypothesis:

Hypothesis (Shadow Junior Minister). *Compared to bills that are drafted without the participation of a shadow junior minister, when a bill is drafted by a ministry that contains a shadow JM, greater policy divisions between coalition partners and the proposing minister:*

- *should lead to a less dramatic, or even no, increase in the length of time a bill spends in the legislative process,*
- *should lead to a similar number of changes made to the bill.*

5.2 THE IMPACT OF THE OPPOSITION

As discussed in Chapter 4, a rich tradition in political science has called attention to the opportunities for policy influence that the legislative process—especially in the presence of strong committee systems—affords to parties that are in opposition. Most prominently, Kaare Strøm's work on minority governments highlights the connection between the opposition's ability to influence policy, and the likelihood that (some) parties will choose not to enter government. As Strøm (1990*b*: 70) points out:

> The predicament of the opposition depends on a number of factors. Among these are the internal structure and procedures of the legislature, as well as its role in the larger political system. Internally, a strong and decentralized committee structure offers much better prospects for oppositional influence than the more centralized and less deliberative mode of decision making traditionally found in such parliaments as the British House of Commons. The greater the potential influence of the opposition, then, the lower the relative benefit of governing, and the higher the probability of minority governments.

To measure the influence of opposition parties in a political system, Strøm constructs an index of the strength of parliamentary committees that focuses on some of the same features that we have identified as components of a strong committee system—most importantly, standing committees that correspond to ministerial jurisdictions. His analysis of government formation suggests that the potential for opposition influence as measured by the strength of legislative committees has a significant and positive effect on the likelihood that minority governments will form. Similarly, in his seminal analysis of the connection between electoral systems and the representativeness of legislatures, Powell (2000: 32–3), taking Strøm's work as a point of departure, argues that strong legislative committees facilitate opposition influence.

The possibility that opposition parties can make use of strong committee systems to exercise influence does not, of course, conflict with the argument that these same committee systems provide coalition parties with an institutional mechanism to "keep tabs" on their partners. If an institutional structure makes legislative influence possible, then legislators of all stripes (and parties) may be able to take advantage of it to advance their goals. In this sense, the analysis of Strøm and Powell is orthogonal to the claims that we are attempting to assess. However, these arguments suggest that we need to control for, and explore, another factor that might have a significant impact on the duration of the legislative process and the extent to which government bills are amended. If these conventional views are correct, then as the bill under consideration becomes more divergent from the preferences of opposition parties, we should expect that these parties will be able to delay and even force changes to the bill.

Such opposition influence should be particularly evident for "pivotal" opposition parties in situations of minority government. Minority governments are, by definition, dependent on the support of *some* opposition parties to advance their legislative agenda. From the coalition's point of view, the most attractive parties for such a "support" role are those parties that are ideologically most compatible with the coalition on the issues at hand. In other words, we would expect that under minority government, those opposition parties most likely to be influential are the opposition parties that are closest to the position of the minister and whose support lifts the coalition above the 50 percent threshold required for passing legislation. As we discussed in Chapter 4, we identify these parties as the "pivotal" opposition parties. All other parties (including all opposition parties in situations of majority government) we treat as "non-pivotal" opposition parties. In short, one lesson from the work of Strøm and Powell is that the preferences of opposition parties may play an important role in understanding the dynamics of legislative politics, especially when those parties play a pivotal supporting role in periods of minority government. We investigate this possibility by including measures of the divisiveness of the issues under consideration from the point of view of pivotal and non-pivotal opposition parties.

5.3 ANALYSIS AND FINDINGS

On September 2, 1999, the Social Democratic/Green coalition in Germany introduced a draft bill entitled, "Law for the Continuation of Environmental Tax Reform," in the Bundestag. The purpose of the bill—as stated in the cabinet letter accompanying the proposal—was to continue tax reforms that the coalition had begun after taking office in 1998 in an effort to "create lasting redirection of consumer demand towards energy- and resource-efficient products, and to provide incentives for the development of environmentally-friendly technology and production methods."[2] In other words, although technically a tax bill—and therefore drafted by the Ministry of Finance—the bill was, at its core, designed to use the tools of the tax code to promote a specific environmental policy.

[2] The German legislative process requires government bills to be submitted to the Bundesrat for comment before they can be introduced in the Bundestag. This bill was submitted to the Bundesrat on August 27, 1999 (Document No. 474/99). As we discussed in the last chapter, to speed up the legislative process, German cabinets often circumvent this requirement by having the coalition parties in the Bundestag introduce the same bill in parallel to the Bundesrat process. This is what happened in the current case. The bill was introduced by the SPD/Green party factions on September 2 (Document BT 14/1524), and committee deliberations began. When the Bundesrat comments were received at the end of September, the cabinet officially "introduced" the bill in the Bundestag on September 29 (Document BT 14/1668), and the government bill "replaced" the party-introduced bill. The quote in the text is taken from the cabinet letter accompanying the bill at the end of September.

At the time, environmental policy was a hotly contested issue within the Social Democratic/Green coalition. While both parties were sympathetic to some increased regulation to protect the environment, the SPD—with a broader constituency, including connections to industry and labor—was keenly aware of the trade-offs involved in environmental policies that had the potential to hurt German economic competitiveness or affect employment. The Greens, facing a constituency that placed high value on ecological protection, were eager to engage in more aggressive environmental policy. It is not surprising that the "Eco-Tax" caused considerable tension. The Greens—who did not have a JM placed in the Ministry of Finance at the time—had good reason to be skeptical of a bill drafted by Minister Hans Eichel, a Social Democrat suspected—like Chancellor Schröder—to be sensitive to the interests of business.[3] Was the draft bill as aggressive as the Greens might hope in pursuing environmental goals, and did it accurately reflect coalition agreements?

Not surprisingly, the proposal was subjected to intense scrutiny in parliament. After its introduction, the bill was referred to twelve committees, with the Finance Committee playing the lead role. In addition to eleven committee meetings by other committees, the Finance Committee held four committee meetings (September 9, October 27, November 3, and November 5) as well as a public hearing (October 4). During the public hearing, seven expert witnesses testified, and fifty-one interest groups and organizations provided input for committee deliberations. Although the original bill was relatively short—thirteen articles on barely six pages—these deliberations, which took more than two months, resulted in a substantial re-drafting of the bill. By the time the bill emerged from committee, nine of the original articles had been amended, and three more articles had been added.

More importantly, the report issued by the Finance Committee—as well as contemporary news coverage—provides a telling account of the changes adopted by the committee. All proposals for change introduced by the opposition parties—most notably, the Christian Democrats and the Free Democrats—were rejected. Instead, the changes that were incorporated emerged from within the coalition. While the report does not attribute amendments to individual parties and simply states that they were agreed to by "the coalition parties," the nature of the changes strongly suggests that the committee version of the bill was moved considerably in a direction favored by the Greens and away from the preferences of the Social Democratic minister who had drafted the bill. Most importantly, the final version of the bill provided significant tax exemptions for highly efficient natural-gas power plants—a policy that the Greens had long favored, and that had been hinted at obliquely in the coalition agreement signed by the SPD and Greens in 1998.[4]

[3] See "Hans Eichel, Stodgy but Safe," in *The Economist*, March 20, 1999.

[4] Specifically, in discussing the planned environmental tax reform, the coalition contract stated that the partners "will create incentives for the production of electricity in highly-efficient power plants"

Indeed, the addition of this provision was so controversial from the perspective of the Social Democrats (who viewed it as a direct threat to the competitiveness of the coal industry) that prominent SPD politicians, including the premiers of two Länder highly dependent on coal production (North-Rhine Westphalia and Saxony), openly denounced the agreement and engaged in a last-minute effort to block the bill. Nevertheless, the proposal was passed by the Bundestag with all committee changes in place in a roll call vote on November 11, 1999.

This vignette is suggestive. A bill dealing with an issue that is divisive within the coalition is subjected to intense parliamentary scrutiny. Attempts by opposition parties to shape the content of the bill are systematically defeated by the coalition majority. The changes that are introduced as a result of the committee deliberations are proposed by the coalition parties, and passed without the votes of the opposition. Moreover, a plausible case can be made that the bill is amended in ways that better reflect the coalition compromise, and that move policy from the position of the minister toward the position of the coalition partner. At least in the example, therefore, strong parliamentary institutions appear to benefit *coalition* parties—especially those that do *not* control the ministry proposing the bill. The influence of the opposition appears to be muted at best. But how typical is this example? Is it representative of more systematic trends in the parliamentary treatment of government legislation? To answer these questions, we turn to a statistical analysis of more than 1,000 government bills in the three strong legislatures in our study.

5.3.1 *Statistical Techniques*

We begin our analysis by describing the statistical techniques we employ here and in the next chapter, and then discuss our strategy for assessing the substantive importance of the findings. To examine the length of legislative deliberations, we employ survival analysis (also known as event history or duration analysis), the usage of which has become increasingly common in political science research over the past two decades.[5] Survival models are appropriate when the variable of interest is the amount of time that a unit (for us, a government bill) spends in a particular state (e.g., legislative deliberations) before it transitions out of that state.[6] The primary quantity of interest in survival analysis is the *hazard*

(p. 16). While this language is not restricted to natural gas powered plants, traditional coal-powered plants were incapable of achieving the efficiency standards incorporated into the bill for natural gas plants to receive favorable tax status.

[5] Box-Steffensmeier and Jones (2004) provide a very lucid guide to event history modeling. For some applications in comparative politics, see King *et al.* (1990), Warwick (1994), Diermeier and Stevenson (2000), Martin and Vanberg (2003), and Martin and Vanberg (2004).

[6] As we pointed out in the previous chapter, almost all government bills in our data "transitioned out" of the legislative process by being passed (albeit most in amended form). Recall that a few bills,

rate, which is defined as the probability that an event (such as the passage of a bill) will occur at a particular point in time, given that it has not yet occurred. The hazard rate has two components. The first is a set of covariates, or independent variables, that are believed to have some systematic impact on the timing of an event. The second component is an underlying baseline hazard function that represents how the rate of event occurrence changes with respect to time, conditional on the covariates included in the model. One of the major issues involved in choosing among the wide variety of survival models that are available concerns how to parameterize the baseline hazard rate, or equivalently, how to specify the distributional form of time dependence.[7] Deciding on how to address this issue is important because an incorrect parameterization of the baseline hazard rate can lead to inconsistent coefficient estimates and incorrect standard errors.

There are two general approaches we could take to address this issue. The first is to use a model that leaves the distributional form of time dependence unspecified. The most popular model of this type is the semi-parametric Cox model, which makes no assumptions about the shape of the distribution of the baseline hazard rate. It assumes only that the hazard rate for any observation, whatever the distribution of the baseline hazard, is proportional over time. Thus, the key advantage of the Cox model is that the estimates of the covariates do not depend on a distributional assumption that might turn out to be incorrect. There are also two notable disadvantages to this model. First, if it were possible to specify the correct distributional assumption in a fully parametric model, this model would produce more precise estimates than the Cox model—that is, the Cox model would be inefficient relative to the parametric alternative (Collett, 1994). Second, because the Cox model only models the hazard rate, not duration times, it is not possible to use the estimates from this model to generate predictions about how long government bills spend in the legislative process.

The second approach is to use a fully parametric model that specifies the distributional form of time dependence. The key advantages of a parametric model are that it may yield efficiency gains relative to a semi-parametric model and that it allows predictions about the length of legislative scrutiny. The major

however, prematurely "died" before they made it to the voting stage because of the expiration of the parliamentary session, while a few others we treat as though they had died because there was a change in government while the bills were still under consideration. In the language of survival analysis, all these bills are "right-censored"—that is, the length of time they spent in the legislative process was observed only up to a point. One nice feature of survival models is that the estimates of the independent variables and standard errors they produce are adjusted to take into account the fact that we have only limited information on the length of deliberation for these observations.

[7] Because time dependence (also called duration dependence) is conditional on the specification of the systematic component of the model, it is perhaps best thought of as a statistical "nuisance" (Box-Steffensmeier and Jones, 2004: 21–2), that is, something that represents model misspecification rather than a "true" dependency of observed durations on time.

disadvantage is that, if the posited distributional form is incorrect, it is possible to draw mistaken inferences about the effects of the covariates.

With this trade-off in mind, we believe the most prudent route is to estimate the semi-parametric Cox model and a wide array of fully parametric models (each of which makes different distributional assumptions about time dependence) and then choose the model that provides the most accurate representation of the data in our study. As we would like to preserve the ability to make predictions about the length of legislative scrutiny a bill will undergo, and since we obviously would desire a more efficient model to a less efficient one, our preference is to find an appropriate parametric specification *if* such a specification does not result in estimates of the covariates that diverge substantially from those of the semi-parametric approach. For interested readers, we provide the results of our model comparisons in the Appendix to this chapter. There, we also discuss the problem of unobserved heterogeneity in our data and our solution for dealing with it. The final model we settle on is a log-logistic shared gamma frailty model, a parametric non-proportional hazards model that can account for unobserved heterogeneity. As we show, the covariate estimates from this model are virtually identical to those from the Cox model, while the standard errors are generally smaller (i.e., our chosen parametric model is more efficient than the Cox model). Most importantly, our parametric model provides a substantially better fit to the data.

To examine the extent of changes made to government bills in the legislative process, we employ an event count model. Event count models have become the standard approach in political science applications where the variable of interest is the number of events that occur over a particular period of time. In most event count formulations, the primary quantity of interest is the rate of event occurrence, or *incidence rate*, over an observation period, which has a systematic component that is usually expressed as an exponential function of a set of covariates. The stochastic component is most often assumed to follow the Poisson distribution, which implies that the events accumulating during the observation period are conditionally independent and that the rate of event occurrence is homogenous across a given time period. These are strong assumptions that are probably violated in our case. In particular, we expect that once party groups have expended the legislative resources to make one substantive change to a draft bill, it is marginally less costly to make several more changes. If this is the case, then the number of changes will exhibit *positive contagion*. This results in overdispersion in the observed number of events, and consequently, standard errors that are biased downward (King, 1989). The general solution for problems of heterogeneity and positive contagion in event count models is to assume that the stochastic component of the count process follows the negative binomial distribution, which allows the incidence rate to vary across an observation period. For the analysis in this chapter and the next, we therefore use the negative binomial model to examine the changes made to government bills.

5.3.2 Legislative Scrutiny

We begin with an analysis of the length of legislative deliberations—our proxy for the level of scrutiny to which a bill is subjected. Table 5.1 reports the results from our analysis of the length of legislative review.[8] Note that coefficient estimates in the table reflect their effects on the (logged) length of legislative review. Thus, a positive coefficient indicates that an increase in the value of a covariate for a given bill leads to a lengthier period of review for the bill in the legislative process.

The most important feature we are interested in concerns the impact of government issue divisiveness on the length of legislative review. We expect that this effect depends on whether a coalition partner has a JM in the department of a hostile minister. If the coalition partner does not control a shadow JM, then as the partner party becomes more divided from the party of the proposing minister on the issues addressed in a bill, the bill should receive a greater amount of parliamentary scrutiny. The partner is taking advantage of the resources associated with a strong committee system to become informed about the minister's proposal, and potential alternatives to it. If the coalition partner does control a shadow JM, however, there is less need to scrutinize legislation at the committee stage. The task of gathering information, and passing this information on to party leaders, can be performed prior to bill introduction by the shadow JM, and party groups need not rely on legislative committees to do so. As a result, the effect of coalition issue divisiveness should be suppressed in the presence of a shadow JM.

The results in Table 5.1 support our expectations.[9] As shown by the estimate on *Government Issue Divisiveness*, if a bill is proposed by a minister who is not constrained by the watchful eye of a shadow JM, the bill is expected to spend an increasingly long time in the legislative process the greater the divisiveness of the issues addressed in the bill. This finding is clearly consistent with the notion that when partners are unable to draw on "inside information" coming out of a ministry, they rely on parliamentary inquiry to review draft proposals to mitigate the risk of ministerial drift.

The data tell a dramatically different story when a JM is present.[10] In the presence of a shadow JM, the coefficient on *Government Issue Divisiveness*

[8] There are more observations in Table 5.1 than in Table 5.2 (where we present our analysis of legislative amendments) because of the presence of a few "split" bills in the sample. Bills that were split at the committee stage were divided into components that were passed at different times in the legislative process. Rather than lose information on the scrutiny of these split bills (by using their average time in the process, for example), we treat them as separate units in the analysis.

[9] Estimates for the shape parameter and frailty variance are shown in the Appendix to this chapter.

[10] Because junior minister posts do not exist in Denmark, and because we include country indicators in the model, the coefficients on the shadow JM variable and the JM–divisiveness interaction (in this table and the next) necessarily indicate the effects of these variables *only* in junior minister systems (i.e., Germany and the Netherlands).

TABLE 5.1 Length of Legislative Review, Strong Committee Systems

Variables	Estimates
Government Issue Divisiveness	0.075**
	(0.032)
Government Issue Divisiveness × Shadow JM	−0.107**
	(0.048)
Shadow JM	−0.286
	(0.181)
Non-Pivotal Opposition Issue Divisiveness	−0.013
	(0.020)
Pivotal Opposition Issue Divisiveness	−0.012
	(0.022)
Minority Government	−0.028
	(0.165)
Number of Committee Referrals	0.018
	(0.021)
Number of Subarticles in Draft Bill (Logged)	0.201***
	(0.027)
Germany	0.122
	(0.175)
The Netherlands	1.158***
	(0.200)
Industry and Markets Policy	0.458***
	(0.092)
Social Policy	1.290***
	(0.199)
Regional Policy	0.506***
	(0.186)
Environmental Policy	0.379***
	(0.110)
Intercept	3.318***
	(0.237)

Log-logistic shared frailty model. $N = 1128$. Significance levels: *, 10%; **, 5%; ***, 1%.

is given by the combination of the original coefficient and the coefficient on the interaction term: $0.075 - 0.107 = -0.032$, which is not statistically different from zero at conventional levels ($p > 0.40$). In other words, an increase in policy divisions within the coalition results in no additional amount of scrutiny when coalition partners control a shadow JM.

The coefficient on the interaction term also shows that the degree to which the presence of a shadow JM suppresses the level of legislative scrutiny of a proposal grows as divisiveness within the coalition on the proposal increases. For every standard deviation increase in government issue divisions for a bill, the amount of time the bill spends in the legislature falls by about 20 percent if coalition partners have a shadow JM in the ministry.[11] This suggests that JMs work much harder gathering information on legislation that greatly divides their party from the party of the proposing minister.

To develop a better sense of the magnitude of these effects, we examine their impact on the expected length of legislative review more directly. The conventional way to do this would be simply to use the coefficient estimates to predict the length of legislative review for certain values of the covariates, and then compare across predictions. However, in generating these predictions, we would only be making use of the coefficient point estimates. We would be ignoring the uncertainty surrounding the estimates (reflected in the standard errors). This obscures information concerning the variable nature of our predictions and thus our level of confidence in the comparisons we make.

Consequently, we use a slightly different strategy. Because we would like our illustration of substantive effects to reflect not only the coefficient estimates themselves but also the level of uncertainty associated with them, we employ statistical simulations that allow us to incorporate both pieces of information. To perform the simulations, we first draw 1,000 simulated values of the main and ancillary parameters of our model from a multivariate normal distribution (where the mean is equal to the vector of parameter estimates and the variance is equal to the estimated variance–covariance matrix). Next, we use the simulated parameters to produce 1,000 expected values for the length of legislative scrutiny of a hypothetical bill under various scenarios.[12]

In systems where JM posts exist—which, in our set of strong legislatures, are Germany and the Netherlands—we consider four scenarios. These are defined by whether the hypothetical bill deals with relatively non-divisive issues or with relatively contentious ones, and by whether the hypothetical bill comes from a ministry where the coalition partner controls a shadow JM (we refer to such a party as a "shadow partner") or one where it does not (we refer to this type of party as a "common partner").[13] In Denmark, a system where JM posts do not exist, we examine only two scenarios: one in which the hypothetical bill deals

[11] This is simply the product of the time ratio of the interaction coefficient (i.e., its inverse log) and the standard deviation of government issue divisiveness.

[12] We produced the simulated parameter estimates with the simulation utility in Clarify (King *et al.*, 2000), but because the prediction utility in Clarify does not support some of the models in our study (including the log-logistic shared frailty model in Table 5.1), we use software we have written to generate expected values for all the models in this chapter and the next.

[13] We define a bill dealing with issues of "low divisiveness" as one with a value of *Government Issue Divisiveness* that is in the lower 10 percent of the sample of bills from our full set of legislatures, and a bill dealing with issues of "high divisiveness" as one with a value in the upper 10 percent of bills. The difference between the two values is roughly two standard deviations.

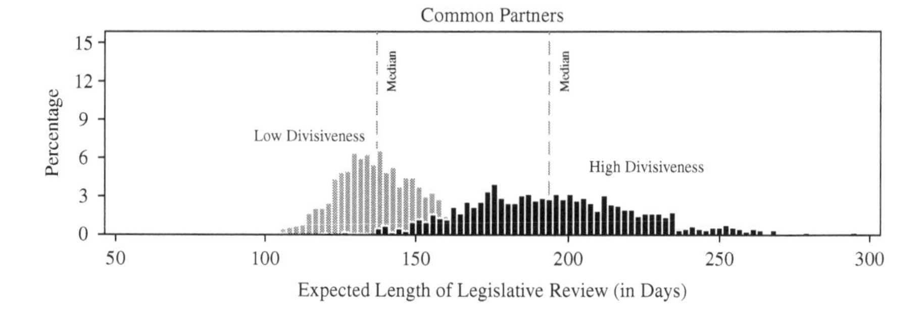

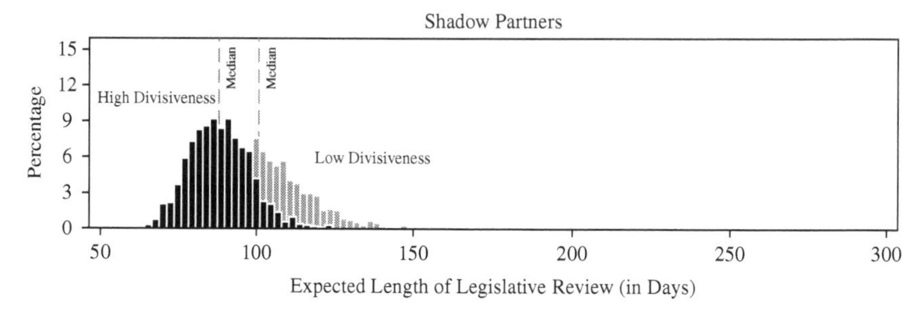

FIGURE 5.1 Government Issue Divisiveness and Legislative Scrutiny in Junior Minister Systems: Strong Legislatures

Note: All other covariates set at their mean sample values for junior minister systems.

with issues that divide coalition partners and one in which the bill deals with issues that are relatively noncontroversial.[14]

We begin with our findings from the two JM systems, which we present in Figure 5.1. For each of the four hypothetical scenarios described above, this figure shows the *frequency distribution* of simulated values of the expected length of legislative scrutiny of a government bill. To facilitate our comparisons across scenarios, we have drawn dashed reference lines indicating the central tendency of each distribution. Specifically, the lines indicate the *median number of days* each hypothetical bill is expected to spend in the legislative process. The shape of each distribution conveys information about the certainty of our inferential comparisons—a distribution tightly centered around its median reference line indicates a relatively high degree of certainty in our expectations, while a "flat" distribution indicates relatively less certainty.

We first consider the impact of issue divisiveness on legislative scrutiny for common partners in these systems, shown in the top pane of the figure. We see immediately that as issue divisiveness increases for a bill in this scenario, so too does the amount of time the bill is expected to spend in the legislative process. The

[14] For each figure in this chapter and the next, we hold all other variables at their mean sample values, where the sample is defined by the type of system or situation being examined in the figure.

median predicted review time for a relatively non-divisive bill is approximately 137 days, compared to almost 194 days for a relatively divisive bill, a difference of roughly two months. Put another way, when a coalition partner has no shadow JM placed in the proposing ministry, bills that severely divide them from the proposing minister are expected to spend about 40 percent longer in the legislative process than bills that do not divide them.[15]

In contrast, we see that when coalition partners have a JM who can effectively "keep tabs" on the proposing minister, increasing divisiveness has virtually no impact on the length of legislative scrutiny. The median predicted review times for divisive and non-divisive bills are virtually the same, 87 days versus 101 days, respectively, a small difference that is not statistically significant.[16] The figure also demonstrates that as divisiveness grows, the suppressive impact of shadow JMs on legislative scrutiny becomes more pronounced. For example, on a non-divisive bill, when coalition partners can rely on a shadow JM to gather information, the bill is expected to spend about a month less in the legislature than when they do not control a JM (a reduction in review time of roughly 25 percent).[17] The effect is clearly much more pronounced when a bill is highly divisive. In this case, having a shadow JM cuts the amount of legislative review time in more than half, from a median expected time of 194 days to 87 days, a period of more than three months.

In Figure 5.2, we present our findings for the non-junior-minister system in Denmark, where coalition partners do not enjoy the luxury of having a shadow JM to gather policy information. One important point to note when comparing this figure to the previous one is that bills in Denmark, on average, take much less

[15] The distribution of expected values for highly divisive bills in this scenario is relatively flat, which owes primarily to the fact that in junior minister systems, very few highly divisive bills come from ministries without a shadow JM (recall our analysis in Chapter 4). In Germany and the Netherlands, fewer than 5 percent of bills reviewed by common partners have issue divisiveness scores greater than the average issue divisiveness score for bills reviewed by shadow partners. Thus, we have relatively less information available to us to make inferences about expected review times for highly divisive bills in this scenario. Even so, the figure shows that we can be quite confident that the difference in median predicted review times for divisive and non-divisive bills for common partners is statistically different from zero. A mere 0.8 percent of expected review times for highly divisive bills are less than or equal to the median predicted review time for non-divisive bills, while no expected review times for non-divisive bills are greater than or equal to the median predicted review time for divisive bills.

[16] The lack of statistical significance between these expected times is reflected visually in the high degree of overlap between the two distributions. Approximately 10 percent of the predicted review times for highly divisive bills in the shadow partner scenario are greater than or equal to the median predicted time for non-divisive bills; similarly, 15 percent of the predicted review times for non-divisive bills are less than or equal to the median predicted time for highly divisive bills.

[17] This is a statistically significant difference: Only 1.1 percent of expected review times for "low divisiveness" bills in the shadow partner scenario are greater than or equal to the median expected review time for such bills in the common partner scenario, while 0.2 percent of expected review times for "low divisiveness" bills in the common partner scenario are less than or equal to the median review time of such bills in the shadow partner scenario.

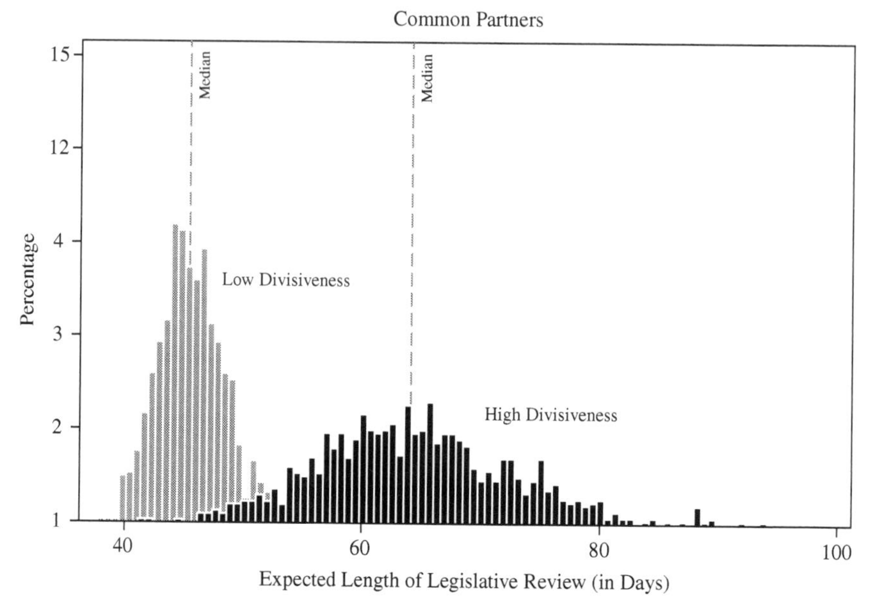

FIGURE 5.2 Government Issue Divisiveness and Legislative Scrutiny in Non-Junior-Minister Systems: Strong Legislatures

Note: All other covariates set at their mean sample values for non-junior-minister systems.

time to review than bills in the Netherlands and Germany. This is not necessarily indicative of less scrutiny, however. First, as we showed in Chapter 4, about three-quarters of bills in Denmark deal with tax and welfare policy, which (as the results from Table 5.1 indicate) take less time to consider than bills dealing with any other type of issue, holding country-specific differences constant. Moreover, Danish governments tend to introduce bills that are limited in scope, and often "split" policy changes that would be accomplished in perhaps only one bill in the Netherlands or Germany across several bills. This accounts for the high number of bills in Denmark relative to the other countries, as well as for the shorter average length of these bills (13 subarticles per bill versus 23 and 50 subarticles per bill in Germany and the Netherlands, respectively).[18] On a per-subarticle basis, Danish bills consume an average of eleven days in the legislature, which is less than Dutch bills (29 days per article), but actually more than German bills (7 days per article).

This matter aside, Figure 5.2 paints very much the same picture as Figure 5.1. There is a clear relationship between how long Danish bills are expected to spend

[18] The coefficient on bill size indicates that for every additional log-increase in the number of subarticles (i.e., for every 2.72 additional subarticles), a bill spends over 20 percent longer in the legislative process.

in the legislature and how divisive these bills are for the coalition. A typical Danish bill dealing with non-divisive issues has a median expected review time of forty-five days in the Folketing, while a bill dealing with highly divisive issues is expected to undergo sixty-four days of review, a difference of approximately 42 percent.

These findings strongly support our central argument. In strong committee systems, coalition partners engage in more legislative scrutiny the greater the potential for ministerial drift. This is particularly true when they do not control a JM in the relevant ministry, and thus have limited opportunities for gathering information at the cabinet or department level. Of course, scrutiny is only part of the story. Just because coalition partners spend more time reviewing a bill does not necessarily imply that they will find evidence that ministers have reneged on the coalition bargain. And even if they do, they may not be able to come up with feasible alternatives or be in a position to modify the proposal by forcing changes. To assess whether strong committees also provide coalition partners an opportunity to engage in meaningful amendment, we turn to an investigation of the changes that bills undergo as they increasingly divide coalition partners from the proposing minister.

5.3.3 Amendment of Ministerial Proposals

We expect that an increase in divisions between coalition partners will lead to more extensive changes to government bills in the legislature. Moreover, in contrast to the "substitution effect" of shadow JMs with respect to legislative scrutiny, the relationship between increasing divisions and increasing change should hold *regardless* of whether coalition partners control a shadow JM. The reason for this contrast is that—even if they do not expect to see their draft bill adopted—ministers are motivated by the policy-signaling benefits of bill introduction and should therefore not adjust a bill preemptively even if they are monitored by a partner's JM. As a result, we expect that divisive bills will be amended at roughly the same rate independent of whether the information necessary to do so comes primarily from a shadow JM or a parliamentary committee.

The findings in Table 5.2 bear out these expectations. A positive coefficient indicates that an increase in the value of a covariate leads to a greater number of changes in a bill, while a negative coefficient indicates a decrease in the number of changes.[19] As the results show, as the issue divisions between coalition partners and the proposing minister grow larger, the bill is likely to be changed more extensively in the legislative process. Further, as revealed by the coefficient estimate and standard error on the interaction between coalition issue divisiveness and the

[19] The dispersion parameter is not presented in the table, but it indicates substantial overdispersion in the number of changes made to bills.

TABLE 5.2 Extent of Legislative Alterations, Strong Committee Systems

Variables	Estimates
Government Issue Divisiveness	0.072**
	(0.036)
Government Issue Divisiveness × Shadow JM	0.067
	(0.052)
Shadow JM	−0.155
	(0.183)
Non-Pivotal Opposition Issue Divisiveness	−0.032
	(0.020)
Pivotal Opposition Issue Divisiveness	0.008
	(0.023)
Minority Government	−0.203
	(0.198)
Number of Committee Referrals	0.036
	(0.026)
Number of Subarticles in Draft Bill (Logged)	0.966***
	(0.034)
Expiration of Bill before Plenary Vote	−1.298***
	(0.171)
Length of Legislative Review	0.002***
	(0.000)
Germany	0.515**
	(0.208)
The Netherlands	−0.150
	(0.233)
Industry and Markets Policy	−0.438***
	(0.111)
Social Policy	−0.266
	(0.225)
Regional Policy	−0.202
	(0.223)
Environmental Policy	−0.142
	(0.129)
Intercept	−1.280***
	(0.278)

Negative binomial model. $N = 1109$. Significance levels: *, 10%; **, 5%; ***, 1%.

shadow JM indicator, this is the case regardless of whether a coalition partner has a JM placed in the proposing ministry. The coefficient on *Government Issue Divisiveness* when a coalition partner controls a JM is $0.072 + 0.067 = 0.139$. This is statistically significant from zero at $p < 0.01$, but not significantly different from the estimated coefficient when the coalition partner has no shadow JM available.

This is an important finding. As we argued in Chapters 2 and 3, there are good reasons to suspect that cabinet-level institutions on their own—particularly JMs—are insufficient for controlling ministerial discretion. The position-taking incentives confronting ministers imply that they will often have good reason not to adjust their proposals preemptively (i.e., before bill introduction), even if they expect that a draft bill will ultimately be amended as it winds its way through the policymaking process. The effect we observe in our data is clearly consistent with this dynamic. If shadow JMs could serve as effective substitutes for legislative committees in amending ministerial proposals, we should observe this "substitution effect" at the legislative stage. The impact of divisions on change should be suppressed or even absent when a shadow JM is placed in the ministry, since the necessary changes would have already been made before the introduction of the proposal to parliament. In other words, we should see the same relationship between coalition divisiveness and amendments that we saw in the relationship between divisiveness and the length of legislative scrutiny. Clearly, this is *not* what we observe—bills originating in ministries that are "shadowed" by a partner's JM are just as heavily amended in the legislative process as bills that are not.[20]

We illustrate these findings in Figure 5.3, focusing again on the two JM systems of Germany and the Netherlands. Analogous to the previous figures, this graph displays the simulated distributions of the expected number of changes made to divisive and non-divisive bills, for both common partners and shadow partners. The figure suggests several interesting points. First, it is immediately clear that an increase in the issue divisiveness of a bill for the government leads to more extensive amendment of the bill in the legislative process. For common partners, the median number of expected changes made to a non-divisive bill is ten articles (for a bill of average size in these systems, thirty-five articles). For divisive bills, the median number of expected changes rises to fourteen articles—an increase of 40 percent.[21] For shadow partners, the median number of expected changes is nine articles for non-divisive bills and seventeen articles for divisive bills—an increase of almost 90 percent. These are substantively large effects that support our argument that, in strong committee systems, coalition partners are able to use the legislative process to control the problems of ministerial drift. The figure also illustrates that JMs—although important in scrutinizing legislation—do

[20] Before moving to a discussion of substantive effects with respect to legislative amendments, we note one other interesting finding from Table 5.2, which is that bills that spend a longer time in the legislative process, all else equal, are changed to a greater degree. This suggests that the time spent by bills in the legislative process (the dependent variable in Table 5.1) is a reasonable proxy for the amount of legislative scrutiny. If time consumed in the legislative process were just indicative of efforts to delay rather than efforts to scrutinize, then we would expect to see *no* relationship between the amount of time a bill spends in the process and the number of amendments made to it.

[21] Again, we note that, even though we have relatively less information on highly divisive bills for common partners, we are still confident that the difference between the median number of expected changes for divisive and non-divisive bills is statistically distinguishable from zero. Only 2.7 percent of the simulations of the expected number of changes for highly divisive bills are less than or equal to the median predicted number of changes for non-divisive bills, while no simulations of the expected number of changes for non-divisive bills are greater than or equal to the median expected number for divisive bills.

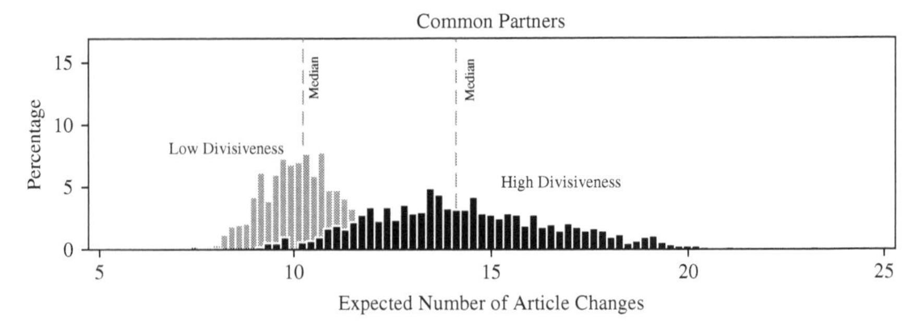

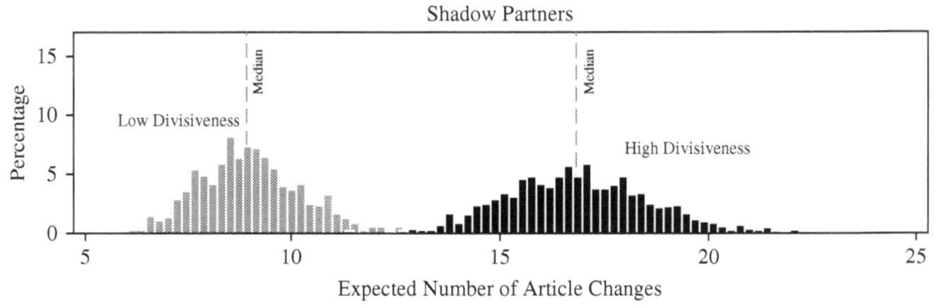

FIGURE 5.3 Government Issue Divisiveness and Legislative Amendment in Junior Minister Systems: Strong Legislatures

Note: All other covariates set at their mean sample values for junior minister systems, for bill of average size (thirty-five articles).

not serve as a substitute for the legislative process in *amending* legislation. A vertical comparison of the common partner and shadow partner panes reveals a substantial overlap between the distributions of non-divisive bills and between the distributions of divisive bills.[22] That is, whatever their level of divisiveness, bills are predicted to be amended to roughly the same degree regardless of whether the proposing minister is shadowed by a JM.

In Figure 5.4, we show the effects of coalition issue divisiveness on legislative amendment for the non-junior-minister system of Denmark. Again, we note that bills in Denmark are smaller, on average, than bills in the other strong legislatures, and so naturally have fewer articles amended. Yet the effect of government divisiveness on the level of legislative amendment is just as clear. Highly divisive bills coming to the Folketing receive almost 40 percent more changes than non-divisive bills. Together with the findings above, these results strongly suggest that, at least in strong legislatures, coalition partners are able to use parliamentary institutions and procedures to help contain policy drift by ministers.

[22] For example, the figure shows that, for non-divisive bills, almost 17 percent of the distribution of expected changes for shadow partners lies to the right of the median number of expected changes for common partners. Similarly, for divisive bills, 17 percent of the distribution of expected changes for common partners lies to the right of the median number of expected changes for shadow partners.

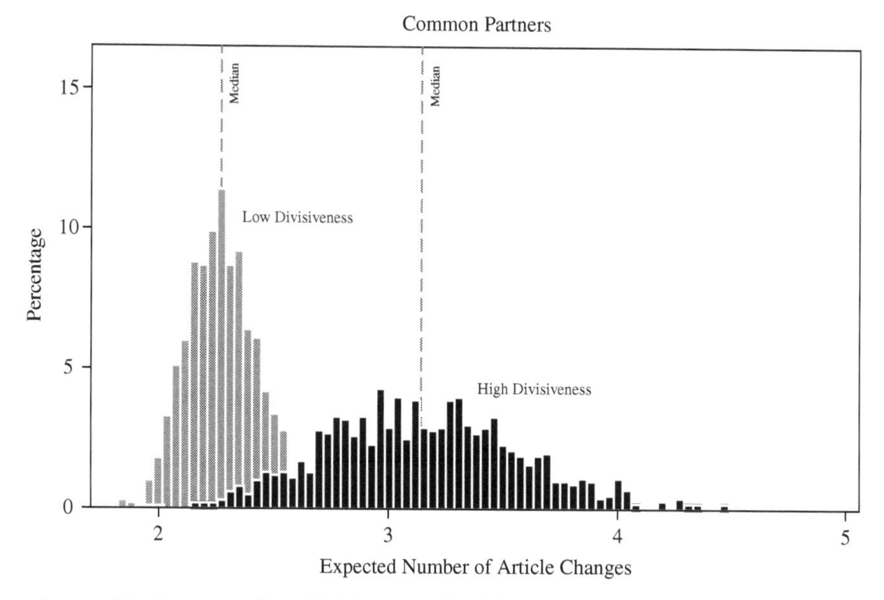

FIGURE 5.4 Government Issue Divisiveness and Legislative Amendment in Non-Junior-Minister Systems: Strong Legislatures

Note: All other covariates set at their mean sample values for non-junior-minister systems, for bill of average size (thirteen articles).

5.3.4 Opposition Influence

A number of scholars have also highlighted the potential value of the legislative process in strengthening the influence of members of the *opposition*. Our analysis allows us to assess these arguments. If the preferences of opposition parties matter directly for policymaking, we should find that government proposals receive a greater amount of scrutiny, and experience a greater degree of change, the more distant these parties are from the preferred policy of the proposing minister.

The results reported in Table 5.1 indicate that issue divisions between opposition parties and the proposing minister have virtually no impact on the length of time a government bill is scrutinized in the legislature. The coefficient estimates on issue divisiveness for "pivotal" opposition parties (those opposition parties in periods of minority government that are ideologically most compatible with the coalition on the issue at hand and bring the coalition to a legislative majority) and for "non-pivotal" opposition parties are not statistically different from zero.[23] They are also in the *opposite* direction expected by earlier scholarship.

[23] In our sample of strong legislatures, only Denmark has minority governments. Because we include country indicators in the model, the coefficients on the minority government variable in Tables 5.1 and 5.2 indicate how scrutiny and change differ between minority and majority governments in Denmark. Similarly, the coefficients on the pivotal opposition issue divisiveness variable (which, by

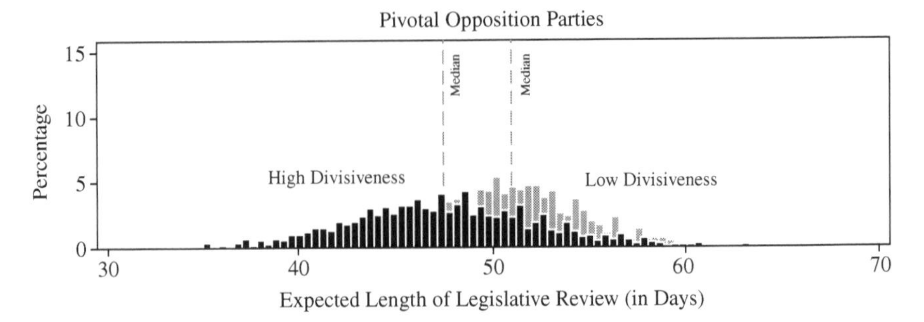

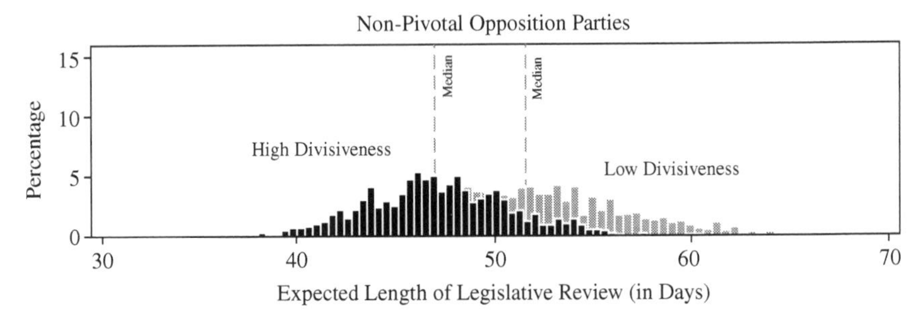

FIGURE 5.5 Opposition Issue Divisiveness and Legislative Scrutiny in Minority Government Situations: Strong Legislatures

Note: All other covariates set at their mean sample values for minority government situations.

To examine the substantive impact of the opposition thoroughly, we examine four different hypothetical scenarios. The scenarios are defined by whether there is a minority or majority government in power, and by whether the bills under review greatly divide opposition parties from the proposing minister or not.[24] In the case of minority governments (present only in Denmark), we examine the effects of opposition issue divisiveness separately for pivotal and non-pivotal opposition parties.

In Figure 5.5, we present the simulated distributions of predicted legislative review times for the different levels of opposition divisiveness when a minority government is in power. In stark contrast to our findings with respect to government parties, we see no appreciable difference between how long divisive

construction, is non-zero only for minority governments) represents the impact of an increase in this variable on scrutiny and change for Danish minority governments.

24 Analogous to our definition for government issue divisiveness, our definition of a bill dealing with issues of "low divisiveness" for the opposition is one with a value that is in the lower 10 percent of our sample of bills (for either non-pivotal or pivotal opposition parties, as appropriate), and a bill dealing with issues of "high divisiveness" as one with a value in the upper 10 percent of the sample. The difference between the two values for each opposition variable in this case is roughly three standard deviations. All other variables are set at their sample means.

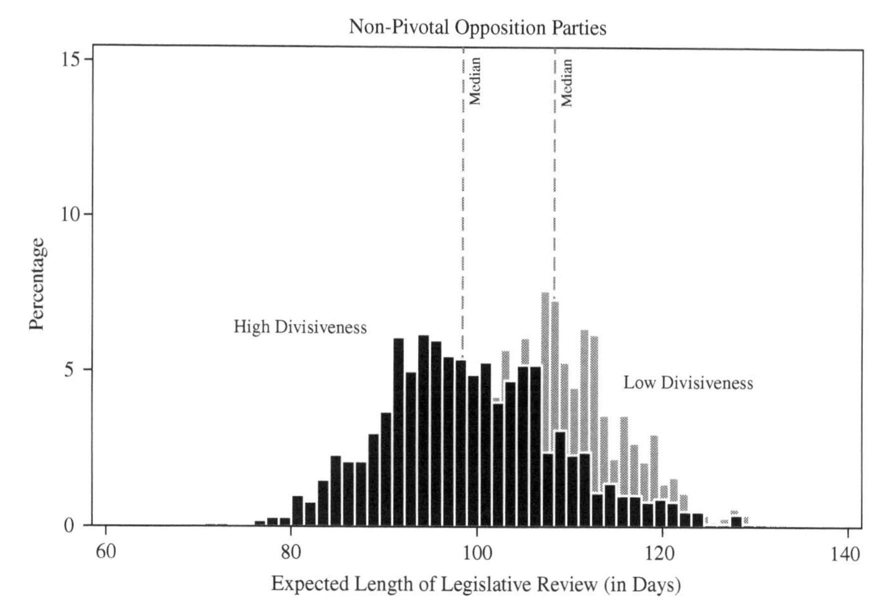

FIGURE 5.6 Opposition Issue Divisiveness and Legislative Scrutiny in Majority Government Situations: Strong Legislatures

Note: All other covariates set at their mean sample values for majority government situations.

bills and non-divisive bills (from the point of view of the opposition) spend in the legislative process. Moreover, whether opposition parties are the natural pivotal support parties for the minority coalition or not makes no difference to the level of scrutiny a minister's bill receives. The typical bill is expected to spend approximately fifty days in the Folketing in a period of minority government regardless of how divisive it is for either type of opposition party.

In Figure 5.6, we examine the effect of divisiveness on legislative scrutiny for opposition parties in periods of majority government (which occurred in all the strong legislatures in our sample), which are (by definition) non-pivotal for the majority status of the coalition. The pattern is clearly the same under both minority and majority scenarios. Issue divisions between the proposing minister and the opposition have no impact on the legislature's scrutiny of his proposals.

These findings obviously do not bode well for parties in the opposition. Nonetheless, it is possible that, while bills that diverge from the preferences of the opposition do not experience a greater amount of scrutiny than non-divergent bills, opposition parties manage to force more changes in these bills in the legislative process. The results from Table 5.2, however, provide little evidence that opposition parties are able to use the legislative process in this way. For pivotal opposition parties, the coefficient estimate on divisiveness is positive,

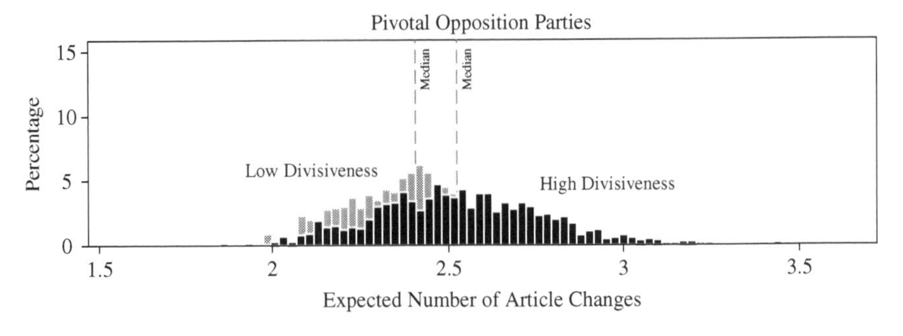

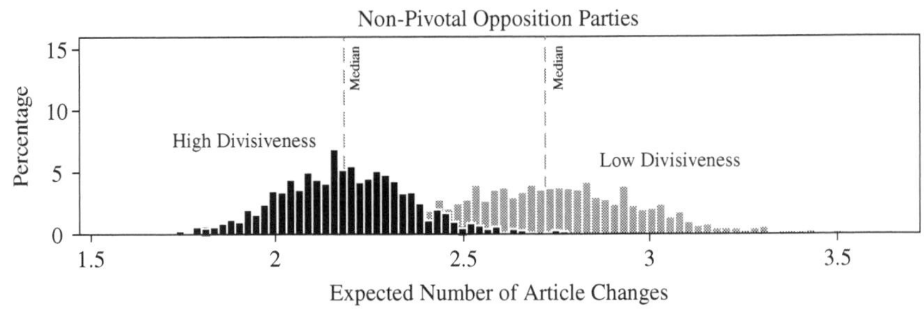

FIGURE 5.7 Opposition Issue Divisiveness and Legislative Amendment in Minority Government Situations: Strong Legislatures

Note: All other covariates set at their mean sample values for minority government situations, for bill of average size (thirteen articles).

but it is quite small and not statistically different from zero ($p > 0.70$). And for non-pivotal opposition parties, the impact of divisiveness is in the *opposite* direction expected by previous scholarship, which is close to statistical significance at conventional levels ($p = 0.11$).

We examine this possibility more closely in Figure 5.7, where we again look at a hypothetical bill in minority government situations. For the first time, we see a clear—and interesting—difference between pivotal and non-pivotal opposition parties. As the bottom pane of the figure shows, for those opposition parties that are not the natural support parties for the ruling minority coalition, a bill is predicted to have roughly 20 percent *fewer* amendments made to it if the issues it addresses divide these parties from the proposing minister.[25] Thus, even when legislative institutions are strong, and even in periods of minority government, opposition parties—if they are not ideologically close to the government and necessary for the government's ability to pass legislation—have little influence in containing ministers with whom they disagree. Notably, the situation is better

[25] For these levels of opposition issue divisiveness, this is a statistically significant difference. Less than 1 percent of each distribution is on the other side of the median expected review time of the other distribution.

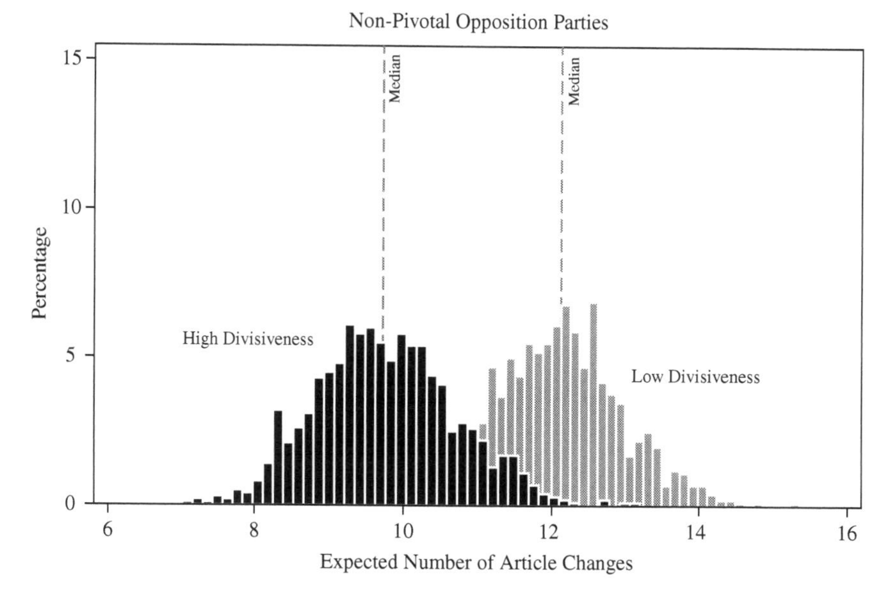

FIGURE 5.8 Opposition Issue Divisiveness and Legislative Amendment in Majority Government Situations: Strong Legislatures

Note: All other covariates set at their mean sample values for majority government situations, for bill of average size (thirty-three articles).

for pivotal opposition parties. As the top pane of the figure shows, highly divisive legislation from their point of view is no *less* likely to be amended in the legislature, although unlike with government parties, such legislation is no more likely to be amended either.[26]

If non-pivotal opposition parties find themselves in such unhappy circumstances under minority government, we certainly do not expect them to fare any better under majority government. In Figure 5.8, we examine this possibility, and indeed, see essentially the same results. Highly divisive bills from the

[26] We remind readers that we have defined pivotal opposition parties in Denmark as those parties ideologically closest to the government that collectively put the government above the majority threshold. This treatment is consistent with most scholarly accounts of how minority governments operate in Denmark—that is, by building ad hoc, issue-based legislative coalitions with different opposition parties. In other countries (e.g., Norway and Sweden for most of the post-war period), minority governments typically relied on a single party (or small set of parties) for support on all issues (Strøm, 1990*b*). Occasionally, this relationship is enshrined in a formal agreement before the minority government takes office. In such cases, it would be reasonable to treat the formal support party (or parties) as pivotal on all issues, regardless of whether it is ideologically close to the government on any particular issue. We suspect that opposition parties in this type of relationship with a minority government would more closely resemble coalition parties with respect to their power to police ministers. This possibility would be useful to explore in future research.

perspective of the opposition are expected to receive approximately 20 percent fewer legislative amendments in majority government situations.[27] In short, these findings suggest that while strong legislative institutions clearly make meaningful scrutiny and change of ministerial proposals possible, such influence is restricted to those parties that participate in government. Parties that occupy the opposition benches appear unable to take advantage of strong committee systems to press their perspective on government-sponsored legislation.

5.4 CONCLUSION

The data presented in this chapter provide substantial evidence that strong legislative institutions are used by coalition governments to confront and resolve the agency problems that derive from the need to delegate to cabinet ministers in drafting policy, and the incentives confronting these ministers to (ab)use their discretion in order to appeal to their party's constituents. Importantly, we were able to demonstrate that the legislative process is used not only to gather information—that is, to scrutinize bills—but also to force change to ministerial proposals. As we argued at the end of Chapter 3, it is the combination of both elements that strongly suggests that the legislative process is crucial to the ability of government partners to police the coalition bargain.

We return to discussing the broader implications of these findings in more detail in Chapter 7. For the moment, we simply note that these results point toward a new perspective on the role of legislative institutions in parliamentary democracies. Traditional accounts have focused on the importance of strong committee systems in allowing members of parliament to hold "the government" accountable. Similarly, scholars have argued for the importance of strong legislatures in providing opposition parties with avenues for exercising influence. In contrast, we suggest that strong legislative institutions are critical in solving *intra-coalition* tensions. Rather than facilitating oversight by parliament over the cabinet as a whole, these institutions facilitate oversight by one coalition partner over another. In the next chapter, we turn to the flip-side of the argument. If strong legislative institutions are not only sufficient but *necessary* to allow coalition parties to use parliament to police the coalition bargain, an analysis of the legislative process in an environment of weak legislative institutions should *not* reveal the same patterns we have found here.

[27] As in the previous figure, for these levels of opposition issue divisiveness, this difference is statistically significant. Less than 1 percent of each distribution is on the other side of the median expected review time of the other distribution.

5.A APPENDIX

As we discussed in Section 5.3, a variety of survival models could be used to model the length of time to an event. One key difference between survival models involves the parametric assumptions they make about the baseline hazard rate, which reflects the form of time dependence, or duration dependence, present in the data after conditioning on the set of covariates. One type of model, the semi-parametric Cox model, makes no assumptions about the distributional form of time dependence. Rather, it assumes that, whatever the distribution of the baseline hazard, the effect of covariates on the hazard rate for any unit (in our case, a government bill) is proportionate over time. Another set of models makes specific assumptions about the form of (conditional) time dependence in the data. These fully parametric models include the Weibull, the exponential (which is a special case of the Weibull), the Gompertz, the log-logistic, and the log-normal models. Another important difference between survival models has to do with the interpretation of their coefficient estimates. Specifically, models are either proportional hazards (PH) models, in which the response variable is the hazard rate and so the effects of the covariates are interpreted in terms of whether they increase or decrease the hazard rate; or they are accelerated failure time (AFT) models, in which the response variable is survival time, and so the effects of the covariates are interpreted in terms of whether they increase or decrease the duration of time to an event. The Cox and Gompertz models are exclusively PH models, the log-logistic and log-normal models are exclusively AFT models, and the Weibull and exponential models can be specified in either metric.

Naturally, our desire is to choose a survival model that gives us accurate estimates of the effects of the covariates and simultaneously minimizes our uncertainty about these effects. As we pointed out in Section 5.3, one potential problem in choosing among survival models is that an incorrect choice of parameterization of the baseline hazard rate threatens the accuracy of the estimates. This concern would incline us to choose the Cox model, since the assumptions it makes about the baseline hazard are minimal. On the other hand, if it were possible to make a reasonably good assumption about the shape of the baseline hazard, then this would incline us to choose a parametric model since we would be improving model efficiency (i.e., reducing our standard errors) by incorporating relevant information into the model without sacrificing the accuracy of our estimates.

Faced with these potential trade-offs, we believe the most prudent course of action is to estimate the semi-parametric Cox model and all the fully parametric models noted above, and then compare them to see which one provides the best representation of the legislative data in our study. Below, we compare estimates of the covariates across models (that are on the same metric) to investigate whether different distributional assumptions lead to dramatically different findings, we compare standard errors across models to assess whether some models lead to more certain inferences than others, and we evaluate overall goodness-of-fit of the various models to our data.

We also address the issue of unobserved heterogeneity in our discussion. Heterogeneity occurs when relevant covariates are excluded from the systematic component of the model, and it has the potential to lead to inconsistent parameter estimates and incorrect standard errors (Box-Steffensmeier and Jones, 2004). A large body of research in survival analysis has been dedicated to finding techniques to deal with heterogeneity problems (e.g., see Hougaard, 2000), the most popular of which involves the use of "frailty" models. These types of models introduce into the hazard rate a random parameter that accounts for the possibility that, conditional on the covariates in the model, some observations are more likely to experience an event at a given time than other observations (i.e., some observations may be more "frail" than others). These frailties may be specific to individual observations or to subgroups of observations. In our case, we believe that the types of factors that are most likely to affect the degree to which government bills are scrutinized in the legislature, but which are unobserved and thus not modeled by us, are at the level of the government ministry. Such factors might include the workload and capacity of the ministry, the professionalization of its civil servants, the personal characteristics of the minister, and so forth. Given this, we estimate "shared frailty" models that can account for possible heterogeneity between groups of bills, where the groups are defined by the specific ministry in a given government that drafted the bills.[28] Below we compare the results from the shared frailty models to those that assume no heterogeneity.

We begin with a comparison of the covariate estimates from the PH models (with the assumption of no heterogeneity), which are shown in Table 5A.1.[29] We draw attention to a couple of points. First, the coefficient estimates generally appear to be robust to model choice, though notably, several of the coefficients in the Weibull model are larger in magnitude than in the other models. Second, no model is clearly preferable to another in terms of efficiency, as the standard error estimates are virtually identical across specifications. In Table 5A.2, we present a comparison of the AFT models.[30] As with the PH models, we see very little

[28] To estimate frailty models, one must make parametric assumptions about the distribution of the frailties. The most commonly adopted distribution is the gamma (Klein and Moeschberger, 1997), which we use as well. In ancillary analysis, we assume an inverse Gaussian distribution instead of the gamma but find virtually no difference in the results.

[29] Because the response variable in PH models is the hazard rate, a negative coefficient implies that an increase in the value of the covariate reduces the probability that a unit will experience an event, thus implying a *longer* duration. In contrast, in AFT models, where the response variable is duration, a negative coefficient means that an increase in the value of the covariate leads to a *shorter* duration.

[30] Because the AFT metric is different from the PH metric, we cannot directly compare the coefficient estimates from the log-logistic and log-normal models to those from the Cox and Gompertz models. We can, however, make indirect comparisons by virtue of the fact that the AFT coefficients from the exponential and Weibull models are a simple mathematical transformation of their

TABLE 5A.1 Estimates from Proportional Hazards Models of Length of Legislative Review, Strong Committee Systems (Assumption of No Heterogeneity)

Variables	Cox	Exponential	Weibull	Gompertz
Government Issue Divisiveness	−0.098***	−0.094***	−0.104***	−0.094***
	(0.034)	(0.034)	(0.034)	(0.034)
Government Issue Divisiveness × Shadow JM	0.107**	0.108**	0.121**	0.107**
	(0.048)	(0.048)	(0.048)	(0.048)
Shadow JM	0.208	0.198	0.192	0.198
	(0.171)	(0.169)	(0.169)	(0.169)
Non-Pivotal Opposition Issue Divisiveness	−0.014	−0.013	−0.013	−0.013
	(0.018)	(0.018)	(0.018)	(0.018)
Pivotal Opposition Issue Divisiveness	−0.052***	−0.053***	−0.061***	−0.053***
	(0.019)	(0.019)	(0.019)	(0.019)
Minority Government	0.009	0.034	0.031	0.034
	(0.167)	(0.167)	(0.167)	(0.167)
Number of Committee Referrals	−0.023	−0.025	−0.031	−0.025
	(0.022)	(0.022)	(0.022)	(0.022)
Number of Subarticles in Draft Bill (Logged)	−0.133***	−0.119***	−0.129***	−0.119***
	(0.029)	(0.029)	(0.029)	(0.029)
Germany	−0.477***	−0.453**	−0.526***	−0.452**
	(0.183)	(0.182)	(0.182)	(0.182)
Netherlands	−1.470***	−1.458***	−1.649***	−1.454***
	(0.200)	(0.196)	(0.200)	(0.199)
Industrial Policy	−0.473***	−0.468***	−0.524***	−0.467***
	(0.102)	(0.101)	(0.102)	(0.101)
Social Policy	−1.231***	−1.246***	−1.375***	−1.243***
	(0.208)	(0.205)	(0.207)	(0.207)
Regional Policy	−0.557***	−0.537***	−0.573***	−0.537***
	(0.199)	(0.199)	(0.199)	(0.199)
Environmental Policy	−0.338***	−0.331***	−0.352***	−0.331***
	(0.120)	(0.119)	(0.120)	(0.119)
Intercept		−3.376***	−3.924***	−3.375***
		(0.240)	(0.262)	(0.240)
Shape Parameter		[1.000]	1.141***	−0.000
			(0.027)	(0.000)

$N = 1128$. Significance levels: *, 10%; **, 5%; ***, 1%.

change in most of the coefficient estimates (or standard errors) across models (although the effects of the government divisiveness variable and its interaction with the shadow JM indicator is slightly smaller in the log-logistic and log-normal models). One interesting exception is the coefficient on *Pivotal Opposition Issue Divisiveness*. The effect of this variable is positive and statistically significant ($p < 0.01$) in the Weibull and exponential specifications—meaning that as pivotal

PH coefficients—the PH coefficient on a variable in these models can be derived by dividing the corresponding AFT coefficient by the negative of the AFT shape parameter.

TABLE 5A.2 Estimates from Accelerated Failure Time Models of Length of Legislative Review, Strong Committee Systems (Assumption of No Heterogeneity)

Variables	Exponential	Weibull	Log-logistic	Log-normal
Government Issue Divisiveness	0.094***	0.091***	0.078***	0.082**
	(0.034)	(0.030)	(0.030)	(0.032)
Government Issue Divisiveness × Shadow JM	−0.108**	−0.106**	−0.111**	−0.094**
	(0.048)	(0.042)	(0.044)	(0.045)
Shadow JM	−0.198	−0.168	−0.259	−0.314*
	(0.169)	(0.149)	(0.165)	(0.166)
Non-Pivotal Opposition Issue Divisiveness	0.013	0.011	0.000	0.009
	(0.018)	(0.016)	(0.017)	(0.018)
Pivotal Opposition Issue Divisiveness	0.053***	0.054***	0.013	0.035*
	(0.019)	(0.017)	(0.018)	(0.019)
Minority Government	−0.034	−0.027	−0.058	−0.184
	(0.167)	(0.146)	(0.150)	(0.167)
Number of Committee Referrals	0.025	0.027	0.011	0.011
	(0.022)	(0.019)	(0.021)	(0.023)
Number of Subarticles in Draft Bill (Logged)	0.119***	0.113***	0.192***	0.181***
	(0.029)	(0.026)	(0.026)	(0.028)
Germany	0.453**	0.461***	0.226	0.323*
	(0.182)	(0.160)	(0.163)	(0.180)
Netherlands	1.458***	1.445***	1.244***	1.288***
	(0.196)	(0.172)	(0.180)	(0.194)
Industrial Policy	0.468***	0.459***	0.462***	0.372***
	(0.101)	(0.089)	(0.091)	(0.096)
Social Policy	1.246***	1.205***	1.314***	1.154***
	(0.205)	(0.180)	(0.189)	(0.187)
Regional Policy	0.537***	0.502***	0.580***	0.676***
	(0.199)	(0.175)	(0.175)	(0.191)
Environmental Policy	0.331***	0.308***	0.401***	0.464***
	(0.119)	(0.105)	(0.105)	(0.114)
Intercept	3.376***	3.439***	3.166***	3.085***
	(0.240)	(0.211)	(0.215)	(0.232)
Shape Parameter	[1.000]	0.876***	0.548***	0.995
		(0.020)	(0.014)	(0.022)

$N = 1128$. Significance levels: ∗, 10%; ∗∗, 5%; ∗∗∗, 1%.

opposition parties in periods of minority government become more divided from the party of the proposing minister on a bill, the bill will spend more time in legislative deliberations. The effect is quite a bit smaller, though still statistically significant at $p < 0.10$, in the log-normal model. The magnitude of the effect drops further still in the the log-logistic specification, where the coefficient is no longer statistically discernible from zero ($p > 0.40$). The chief differences between the latter two models, the log-logistic and log-normal, and the others we have discussed is that the log-logistic and log-normal do not assume proportionality or monotonicity of the hazard rate. These differences could account for the changes in parameter estimates we see on some of the coefficients, though as we shall show, once heterogeneity is taken into account, many of the differences between parameter estimates across models disappear.

In Table 5A.3, we present results from the four PH models assuming subgroup heterogeneity, where the groups, as discussed above, are defined by the individual ministries for each government in the sample that introduced the bills. The estimate of the frailty variance is at the bottom of the table. An estimate of zero would indicate the absence of heterogeneity, which would imply that taking heterogeneity into account does not significantly improve the fit of the model. As the estimates of the frailty parameter show, heterogeneity is present in our data. That is, we can safely reject the notion that there are no unmeasured factors at the ministry level that have an impact on the length of legislative review. The problem is especially apparent in the Weibull specification, where the estimated frailty variance is substantially larger than in the other models. Importantly, we see that the estimates on our key theoretical variables (government issue divisiveness and its interaction with the shadow JM indicator) continue to be in the expected direction and statistically significant (indeed, larger in magnitude by 10–20 percent across the four models) once heterogeneity is taken into account. We also now see that the coefficient on *Pivotal Opposition Issue Divisiveness*, which had been statistically significant across the models in Table 5A.1, drops sufficiently in magnitude that it is no longer statistically discernible from zero for any of the models. This suggests that the presence of unmodeled heterogeneity was largely responsible for the previous results on this variable.

This also appears to be the case in Table 5A.4, where we present the results for the AFT models with subgroup heterogeneity. We note that heterogeneity is also present in the log-logistic and log-normal models. Interestingly, though, we note that for these two models, incorporating heterogeneity has little impact on the coefficient estimates for the government issue divisiveness variable and its interaction with the shadow JM indicator. That is, while taking account of heterogeneity moves these coefficients by about 10–20 percent for all other models, the change in their magnitude in these two models is a mere 1–4 percent. This suggests that the log-logistic and log-normal specifications, which relax the assumptions of monotonicity and proportionality of the hazard rate, may ameliorate the problems caused by heterogeneity in our case. Finally, we note that, for *all* the explanatory variables, the standard errors in the log-logistic model are smaller than in any other model. This suggests to us that the log-logistic shared frailty specification may be preferable to all other models on efficiency grounds. A comparison of model fit, to which we now turn, reveals even more clearly that the log-logistic is the best specification for the data in our study.

We evaluate goodness-of-fit in two ways. First, we evaluate the Akaike Information Criterion (AIC) across the models. The AIC allows us to compare our competing models (some of which are non-nested) on the basis of their log-likelihoods, where each log-likelihood is "penalized" for the number of parameters estimated in the model. The best-fitting model is the one with the lowest AIC.

TABLE 5A.3 Estimates from Proportional Hazards Models of Length of Legislative Review, Strong Committee Systems (Shared Gamma Frailty)

Variables	Cox	Exponential	Weibull	Gompertz
Government Issue Divisiveness	−0.114***	−0.105***	−0.124***	−0.107***
	(0.043)	(0.040)	(0.046)	(0.041)
Government Issue Divisiveness	0.116*	0.112**	0.134**	0.114**
× Shadow JM	(0.059)	(0.055)	(0.064)	(0.057)
Shadow JM	0.221	0.202	0.205	0.212
	(0.214)	(0.196)	(0.233)	(0.202)
Non-Pivotal Opposition Issue	0.002	−0.005	0.011	−0.002
Divisiveness	(0.024)	(0.023)	(0.027)	(0.024)
Pivotal Opposition Issue Divisiveness	−0.021	−0.031	−0.022	−0.030
	(0.026)	(0.024)	(0.028)	(0.025)
Minority Government	−0.057	−0.015	−0.047	−0.016
	(0.215)	(0.200)	(0.235)	(0.206)
Number of Committee Referrals	−0.038	−0.033	−0.049*	−0.037
	(0.026)	(0.025)	(0.027)	(0.025)
Number of Subarticles in	−0.148***	−0.123***	−0.151***	−0.127***
Draft Bill (Logged)	(0.031)	(0.030)	(0.032)	(0.031)
Germany	−0.347	−0.356*	−0.328	−0.348
	(0.228)	(0.214)	(0.250)	(0.221)
Netherlands	−1.482***	−1.409***	−1.662***	−1.463***
	(0.252)	(0.230)	(0.275)	(0.240)
Industrial Policy	−0.483***	−0.462***	−0.533***	−0.475***
	(0.112)	(0.108)	(0.117)	(0.110)
Social Policy	−1.227***	−1.213***	−1.368***	−1.255***
	(0.234)	(0.222)	(0.246)	(0.227)
Regional Policy	−0.512**	−0.509**	−0.506**	−0.507**
	(0.239)	(0.226)	(0.257)	(0.232)
Environmental Policy	−0.300**	−0.308**	−0.275*	−0.301**
	(0.140)	(0.134)	(0.151)	(0.137)
Intercept		−3.420***	−4.399***	−3.449***
		(0.283)	(0.359)	(0.293)
Shape Parameter		[1.000]	1.227***	0.000
			(0.032)	(0.000)
Frailty Parameter	0.093***	0.055***	0.151***	0.070***

$N = 1128$. Shared frailty models grouped on country, government, and ministry. Number of groups = 203. Significance level of frailty parameter based on a log-likelihood test against a model where the parameter is constrained to equal zero. Significance levels: ∗, 10%; ∗∗, 5%; ∗∗∗, 1%.

In Table 5A.5, we present the AIC statistics for all the models we have estimated. We should note that the AIC for the two Cox models cannot be compared to the AIC from the fully parametric models but can be compared to each other.[31] Below, we conduct a residuals-based test in which the Cox model can be (visually)

[31] The Cox model is often referred to as a "partial-likelihood" model because it only uses information on the *order* of duration times, rather than exact duration times, which is why it does not require

TABLE 5A.4 Estimates from Accelerated Failure Time Models of Length of Legislative Review, Strong Committee Systems (Shared Gamma Frailty)

Variables	Exponential	Weibull	Log-logistic	Log-normal
Government Issue Divisiveness	0.105***	0.101***	0.075**	0.083**
	(0.040)	(0.037)	(0.032)	(0.035)
Government Issue Divisiveness	−0.112**	−0.109**	−0.107**	−0.088*
× Shadow JM	(0.055)	(0.052)	(0.050)	(0.050)
Shadow JM	−0.202	−0.167	−0.286	−0.353*
	(0.196)	(0.190)	(0.181)	(0.183)
Non-Pivotal Opposition Issue	0.005	−0.009	−0.013	−0.001
Divisiveness	(0.023)	(0.020)	(0.018)	(0.021)
Pivotal Opposition Issue	0.031	0.018	−0.012	0.017
Divisiveness	(0.024)	(0.023)	(0.022)	(0.023)
Minority Government	0.015	0.038	−0.028	−0.202
	(0.200)	(0.191)	(0.165)	(0.186)
Number of Committee Referrals	0.033	0.040*	0.018	0.018
	(0.025)	(0.022)	(0.021)	(0.023)
Number of Subarticles in	0.123***	0.123***	0.201***	0.188***
Draft Bill (Logged)	(0.030)	(0.027)	(0.027)	(0.028)
Germany	0.356*	0.267	0.122	0.240
	(0.214)	(0.204)	(0.175)	(0.195)
Netherlands	1.409***	1.354***	1.158***	1.204***
	(0.230)	(0.222)	(0.200)	(0.215)
Industrial Policy	0.462***	0.434***	0.458***	0.359***
	(0.108)	(0.095)	(0.092)	(0.099)
Social Policy	1.213***	1.115***	1.290***	1.095***
	(0.222)	(0.200)	(0.199)	(0.201)
Regional Policy	0.509**	0.412**	0.506***	0.645***
	(0.226)	(0.210)	(0.186)	(0.204)
Environmental Policy	0.308**	0.224*	0.379***	0.455***
	(0.134)	(0.123)	(0.110)	(0.120)
Intercept	3.420***	3.585***	3.318***	3.208***
	(0.283)	(0.270)	(0.237)	(0.258)
Shape Parameter	[1.000]	0.815***	0.527***	0.967
		(0.021)	(0.015)	(0.023)
Frailty Parameter	0.055***	0.151***	0.070***	0.063***

$N = 1128$. Shared frailty models grouped on country, government, and ministry. Number of groups = 203. Significance level of frailty parameter based on a log-likelihood test against a model where the parameter is constrained to equal zero. Significance levels: *, 10%; **, 5%; ***, 1%.

compared to the rest. The AIC comparisons are nonetheless informative. First, they show that, for each specification, taking heterogeneity into account improves the explanatory power of the model. They also show that, among the parametric models, the log-logistic model provides the best fit to the data.

parameterization of the baseline hazard rate (Collett, 1994). Because of this, the likelihood from the Cox model is not conformable to those from the (maximum likelihood) parametric models.

TABLE 5A.5 Comparisons of Akaike Information Criterion across Survival Models, Strong Legislatures

Model	AIC
Cox model	12547.47
Exponential model	3202.55
Weibull model	3174.52
Gompertz model	3204.53
Log-logistic model	3092.50
Log-normal model	3139.93
Cox shared frailty model	12524.93
Exponential shared frailty model	3190.61
Weibull shared frailty model	3134.43
Gompertz shared frailty model	3190.36
Log-logistic shared frailty model	3074.55
Log-normal shared frailty model	3126.13

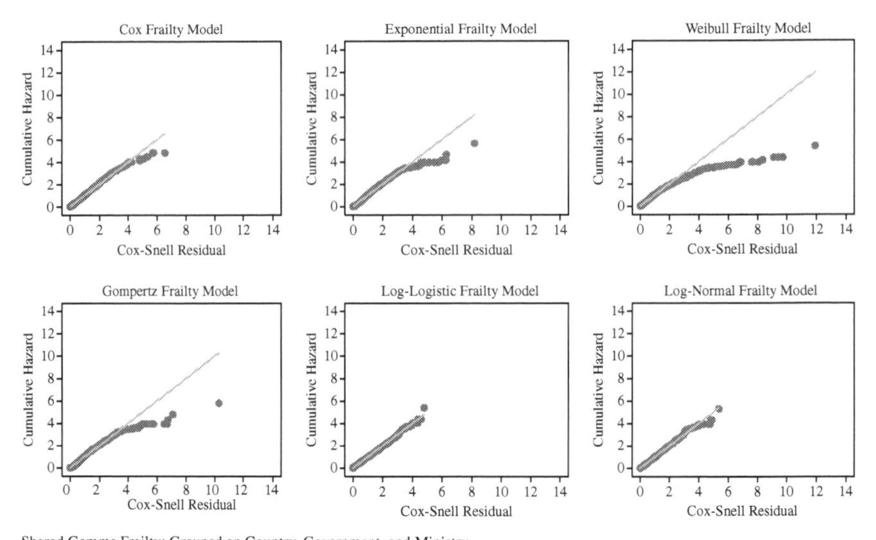

FIGURE 5A.1 Residual Analysis of Survival Models with Heterogeneity, Strong Legislatures

We can also evaluate fit graphically with an analysis of Cox–Snell residuals (for mathematical details, see Cox and Snell, 1968). If we have indeed fit the correct model to the data, then the Cox–Snell residuals will be unit exponentially distributed with a hazard ratio of 1 (Cox and Snell, 1968; Collett, 1994; Klein and Moeschberger, 1997; Box-Steffensmeier and Jones, 2004). We can discern whether this is the case by plotting these residuals against the estimated cumulative (or integrated) hazard rate based on these residuals. If the model in question is a good fit to the data, then the residuals should lie on a 45-degree line through the origin.

Given that we have already established (with the AIC statistics) the superiority of the shared frailty specification for all models, in Figure 5A.1, we plot the Cox–Snell residuals only for the models shown in Tables 5A.3 and 5A.4, all of which assume heterogeneity. As the figure shows, there are obvious differences in model fit across specifications. The Weibull model provides the least reasonable fit to the data, mispredicting the review times of numerous bills, especially those that spent a long time in the legislative process. The exponential and Gompertz models provide a slightly better fit, but still underperform for observations with long durations. Further, we see that while the Cox model provides a noticeably better fit than the other PH models, the Cox–Snell residuals still deviate from the 45-degree line for bills that underwent lengthy legislative review. Clearly, the best-fitting specifications are the two non-PH models, the log-logistic and log-normal, as almost all the residuals lie close to the 45-degree line. The log-logistic model performs slightly better than the log-normal (which was also apparent from the AIC statistics), and thus on the basis of our comparisons, we choose the log-logistic shared frailty model to evaluate our hypotheses concerning the length of the review process in strong legislatures.

6

Weak Legislative Institutions and Multiparty Governance

The last chapter demonstrated that strong parliamentary institutions—which facilitate information-gathering and the amendment of ministerial proposals—allow government parties to police the coalition bargain. In such cases, parliament can serve as an arena for reining in overzealous ministers as they attempt to seize the policy-signaling benefits associated with introducing legislation. In this chapter, we examine whether parliamentary institutions play a similar role in France and Ireland, two countries with exceptionally weak legislatures.

6.1 POLICING IN WEAK LEGISLATURES

In contrast to strong legislatures, committee systems in weak legislatures make it much more difficult to gather policy-relevant information or to counteract initiatives that deviate from the agreed-upon coalition compromise. Legislative committees in these systems are ill-equipped for these tasks because they are few in number, large and unwieldy, and generally do not conform to the jurisdictional boundaries of ministries. In addition, a number of other institutional features, such as the guillotine and urgency procedures, strengthen the hand of ministers and weaken parliamentary influence. In short, the theoretical model presented in Chapter 2, which assumes the existence of an effective institutional mechanism for scrutiny and change, does not apply to weak legislative institutions. Coalition partners should not be able to employ the legislative process in these systems to keep tabs on their partners. Empirically, this implies that we do *not* expect the relationships between issue divisions and the policing of ministers that we observed in the previous chapter.

Hypothesis (Policing). *Under weak legislative institutions, greater policy divisions between coalition partners and the proposing minister on the issues addressed by a bill do not lead to greater policing of the minister in the legislative process.*

The two parliamentary chambers that serve as testing grounds for this expectation are the Irish Dáil and the French Assemblée Nationale. Recall from our discussion in Chapter 3 that the institutional structure of these parliaments conforms well to the the archetypal properties of weak legislatures. Indeed, as our factor analysis in that chapter suggested, among sixteen prominent European legislatures, only the British House of Commons—a notoriously impotent legislature—ranks below the Irish and French parliaments. Thus, these two chambers provide an appropriate forum for evaluating whether strong legislative institutions are a *necessary* precondition for effective use of the parliamentary process as a tool of multiparty governance.

Recall that the concept of "policing" as we use it is quite strict, with important implications for the type of evidence we look for in our empirical evaluation. To conclude that the legislative process is being used to police ministers requires evidence that internal policy divisions induce coalition ministers *both* to scrutinize ministerial proposals to a greater degree *and* to counteract those proposals during the process of legislative review. It is useful to revisit why we require both conditions to be met. Consider, for a moment, what we should conclude if we see no evidence that parties are scrutinizing legislation during the parliamentary process, but that changes are made to ministerial proposals. Such a scenario would be consistent with a policing process in which coalition parties use *extra-parliamentary* resources and institutions to police the coalition bargain and then incorporate the results of that process into proposed legislation at the legislative stage—which would not be surprising, as virtually all legislation requires parliamentary approval. Parliament matters in this scenario—because that is where changes are formally adopted—but it is not the primary forum in which policing takes place.

On the other hand, suppose we observe that divisive legislation is scrutinized more heavily in the legislature, but that parties are ultimately unable to force changes to draft proposals. That is, whether parties are gathering information for the purpose of policing, or for some other purpose, they are unable to use that information to amend a minister's proposal. In this scenario, it would also be inappropriate to conclude that parties use legislative institutions to police the coalition bargain. There are two potential explanations for the lack of observed change: Either proposals already conform to the bargain when they are introduced (which implies that any modifications take place before bill introduction), or parties are unable to actually force change even when they find that proposals deviate from agreed-upon compromises (which also implies that the legislative process is ineffective as a policing tool). In short, to establish the claim that parliament plays a significant role in resolving intra-coalition tensions, we should see evidence of both conditions of policing.

As we have pointed out throughout the book, the legislative process represents only one potential counterweight to ministerial influence; there exists a myriad of other mechanisms that can serve as substitutes or complements to the parliamentary arena. Indeed, our analysis of strong legislatures revealed a conditional relationship between the use of shadow junior ministers (JMs) and legislative scrutiny and the amendment of ministerial proposals. In particular, the results suggested that for *gathering information*, JMs serve as a substitute for parliamentary review. Shadow JMs are in an excellent position to provide detailed information on the content of draft bills and feasible policy alternatives, thereby reducing the need for expansive information-gathering in parliament. As a result, the length of the legislative process for bills that fall under the watchful eye of a JM does not depend on the divisiveness of the bill—parties are already well-informed and need not rely on lengthy committee review.

In contrast, JMs do not substitute for parliamentary committees in amending draft bills. The policy-signaling incentives accruing to ministers, who introduce internally divisive legislation, make it unlikely that JMs will be able to force changes to such legislation before its introduction in parliament. However, once legislation is introduced, coalition partners are able to make use of the information provided by JMs to amend ministerial proposals.

How do our expectations change in the current context? In weak legislatures, we have hypothesized that the parliamentary process is not an effective tool for policing ministers. As a result, we do not expect that shadow JMs "reinforce" legislative oversight: There simply is nothing *to* reinforce. This does not mean that shadow JMs in these systems are unimportant. On the contrary, they may be even more critical. But it does imply that parties cannot take advantage of information provided by a shadow JM to counteract ministerial drift in the legislative arena. As a result, we expect that the legislative treatment of bills that come out of ministries with a shadow JM will not differ in systematic ways from those that do not:

Hypothesis (Shadow Junior Minister). *Under weak legislative institutions, the presence of a shadow junior minister does not improve policing of the proposing minister in the legislative process.*

6.2 THE IMPACT OF THE OPPOSITION

As we discussed in Chapter 4, an important set of arguments in the study of legislatures in parliamentary systems has focused on the potential benefits that can accrue to opposition parties during the legislative process. Most prominently, Strøm (1990*b*) and Powell (2000) have argued that legislative institutions can provide opposition parties influence over the content of policy, especially under minority government. Our analysis in Chapter 5, however, provided little support for these arguments. We found no compelling evidence that opposition parties (regardless of whether they were pivotal to a government's majority) are able to force greater scrutiny of, or more changes to, bills dealing with issues that divide them from the proposing minister.

Given our non-findings in strong legislatures—where opposition strength is presumably at its highest—we would be surprised to find that opposition preferences make a difference to the scrutiny and amendment of government bills in weak legislatures. The absence of strong legislative institutions that opposition parties can use to delay government bills, or that allow them to present alternative policy proposals on which government parties are forced to vote in a public setting, severely limits—perhaps even eliminates—the potential for opposition influence. Government ministers in weak legislatures are in a strong position to ignore opposition concerns, and we expect they will do so.

6.3 ANALYSIS AND FINDINGS

In contrast to strong legislatures, we expect that weak parliaments—such as the Irish Dáil and the French Assemblée Nationale—simply do not provide effective mechanisms for coalition partners to monitor and amend ministerial draft bills. It is not difficult to find suggestive cases in our sample of legislation. For example, the Irish "Rainbow Coalition" of the late 1990s (composed of Fine Gael, the Labour Party, and the Democratic Left) was characterized by pronounced ideological differences, particularly with respect to tax and welfare issues. Indeed, as we showed earlier in Figures 4.17–4.21, no government in our sample was more divided on any issue than this particular government on tax and welfare policy. In late February 1997, the Rainbow Coalition introduced a bill to change existing social welfare law on the provision of state services and benefits.[1] The bill had been drafted under the auspices of the Minister for Social Welfare, and leader of the Democratic Left, Proinsias De Rossa. The bill significantly expanded a variety of benefits and services. It increased unemployment insurance, need-based social assistance payments, child benefit rates, and maternity and adoptive benefits. It also introduced a new "sickness allowance" for those prevented from working due to temporary illness, extended entitlements for occupational injuries benefits, and reduced eligibility requirements for pension payments—all the while reducing worker contributions to social insurance.

As one might imagine for such a bill, the legislative details were highly technical and required extensive changes to previous laws. In total, the bill consisted of eighty-one articles, was nearly fifty pages long, and altered twenty-eight previous acts. But despite its scope, and fundamental policy disagreements between the

[1] This is the Social Welfare Bill, 1997 (Bill Number 10 of 1997).

coalition partners, the bill moved swiftly through the legislative process. Introduced on February 18, the bill was debated on general principles by the Dáil on March 5–6, considered by the Select Committee on Social Affairs for the next five days, and then debated a final time on March 19, when the bill was passed. Thus, the legislative process on this far-reaching, internally divisive bill lasted a mere twenty-nine days. In the end, only six of eighty-one articles were changed (7.4 percent of the bill)—and all of the changes came at the behest (or received the explicit acceptance) of the proposing minister, and dealt with small, technical matters. When the brief, pre-allotted debate time for the bill ran out at 6:45 p.m. on March 19, the guillotine procedure was invoked, and all amendments that had not yet been debated, except for those proposed by the minister himself, were automatically rejected.

In this case, a bill of significant scope, dealing with an issue that was contentious within the coalition, was rushed through the legislature in less than a month and emerged from the process virtually unscathed. A comparison with our strong legislatures puts this outcome in stark relief. Consider a similar bill in Germany or the Netherlands, for example.[2] In Germany, such a bill would be predicted to have spent forty-eight days in the legislature (65 percent longer than in Ireland), with 41 percent of the articles changed. In the Netherlands, the process would be predicted to have lasted 102 days (150 percent longer than in Ireland), with 37 percent of the articles amended. These hypothetical outcomes are clearly quite different from what occurred in the Irish Dáil.

While illustrative, this example merely serves to motivate broader questions: Is this a representative instance of how legislative review operates in weak committee systems? Is there systematic evidence that coalition parties are unable to rely on parliament to police the coalition bargain? As in Chapter 5, our empirical approach to answering these questions focuses on the manner in which policy differences within the governing coalition affect the *length of legislative deliberations* on bills drafted by government ministers and the *extent of changes* made to these bills during the process of legislative review. For the analysis below, we use the same statistical techniques employed in our analysis of strong legislative institutions—a parametric survival model to model the length of deliberations and an event count model to model the number of changes made to ministerial proposals.[3]

[2] By "similar," we mean a bill coming from a ministry with a shadow JM (which is why we exclude Denmark from this comparison), and of similar divisiveness and length (i.e., falling in roughly the same place in the distribution of government divisiveness and article length in the sample of bills from these two legislatures). The government issue divisiveness score for the Social Welfare Bill was at the 92nd percentile of the distribution of all Irish bills, and article length was at the 58th percentile. In Germany, this amounts to a divisiveness score of 1.87 and a length of twenty-six articles. In the Netherlands, the respective values are a divisiveness score of 5.81 and a length of twelve articles.

[3] Unlike in Chapter 5, we find no evidence that unobserved heterogeneity in the length of legislative scrutiny is a problem for the sample of bills from weak legislatures. Therefore, we do not estimate a

6.3.1 Legislative Scrutiny

Table 6.1 reports our findings with respect to the length of legislative review of government bills.[4] The first point to note concerns the impact of internal coalition divisions and the impact of these divisions as they interact with the presence (or absence) of a shadow JM. Are coalition parties more likely to scrutinize bills—thus leading to greater delay in the legislative process—when they are ideologically distant from the proposing minister? The effect of coalition divisions when a coalition partner does *not* control a shadow JM is given by the estimated coefficient on the *Government Issue Divisiveness* variable. As the table reveals, this coefficient is positive and statistically different from zero. As a bill under consideration becomes more divisive for the coalition, the legislative process is more drawn out. Thus, despite the fact that the legislative committee system is weak, it appears that, at least in the absence of a watchdog JM, coalition parties scrutinize ministerial proposals when they are divisive. In contrast, the estimated impact of issue divisiveness in the presence of a shadow JM—given by the combination of the coefficient on government issue divisiveness and the coefficient on the interaction between divisiveness and shadow JMs ($0.188 - 0.154 = 0.034$)—is small and not statistically distinguishable from zero ($p > 0.60$). That is, where partners can rely on a shadow JM, their divisions from the minister have no discernible impact on the length of the legislative process.

These results mirror the pattern we observed in strong legislatures. In both types of parliaments, if a shadow JM is present, the minister's bill does not receive a higher level of scrutiny as the issues it addresses become more divisive. Further, the suppressive effect of a shadow JM on legislative scrutiny increases on the divisiveness of the issues. In weak legislatures, each standard deviation increase in government issue divisions on a bill coming from a shadowed ministry results in a 25 percent reduction in the amount of time the bill spends in the legislative process.[5] This is very similar to the 20 percent reduction in review time in such cases in strong legislatures. However, if coalition partners cannot rely on the services of a JM placed in the ministry, then as they become more divided from the proposing minister, the bill spends substantially *more* time in the legislative process. Indeed, a surface comparison of the coefficient on *Government Issue Divisiveness* (without a shadow JM) to the corresponding coefficient in the previous chapter (0.075) might suggest that divisive bills receive substantially more scrutiny in weak legislatures.

frailty model in the present case. As in the previous chapter, we find that the best-fitting parametric model is the log-logistic. We refer readers interested in our survival model comparisons to the Appendix of this chapter.

[4] The estimate of the shape parameter is shown in the Appendix to this chapter.

[5] Recall that this is simply the product of the time ratio of the interaction coefficient (i.e., its inverse log) and the standard deviation of government issue divisiveness shown in Table 4.1.

TABLE 6.1 Length of Legislative Review, Weak Committee Systems

Variables	Estimates
Government Issue Divisiveness	0.188**
	(0.074)
Government Issue Divisiveness × Shadow JM	−0.154**
	(0.078)
Shadow JM	0.295
	(0.213)
Non-Pivotal Opposition Issue Divisiveness	−0.045
	(0.050)
Pivotal Opposition Issue Divisiveness	−0.034
	(0.146)
Minority Government	0.667**
	(0.287)
Number of Committee Referrals	0.232
	(0.184)
Number of Subarticles in Draft Bill (Logged)	0.335***
	(0.063)
Ireland	−0.223
	(0.355)
Industry and Markets Policy	0.373**
	(0.182)
Social Policy	0.390
	(0.429)
Regional Policy	0.181
	(0.366)
Environmental Policy	1.637***
	(0.426)
Intercept	1.935***
	(0.489)

Log-logistic model. $N = 187$. Significance levels: *, 10%; **, 5%; ***, 1%.

A closer look at the substantive effects, however, reveals that this is not the case. As we did in Chapter 5, we explore the substantive impact of our findings using statistical simulations. Figure 6.1 shows the frequency distribution of simulated values of the expected length of legislative scrutiny (along with reference lines indicating the median expected value of each distribution) in four hypothetical scenarios—which, as before, are defined by whether the hypothetical bill deals with relatively non-divisive issues or with relatively contentious ones, and by whether the hypothetical bill comes from a ministry where the coalition partner controls a shadow JM or one where it does not.[6]

[6] As in Chapter 5, we define a bill dealing with issues of "low divisiveness" as one with a value of *Government Issue Divisiveness* that is in the lower 10 percent of our sample, and a bill dealing with issues of "high divisiveness" as one with a value in the upper 10 percent of the sample, a difference

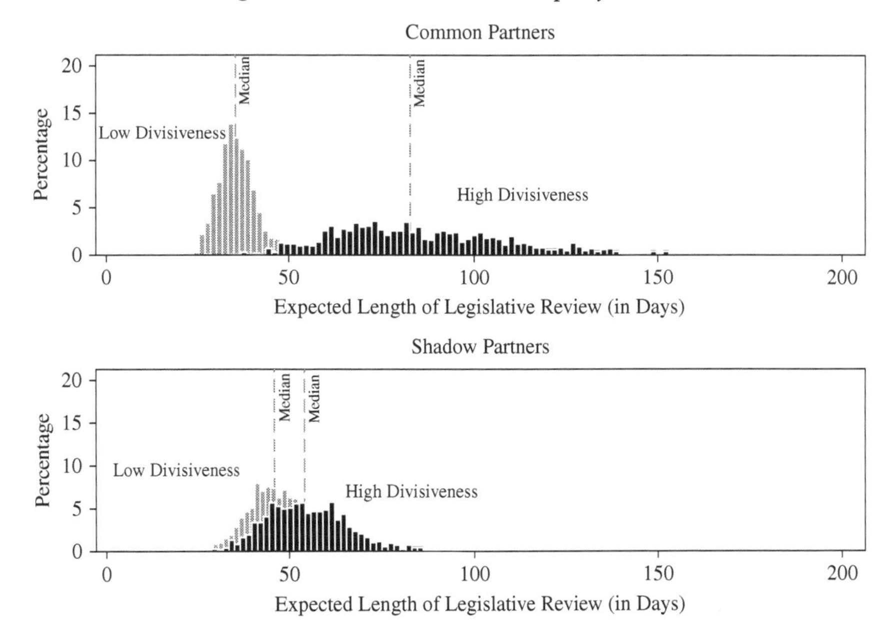

FIGURE 6.1 Government Issue Divisiveness and Legislative Scrutiny: Weak Legislatures

Note: All other covariates set at their mean sample values.

The top pane of the figure shows quite clearly that coalition partners without a shadow JM in place do scrutinize highly divisive bills more intensely than non-divisive ones. The median predicted review time for a relatively non-divisive bill is approximately thirty-five days, compared to eighty-three days for a relatively divisive bill, a difference of forty-eight days. How do these results compare to our findings from strong legislatures? In the previous chapter, we showed that, in JM systems (the appropriate comparison here), when coalition partners lack a shadow JM, a non-divisive bill is expected to spend approximately 137 days in the legislature, while parliamentary review of a divisive bill is expected to last around 194 days, a difference of 57 days. In both types of legislatures, then, moving from a non-divisive to a divisive bill is expected to lengthen the process of parliamentary review for common partners, but the additional amount of review time is actually *greater* in strong legislatures. This comparison also emphasizes how much more limited coalition parties in weak legislatures are, in general, in their ability to engage in legislative scrutiny: The *most* divisive set of bills for common partners in Ireland and France are expected to spend almost *two*

of roughly two standard deviations. In this figure and the others in this chapter, we hold all other variables at their mean sample values, where the sample is defined by the type of system or situation being examined in the figure.

months less time in the legislative process as the *least* divisive set of bills for common partners in Germany and the Netherlands (83 days versus 137 days). Equally telling is the difference between highly divisive bills across the two types of parliaments. Bills that severely divide common partners from the proposing minister are expected to remain in the parliamentary review process over 130 percent longer in strong legislatures than in weak ones—194 days versus 83 days, a difference of almost four months.

Nevertheless, while divisive bills in weak legislatures clearly receive less scrutiny than they do in strong legislatures, such bills are reviewed for significantly *more* time than bills that are non-divisive. Thus, even where parliamentary institutions are "emasculated," there is a systematic relationship between coalition divisiveness and the extent of legislative scrutiny—parties appear to use even weak committee systems to scrutinize cabinet proposals. This conclusion is reinforced by the fact that policy divisions do *not* lead to greater scrutiny when a shadow JM is in place, as shown in the bottom pane of the figure. This is similar to the the results from strong legislative systems. The reason is again immediate: A shadow JM is a ready alternative for the need to gather information and can therefore serve as an effective substitute. If increasing length of the legislative process simply results from the desire to delay legislation—simply a "twiddling of thumbs" while no action is being taken on a bill—then we would expect to see the same delay in the presence of a shadow JM that we observe in its absence. The fact the placement of a shadow JM appears to substitute for greater time in the legislative process strongly suggests that this time is being used for scrutiny, and not simply as a delaying tactic.

6.3.2 *Amendment of Ministerial Proposals*

The results so far demonstrate that coalition parties appear to use the legislative process—even with all the limitations they face in weak committee systems—to scrutinize contentious ministerial proposals. But as we outlined earlier, this is not sufficient evidence to conclude that the parliamentary process serves the function of allowing government partners to police the coalition bargain. Policy-relevant information, once collected, can be used for various purposes by coalition partners. For example, such information can improve the ability to criticize ministerial proposals (or to defend their support of them) in legislative debates or media outlets (e.g., see Martin and Vanberg, 2008). It can also allow parties to develop policy alternatives that can be used in subsequent electoral campaigns. However, such uses of information do not imply that coalition parties are able to control the content of policy proposals emanating from hostile ministries. To conclude that they are actually able to counteract "ministerial drift," we require evidence that policy information, once gathered, can be used effectively to *modify* the actions of ministers who are straying from the coalition compromise. The theoretical model

TABLE 6.2 Extent of Legislative Alterations, Weak Committee Systems

Variables	Estimates
Government Issue Divisiveness	0.019
	(0.059)
Government Issue Divisiveness × Shadow JM	−0.105*
	(0.064)
Shadow JM	0.098
	(0.201)
Non-Pivotal Opposition Issue Divisiveness	−0.029
	(0.049)
Pivotal Opposition Issue Divisiveness	0.119
	(0.131)
Minority Government	0.033
	(0.266)
Number of Committee Referrals	0.325*
	(0.181)
Number of Subarticles in Draft Bill (Logged)	1.011***
	(0.065)
Expiration of Bill before Plenary Vote	−2.489***
	(0.473)
Length of Legislative Review	0.002**
	(0.001)
Ireland	−1.390***
	(0.329)
Industry and Markets Policy	−0.294*
	(0.175)
Social Policy	0.355
	(0.407)
Regional Policy	−0.739**
	(0.336)
Environmental Policy	−0.483
	(0.432)
Intercept	−0.567
	(0.502)

Negative binomial model. $N = 187$. Significance levels: *, 10%; **, 5%; ***, 1%.

presented in Chapter 2 predicts that this should happen with increasing frequency as issues become more divisive.

Table 6.2 reports the results of a negative binomial model of the number of articles changed in a draft bill over the course of the legislative process.[7] Given the institutional structure of weak parliaments, it should generally be difficult for parties to press for changes that are not favored by the minister, and thus coalition

[7] The dispersion parameter is not presented in the table, but it indicates substantial overdispersion in the number of changes made to bills.

partners will generally be in a less favorable position to make substantial amendments to a minister's proposals. As a result, our expectation is that proposals dealing with issues that divide the coalition to a greater extent are no more likely to be changed over the course of the legislative process than proposals dealing with issues that are relatively noncontroversial. Our findings clearly bear this out.

Consider the impact of issue divisiveness on the number of articles changed when coalition partners do not have the services of a shadow JM available. This effect is given by the estimated coefficient on *Government Issue Divisiveness*, which, while positive, is substantially smaller in magnitude than the corresponding coefficient from the analysis in Chapter 5 (approximately 75 percent smaller, in fact) and not statistically different from zero ($p > 0.70$). In the absence of a JM, as the issue divisions between coalition partners and the proposing minister grow, a bill is no more likely to be amended in the legislative process. This contrasts sharply with the results for strong legislatures. Even more conspicuously, the coefficient on *Government Issue Divisiveness* when a shadow JM is present—and recall from Chapter 4 that about 45 percent of bills in weak legislatures come from ministries with a shadow JM—is actually *negative* ($0.019 - 0.105 = -0.086$). In other words, our analysis indicates that in weak committee systems, *there is no systematic relationship between the internal coalition divisions on the issues dealt with in a bill and the extent to which the bill is amended in parliament.* This finding clearly distinguishes coalition policymaking in weak legislatures from coalition policymaking in strong legislatures, where the process of parliamentary review plays a crucial role in containing ministerial policy drift.

We illustrate these findings in Figure 6.2. Analogous to Figure 6.1, this graph displays the simulated distributions of the expected number of changes made to divisive and non-divisive bills, for both common partners and shadow partners. The figure shows quite starkly that there is very little difference between the number of changes made to highly divisive legislation and the number of changes made to non-divisive legislation. When coalition partners have no shadow JM placed in the proposing ministry, the median expected number of articles changed in non-divisive bills is approximately twenty out of eighty-four articles (a bill of average size in these legislatures). By comparison, the median number of expected changes in highly divisive bills is twenty-two articles. As the overlap in the distributions reveal, we cannot reject our hypothesis that government issue divisiveness has no impact on the number of article changes.

More important, however, is a comparison of these results with our findings from strong legislatures. The figure indicates that for a typical bill in weak legislatures, when no shadow JM is present, highly divisive bills receive only 10 percent more amendments than noncontroversial bills (which, again, is not statistically different from zero). In contrast, the analysis in Chapter 5 revealed that in strong legislatures (in JM systems), when no shadow JM is present, highly divisive bills for the coalition receive approximately 40 percent more amendments than noncontroversial bills. In other words, the substantive impact of coalition

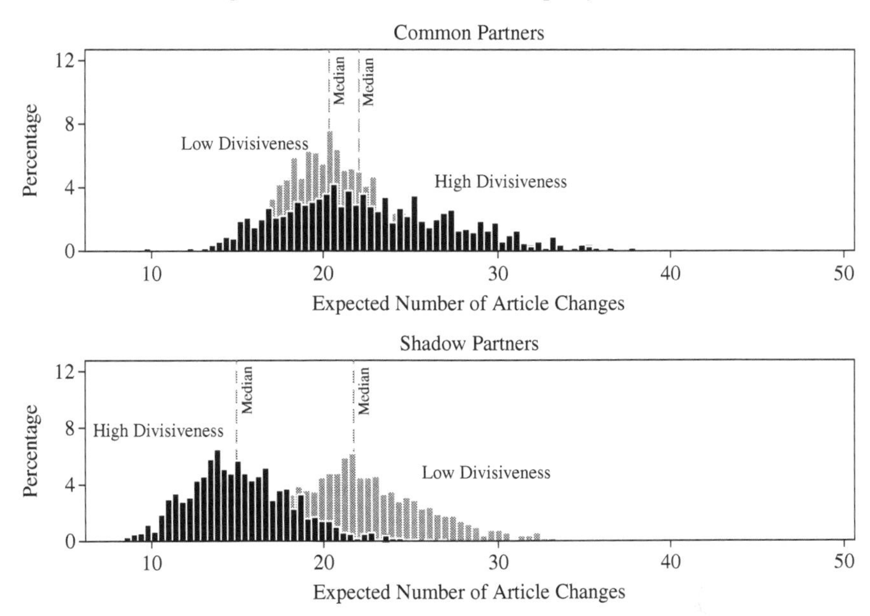

FIGURE 6.2 Government Issue Divisiveness and Legislative Amendment: Weak Legislatures

Note: All other covariates set at their mean sample values, for bill of average size (eighty-four articles).

issue divisions on a typical piece of legislation is approximately *four times larger* under strong legislative institutions.

Perhaps the more striking comparison with our findings from Chapter 5 involves the case in which a coalition partner has a shadow JM placed in the proposing ministry. Recall that in strong legislatures, highly divisive bills coming from a ministry with a shadow JM are amended roughly 90 percent more than non-divisive bills coming from such a ministry. Figure 6.2 paints a very different picture of how cabinet and parliamentary institutions interact in weak legislatures. Even though an analysis of the length of the legislative process in these systems suggests that shadow JMs play an information-gathering role in weak legislatures (which results in a shorter legislative process when a JM is in place), there is no evidence that legislative party groups are able to use this information to amend a minister's policy proposals. Indeed, as we pointed out earlier, the coefficient on government issue divisiveness in the 45 percent of cases where a shadow JM is in place is in a direction that is *inconsistent* with the idea that coalition partners in weak legislatures use the review process to force changes to government bills.[8] Indeed, this finding is more consistent with the idea that,

[8] The lower pane of the figure shows that the substantive impact of increasing divisiveness in this scenario is to *reduce* the number of expected changes from twenty-two articles to fifteen articles, a decrease of over 30 percent. This is a statistically significant difference for these levels of divisiveness:

in weak legislatures, it is the *minister* who receives benefits from the legislative review of his policy proposals. We have argued that ministers can receive policy-signaling benefits from (at least the appearance of) "fighting the good fight" with his coalition partners on the issues that divide them. Just as he can receive such benefits by *introducing* bills on internally divisive issues, he can receive them by actively *preventing* alterations to these bills in the legislative process. The need to do so should be especially pressing in those situations where supporters realize that the minister possesses numerous legislative prerogatives that would allow him to get his way—such as in weak legislatures—*and* where supporters perceive a greater degree of power-sharing—such as when a coalition partner occupies a high-level position in the ministry.

In sum, the conclusion we draw is that when parliamentary institutions are weak, coalition partners are unable to use the legislative process to effectively police hostile government ministers—and this holds true regardless of whether they have access to institutional resources (such as a JM) that operate outside the legislative process. Naturally, this does not imply that coalition partners in these systems do not police the coalition bargain in some other fashion. But it does imply that *parliament* does not play the same central role in this regard as when legislative institutions are strong.

6.3.3 Opposition Influence

A conventional view in the comparative literature portrays parliamentary institutions as one avenue for opposition influence in policymaking. This view is premised on the idea that legislative institutions can be used to shape policy, which is more likely to be the case in strong legislatures. As we saw in Chapter 5, however, even in strong legislative systems, opposition parties appear incapable of using the legislative process in a way that would suggest an ability to translate their policy views into legislation. They cannot systematically slow down bills dealing with issues that greatly separate them from the proposing minister, nor are they able to force changes to those bills. Indeed, we found that opposition parties that are not pivotal for the majority status of the government are *less* likely to be able to amend bills that separate them from the minister. It would be a great surprise if we were to find any other pattern in the weak legislatures under investigation here—after all, these parliaments provide even less influence for opposition parties.

Only 2.6 percent of expected review times for "high divisiveness" bills in the shadow partner scenario are greater than or equal to the median expected review time for "low divisiveness" bills, while only 0.6 percent of expected review times for "low divisiveness" bills are less than or equal to the median review time of "high divisiveness" bills.

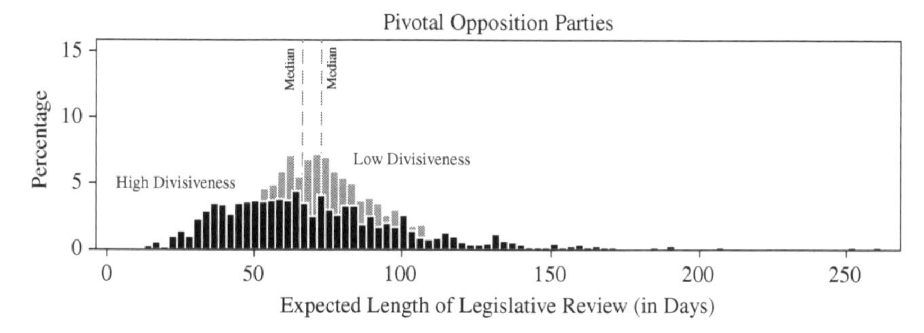

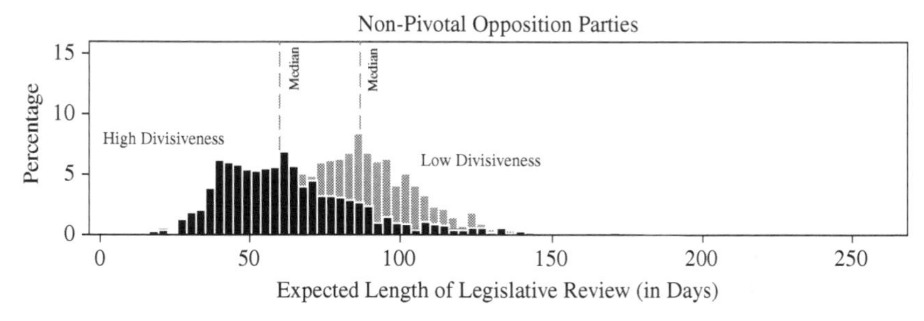

FIGURE 6.3 Opposition Issue Divisiveness and Legislative Scrutiny in Minority Government Situations: Weak Legislatures

Note: All other covariates set at their main sample values for minority government situations.

The coefficient estimates in Tables 6.1 and 6.2 show that this expectation is justified. The policy divisions between both types of opposition parties (pivotal and non-pivotal) and the proposing minister have a slightly negative, and statistically insignificant, impact on the amount of time a bill is deliberated. Moreover, for non-pivotal parties, divisiveness has a slightly negative impact on the degree to which the bill is amended in the review process. For pivotal opposition parties, divisiveness has a positive, but substantively and statistically insignificant, impact on the extent of amendment.[9]

As in Chapter 5, to examine the substantive impact of the opposition thoroughly, we examine four different hypothetical scenarios. The scenarios are defined by whether there is a minority or majority government in power, and by whether the bills under review greatly divide opposition parties from the

[9] In our sample of weak legislatures, only Ireland has minority governments. Thus, because we include country indicators in the model, the coefficients on the minority government variable in Tables 6.1 and 6.2 indicate the difference between minority and majority governments in Ireland on scrutiny and change. Similarly, the coefficients on pivotal opposition issue divisiveness (which, by construction, is non-zero only for minority governments) represents the impact of an increase in this variable on scrutiny and change for Irish minority governments.

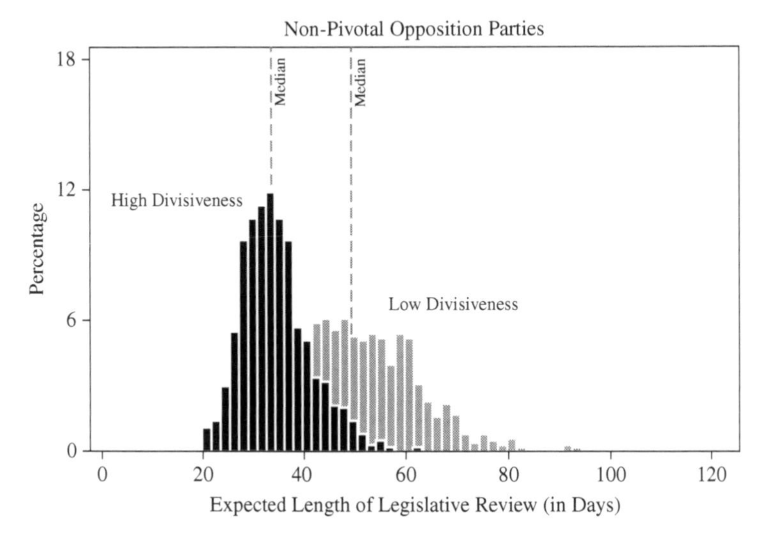

FIGURE 6.4 Opposition Issue Divisiveness and Legislative Scrutiny in Majority Government Situations: Weak Legislatures

Note: All other covariates set at their mean sample values for majority government situations.

proposing minister or do not.[10] In Figure 6.3, we show the effects of divisiveness for pivotal and non-pivotal members of the opposition in minority government situations. The figure shows that regardless of the type of opposition parties confronting the government, their level of disagreement with the proposing minister simply has no significant impact on how long bills are expected to spend in the legislative process.

In Figure 6.4, we examine the effect of divisiveness on scrutiny for non-pivotal opposition parties in majority government situations, the more typical case in weak legislatures. Here, we see a clear difference between the length of parliamentary scrutiny for divisive and non-divisive bills (from the perspective of the opposition), but in a direction *inconsistent* with the idea that opposition parties can use legislative institutions to press their perspective on government policy. In the current scenario, a highly divisive bill for opposition parties is expected to spend two weeks fewer in the legislative process than a non-divisive bill, a decrease in review time of roughly 30 percent.[11]

[10] Analogous to our definition for government issue divisiveness, our definition of a bill dealing with issues of "low divisiveness" for the opposition is one with a value that is in the lower 10 percent of our sample of bills (for either non-pivotal or pivotal opposition parties, as appropriate), and a bill dealing with issues of "high divisiveness" as one with a value in the upper 10 percent of the sample. The difference between the two values for each opposition variable in this case is roughly three standard deviations. All other variables are set at their sample means.

[11] Approximately 6.4 percent of expected review times for "low divisiveness" bills in this scenario are less than or equal to the median expected review time for "high divisiveness" bills, while only 2.7

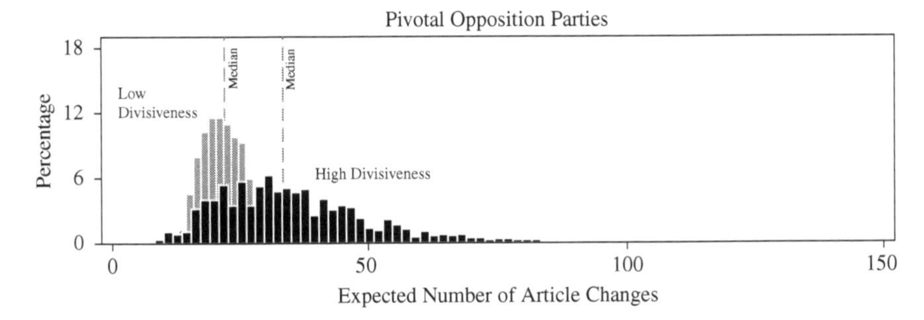

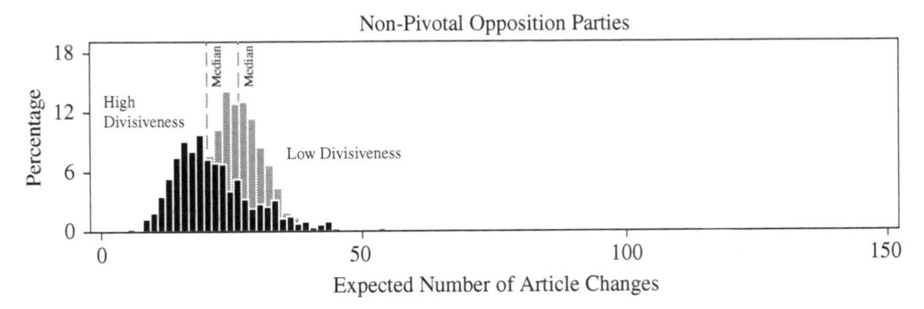

FIGURE 6.5 Opposition Issue Divisiveness and Legislative Amendment in Minority Government Situations: Weak Legislatures

Note: All other covariates set at their mean sample values for minority government situations, for bill of average size (133 articles).

Similarly, Figure 6.5, which shows the expected number of article changes in relation to the divisiveness of a bill from the opposition's perspective (in minority government situations), indicates clearly that greater divisions between opposition parties and a minister make it no more likely that the minister's proposal will be amended in the legislative process. For non-pivotal opposition parties, the effect is in the opposite direction predicted by conventional scholarship, while for pivotal opposition parties (as we saw with strong legislatures), the effect is in the predicted direction, but not statistically significant.

Finally, in Figure 6.6, we examine the effect of divisiveness on legislative amendment for non-pivotal opposition parties in majority government situations. Once again, we see little evidence that opposition parties in weak legislatures, just as we saw in strong legislatures, have any impact on the degree to which they can change government policy.[12] In short, our findings reinforce the results

percent of expected review times for "high divisiveness" bills are greater than or equal to the median review time of "low divisiveness" bills.

[12] Indeed, the figure shows that high divisiveness bills from the perspective of the opposition are likely to experience fewer changes (fifteen articles out of seventy-three) than non-divisive bills (twenty-two articles out of seventy-three). This difference is not statistically significant at conventional

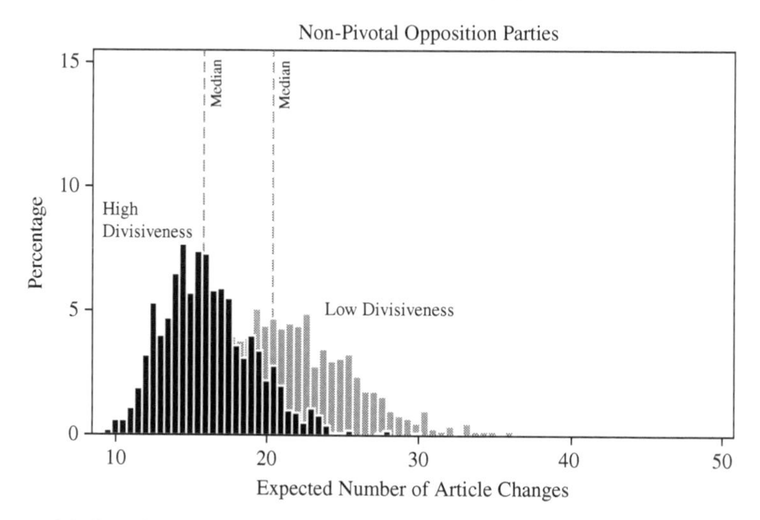

FIGURE 6.6 Opposition Issue Divisiveness and Legislative Amendment in Majority Government Situations: Weak Legislatures

Note: All other covariates set at their mean sample values for majority government situations, for bill of average size (seventy-three articles).

for opposition influence in strong legislatures. There is little empirical support for the claim that legislative institutions are useful to the opposition in exercising direct influence on government policy. Strong legislative institutions only appear to benefit *government* parties in shaping the policies coming out of ministries they do not control, while weak legislative institutions do not even offer government parties an effective means to counteract the policy actions of hostile ministers.

6.4 CONCLUSION

It is not often that the "take-away" point of an empirical analysis in social science is a non-finding—that is, the *absence* of a relationship between two or more variables of interest. And yet, this has been precisely the purpose of this chapter. To demonstrate that strong legislative institutions not only *allow* coalition parties to use the legislative arena to shadow and ultimately control hostile ministers, but that they are in fact *necessary* if parliament is to be used for this purpose, we

levels, however. Approximately 15 percent of expected review times for "low divisiveness" bills in this scenario are less than or equal to the median expected review time for "high divisiveness" bills, while 9.2 percent of expected review times for "high divisiveness" bills are greater than or equal to the median review time of "low divisiveness" bills.

turned to an analysis of the legislative process in weak legislatures. The goal of the analysis was to show that—in contrast to the findings of the previous chapter—when parties only have access to weak legislative institutions, they are unable to police ministers during the process of legislative review.

Our findings leave little doubt that this is the case. While the results suggest that even in the absence of strong legislative committees and procedures, parties attempt to scrutinize bills introduced by hostile ministers, the scope with which they are able to do so (measured by time in the legislative process) is much more limited than in strong committee systems. In addition, the data reveal that even if parties become informed about the policy issues surrounding a minister's bill, they are unable to force change to the bill in the legislative process. It is important to be precise about this claim. We do not argue, and the data presented here do not allow us to conclude, that coalition parties in weak legislative systems are completely unable to police the coalition bargain, and thus are more vulnerable to ministerial subterfuge. We suspect that they may be, however, simply because they lack an important resource for doing so. If this suspicion is correct, then it may be that the distribution of ministerial portfolios has a significantly greater influence on policy in weak legislatures than in strong ones. In any event, confronted with the challenges of coalition governance, parties in systems with weak legislative institutions should look for, and make use of, other mechanisms that can help them police ministers. The conclusion we draw is that coalition partners are not using *parliament* for this purpose. Legislatures with weak institutions simply provide no avenue for placing effective constraints on government ministers.

6.A APPENDIX

As we did at the conclusion of the last chapter, we attempt to demonstrate in this appendix that our choice of the specific survival model used to test our hypotheses about legislative scrutiny in weak legislatures is the appropriate one. Again, our desire is to choose a survival model that gives us accurate estimates of the effects of the covariates and simultaneously minimizes our uncertainty about these effects. Recall that the accuracy and efficiency of survival model estimates depend to some degree on the choice of parameterization of the baseline hazard rate (which reflects the nature of time dependence in the data, conditional on the model covariates), and that different models assume different parameterizations. As we outlined in the last chapter, we believe a reasonable course of action in evaluating the choice of model specification is to estimate the semiparametric Cox model that makes minimal assumptions about the baseline hazard, and then a range of fully parametric models that make distinct assumptions about the form of time dependence. We can then compare these models to see which one provides the best representation of the sample data.

TABLE 6A.1 Estimates from Proportional Hazards Models of Length of Legislative Review, Weak Committee Systems (Assumption of No Heterogeneity)

Variables	Cox	Exponential	Weibull	Gompertz
Government Issue Divisiveness	−0.163**	−0.209***	−0.195***	−0.176***
	(0.066)	(0.065)	(0.066)	(0.066)
Government Issue Divisiveness × Shadow JM	0.123*	0.156**	0.148**	0.125*
	(0.070)	(0.068)	(0.068)	(0.069)
Shadow JM	−0.242	−0.358	−0.326	−0.212
	(0.219)	(0.218)	(0.218)	(0.216)
Non-Pivotal Opposition Issue Divisiveness	0.072	0.102*	0.091*	0.080
	(0.053)	(0.054)	(0.054)	(0.052)
Pivotal Opposition Issue Divisiveness	0.059	0.080	0.070	0.044
	(0.155)	(0.156)	(0.156)	(0.155)
Minority Government	−0.490*	−0.670**	−0.616**	−0.549*
	(0.287)	(0.290)	(0.290)	(0.287)
Number of Committee Referrals	−0.053	0.018	0.001	−0.020
	(0.200)	(0.202)	(0.200)	(0.198)
Number of Subarticles in Draft Bill (Logged)	−0.260***	−0.286***	−0.268***	−0.253***
	(0.067)	(0.066)	(0.067)	(0.066)
Ireland	0.261	0.400	0.355	0.317
	(0.357)	(0.360)	(0.360)	(0.355)
Industrial Policy	−0.251	−0.266	−0.247	−0.224
	(0.177)	(0.172)	(0.173)	(0.174)
Social Policy	−0.766*	−1.073**	−0.960**	−0.818*
	(0.429)	(0.436)	(0.438)	(0.429)
Regional Policy	−0.137	−0.155	−0.136	−0.070
	(0.353)	(0.353)	(0.352)	(0.349)
Environmental Policy	−1.103**	−1.281***	−1.220***	−1.104**
	(0.452)	(0.445)	(0.447)	(0.449)
Intercept		−3.274***	−2.951***	−3.109***
		(0.490)	(0.534)	(0.485)
Shape Parameter		[1.000]	0.926	−0.003***
			(0.051)	(0.001)

$N = 187$. Significance levels: *, 10%; **, 5%; ***, 1%.

We begin by examining estimates from the class of proportional hazards (PH) models, shown in Table 6A.1. As before, we begin by making the assumption that, conditional on the covariates, there is no heterogeneity in the data. We first note that, just as with the PH models estimated for the strong legislatures, the coefficients are roughly similar across models for the government issue divisiveness variable and its interaction with the shadow JM indicator, except for a notable increase in magnitude in the exponential and Weibull specifications (on the order of roughly 25 percent). Indeed, the coefficients on all the explanatory variables for these two models are larger in magnitude than those from the Cox and Gompertz models. We also note that the standard errors are roughly the same across models

TABLE 6A.2 Estimates from Accelerated Failure Time Models of Length of Legislative Review, Weak Committee Systems (Assumption of No Heterogeneity)

Variables	Exponential	Weibull	Log-logistic	Log-normal
Government Issue Divisiveness	0.209***	0.211***	0.188**	0.180**
	(0.065)	(0.070)	(0.074)	(0.072)
Government Issue Divisiveness × Shadow JM	−0.156**	−0.160**	−0.154**	−0.147*
	(0.068)	(0.074)	(0.078)	(0.076)
Shadow JM	0.358	0.352	0.295	0.220
	(0.218)	(0.234)	(0.213)	(0.227)
Non-Pivotal Opposition Issue Divisiveness	−0.102*	−0.098*	−0.045	−0.042
	(0.054)	(0.058)	(0.050)	(0.054)
Pivotal Opposition Issue Divisiveness	−0.080	−0.075	−0.034	−0.010
	(0.156)	(0.168)	(0.146)	(0.160)
Minority Government	0.670**	0.665**	0.667**	0.607**
	(0.290)	(0.311)	(0.287)	(0.294)
Number of Committee Referrals	−0.018	−0.001	0.232	0.268
	(0.202)	(0.216)	(0.184)	(0.203)
Number of Subarticles in Draft Bill (Logged)	0.286***	0.289***	0.335***	0.343***
	(0.066)	(0.071)	(0.063)	(0.068)
Ireland	−0.400	−0.384	−0.223	−0.160
	(0.360)	(0.387)	(0.355)	(0.379)
Industrial Policy	0.266	0.267	0.373**	0.240
	(0.172)	(0.186)	(0.182)	(0.190)
Social Policy	1.073**	1.036**	0.390	0.560
	(0.436)	(0.467)	(0.429)	(0.424)
Regional Policy	0.155	0.147	0.181	0.122
	(0.353)	(0.380)	(0.366)	(0.369)
Environmental Policy	1.281***	1.317***	1.637***	1.559***
	(0.445)	(0.481)	(0.426)	(0.461)
Intercept	3.274***	3.186***	1.935***	1.952***
	(0.490)	(0.530)	(0.489)	(0.514)
Shape Parameter	[1.000]	1.079	0.597***	1.083
		(0.055)	(0.037)	(0.058)

$N = 187$. Significance levels: *, 10%; **, 5%; ***, 1%.

for all variables, suggesting that there would be little to gain in terms of efficiency by choosing one model over another.

In Table 6A.2, we compare estimates across the four Accelerated Failure Time (AFT) models. Again, we note that the exponential and Weibull specifications yield coefficients that are generally larger in magnitude than the coefficients in the other models. This is especially apparent for the coefficients on the non-pivotal opposition issue divisiveness measure, where the coefficients on the exponential and Weibull models (which indicate that bills that divide the opposition from the proposing minister are likely to be expedited in the legislative process) are more than twice as large as the corresponding coefficient from the log-logistic and log-normal models. We also see that (as in Chapter 5) the standard errors

TABLE 6A.3 Estimates from Proportional Hazards Models of Length of Legislative Review, Weak Committee Systems (Shared Gamma Frailty)

Variables	Cox	Exponential	Weibull	Gompertz
Government Issue Divisiveness	−0.172**	−0.243***	−0.265***	−0.190***
	(0.069)	(0.079)	(0.086)	(0.072)
Government Issue Divisiveness × Shadow JM	0.128*	0.165*	0.172*	0.134*
	(0.073)	(0.085)	(0.089)	(0.075)
Shadow JM	−0.252	−0.301	−0.308	−0.228
	(0.232)	(0.283)	(0.300)	(0.237)
Non-Pivotal Opposition Issue Divisiveness	0.073	0.103	0.116	0.082
	(0.056)	(0.066)	(0.071)	(0.056)
Pivotal Opposition Issue Divisiveness	0.069	0.093	0.104	0.057
	(0.160)	(0.183)	(0.192)	(0.164)
Minority Government	−0.548*	−0.870**	−0.962**	−0.636*
	(0.300)	(0.354)	(0.386)	(0.327)
Number of Committee Referrals	−0.039	0.044	0.061	0.000
	(0.207)	(0.230)	(0.238)	(0.210)
Number of Subarticles in Draft Bill (Logged)	−0.271***	−0.317***	−0.340***	−0.268***
	(0.069)	(0.074)	(0.079)	(0.072)
Ireland	0.305	0.580	0.680	0.384
	(0.374)	(0.360)	(0.489)	(0.394)
Industrial Policy	−0.272	−0.333	−0.365*	−0.257
	(0.184)	(0.208)	(0.219)	(0.190)
Social Policy	−0.779*	−0.882*	−0.878	−0.830*
	(0.444)	(0.526)	(0.556)	(0.452)
Regional Policy	−0.134	−0.078	−0.059	−0.067
	(0.368)	(0.430)	(0.449)	(0.373)
Environmental Policy	−1.128**	−1.315***	−1.368***	−1.143**
	(0.461)	(0.498)	(0.519)	(0.466)
Intercept		−3.090***	−3.305***	−3.070***
		(0.600)	(0.688)	(0.522)
Shape Parameter		[1.000]	1.057	−0.003**
			(0.074)	(0.001)
Frailty Parameter	0.030	0.180***	0.238***	0.047

$N = 187$. Shared frailty models grouped on country, government, and ministry. Number of groups = 78. Significance level of frailty parameter based on a log-likelihood test against a model where the parameter is constrained to equal zero. Significance levels: *, 10%; **, 5%; ***, 1%.

in the log-logistic model, for the majority of coefficients, are smaller than those in any other model. This suggests that, if the log-logistic turns out to be a good fit to the data (which we assess below), it may be preferable to other models on efficiency grounds.

In Tables 6A.3 and 6A.4, we reexamine the PH and AFT models, respectively, but this time assuming subgroup heterogeneity, where the groups, as in Chapter 5, are defined by the individual ministries for each government in the sample that introduced the bills. The estimate of the frailty variance is at the bottom of the table. Recall that an estimate of zero would indicate the absence of heterogeneity, which would imply that taking heterogeneity into account does not significantly improve the fit of the model. In this case, unlike what we saw with the sample of bills in strong legislatures, heterogeneity appears to be a problem only in the Weibull and exponential specifications. The estimates of the frailty variance for these two models are rather high and statistically different from zero. For the Cox, Gompertz, log-logistic, and log-normal models, the frailty variance estimate is substantially lower. That is, we do not improve the explanatory power of

TABLE 6A.4 Estimates from Accelerated Failure Time Models of Length of Legislative Review, Weak Committee Systems (Shared Gamma Frailty)

Variables	Exponential	Weibull	Log-logistic	Log-normal
Government Issue Divisiveness	0.243***	0.251***	0.195**	0.189**
	(0.079)	(0.078)	(0.078)	(0.074)
Government Issue Divisiveness	−0.165*	−0.163*	−0.156*	−0.148*
× Shadow JM	(0.085)	(0.084)	(0.081)	(0.079)
Shadow JM	0.301	0.291	0.320	0.212
	(0.283)	(0.284)	(0.224)	(0.241)
Non-Pivotal Opposition Issue	−0.103	−0.110*	−0.048	−0.041
Divisiveness	(0.066)	(0.066)	(0.051)	(0.055)
Pivotal Opposition Issue Divisiveness	−0.093	−0.099	−0.047	−0.019
	(0.183)	(0.181)	(0.146)	(0.161)
Minority Government	0.870**	0.910**	0.739**	0.698**
	(0.354)	(0.353)	(0.301)	(0.311)
Number of Committee Referrals	−0.044	−0.057	0.239	0.278
	(0.230)	(0.225)	(0.186)	(0.205)
Number of Subarticles in	0.317***	0.321***	0.340***	0.350***
Draft Bill (Logged)	(0.074)	(0.072)	(0.063)	(0.068)
Ireland	−0.580	−0.643	−0.286	−0.242
	(0.374)	(0.457)	(0.368)	(0.399)
Industrial Policy	0.333	0.345*	0.403**	0.270
	(0.208)	(0.205)	(0.185)	(0.193)
Social Policy	0.882*	0.831	0.371	0.527
	(0.526)	(0.531)	(0.420)	(0.429)
Regional Policy	0.078	0.056	0.151	0.102
	(0.430)	(0.425)	(0.372)	(0.382)
Environmental Policy	1.315***	1.294***	1.612***	1.531***
	(0.498)	(0.487)	(0.430)	(0.463)
Intercept	3.090***	3.125***	1.910***	1.910***
	(0.600)	(0.595)	(0.497)	(0.529)
Shape Parameter	[1.000]	0.946	0.574***	1.040
		(0.069)	(0.044)	(0.023)
Frailty Parameter	0.180***	0.238***	0.062	0.072

$N = 187$. Shared frailty models grouped on country, government, and ministry. Number of groups = 78. Significance level of frailty parameter based on a log-likelihood test against a model where the parameter is constrained to equal zero. Significance levels: $*$, 10%; $**$, 5%; $***$, 1%.

TABLE 6A.5 Comparisons of Akaike Information Criterion across Survival Models, Weak Legislatures

Model	AIC
Cox model	1540.57
Exponential model	662.10
Weibull model	662.05
Gompertz model	610.93
Log-logistic model	579.56
Log-normal model	585.33
Cox shared frailty model	1540.38
Exponential shared frailty model	615.46
Weibull shared frailty model	616.90
Gompertz shared frailty model	612.43
Log-logistic shared frailty model	580.64
Log-normal shared frailty model	586.06

these models by taking into account the possibility that unmeasured factors at the ministry level could have an impact on the length of legislative review.

We consider goodness-of-fit of the various models (with and without heterogeneity) in more detail in Table 6A.5, where we compare the Akaike Information Criterion (AIC) for each specification. Recall that the AIC statistics allow us to compare our competing models on the basis of their log-likelihoods, where each

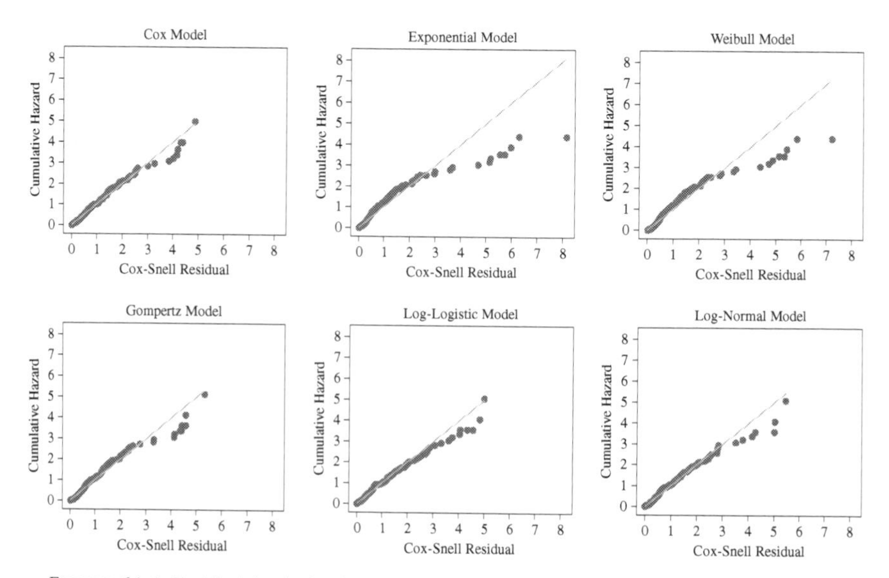

FIGURE 6A.1 Residual Analysis of Survival Models without Heterogeneity: Weak Legislatures

log-likelihood is "penalized" for the number of parameters estimated in the model. The best-fitting model is the one with the lowest AIC.[13]

Two points from this table are immediately apparent. First, if we compare (for each pair of models that make the same assumption about the baseline hazard rate) the model that does not take heterogeneity into account to the one that does, it becomes even clearer that heterogeneity is only an issue for the Weibull and exponential specifications. The AIC statistics for the Cox model and the Cox shared frailty model, for example, are virtually identical, which indicates that the gain in fit from adding the frailty variance parameter to the model does not outweigh the cost of losing an extra degree of freedom. For the Gompertz, log-logistic, and log-normal models, estimating this parameter actually *increases* the AIC slightly. A second notable point is that, of the parametric models, the log-logistic model (with no heterogeneity) produces the lowest AIC, indicating that it provides the best fit to the data.

Recall that another way to evaluate goodness-of-fit across models is to evaluate it graphically with the Cox–Snell residuals. If a model is an adequate fit to the data, then the Cox–Snell residuals will be unit exponentially distributed with a hazard ratio of 1 (i.e., they should lie on a 45-degree line through the origin), which we can easily assess by plotting the residuals against the estimated cumulative hazard rate. Since heterogeneity has been diagnosed as not being a problem for any models except the exponential and Weibull (and since the AIC statistics reveal that these two models even taking heterogeneity into account are not the best-fitting models for the data), we only present the plots for the models that assume no heterogeneity. We do this in Figure 6A.1. For the five parametric models, we see that (just as the AIC statistics show) the log-logistic is the best fit to the data, followed closely by the log-normal, then the Gompertz. As in Chapter 5, we see that the Weibull and exponential specifications are inadequate fits for many of the observations, especially for those bills with relatively longer durations in the legislative process. The log-logistic model also compares favorably to the semiparametric Cox model. The deviations for the log-logistic model appear to be slightly smaller for the longer duration bills than those from the Cox model, but admittedly, the differences between the two are not as clearly perceptible as they were in the case of bills in strong legislatures. We could safely choose either of these specifications, but to facilitate a comparison with our results in Chapter 5—where the coefficients were interpreted in the AFT metric (i.e., in terms of their effects on survival times rather than the hazard rate)—we choose the log-logistic model (with the assumption of no heterogeneity) to evaluate our hypotheses concerning the length of the review process.

[13] Recall also that the AIC statistics for the (semiparametric) Cox models cannot be compared to the fully parametric models.

7

Conclusion

Cooperation and compromise are fundamental to multiparty government. Parties must develop a policy program that strikes an acceptable balance between the competing interests of the partners. Enforcing the coalition compromise in the face of policy delegation to ministers and the pressures of electoral competition poses a formidable challenge. Compromise is only viable in an institutional environment that allows parties to "keep tabs" on hostile ministers (and the departments they oversee). If multiparty governance is to be successful in fostering compromise and protecting against "ministerial drift," it requires mechanisms that allow parties to follow the old Russian proverb, *Doveryai, no proveryai*: Trust, but verify.

Party leaders are not, of course, oblivious to this problem, and they employ numerous devices to supervise the work of their coalition partners. Junior ministers (JMs), who are ostensibly being groomed for future ministerial service, serve as "watchdogs" (Thies, 2001). Other mechanisms to reduce coalition conflict include cabinet committees, inner cabinets, and coalition committees (Müller and Strøm, 2000; Anderweg and Timmermans, 2008; Müller and Strøm, 2008). Similarly, interest groups can serve as "fire alarms." The central argument of this book is that the legislative process provides another device in policing the coalition bargain. Parliaments that feature strong committee systems that are organized along ministerial lines, that have broad investigative powers, and that enable members to present amendments without restriction, allow parties to scrutinize and amend ministerial proposals, thus reducing the threat posed by ministerial discretion. In contrast, legislative institutions that make scrutiny and change more difficult—for example, committees that are not permanent or small in number, with jurisdictions that do not correspond to those of ministries, and restrictive procedures that curb the use of legislative amendments—make it much harder for parties to control ministerial drift.

An important implication of this argument is that strong legislatures play a far more important policy role in parliamentary systems than is often assumed. Moreover, they are important for reasons that differ from most conventional accounts. Historically, parliamentary institutions emerged as institutional checks on the power of unelected monarchs. With the rise of democratic governance, executive powers traditionally exercised by the crown shifted to a prime minister and cabinet. Parliaments came to be viewed as institutions that check, or at least oversee, the work of cabinets—a conception that is still reflected in vote of no-confidence provisions that make the cabinet accountable to the legislature.

This traditional juxtaposition of cabinet and parliament as separate institutions misses an important dimension of parliamentary activity, at least under coalition government. Strong parliaments do not simply serve as "oversight" bodies for the cabinet as a whole. Rather, the legislative process plays a central role in allowing multiparty governments to resolve *intra-government* tensions. Thus, the relevant juxtaposition is not between the cabinet and the parliament that holds "the government" accountable. Rather, it is between coalition parties that use legislative institutions to contain threats posed by the discretionary powers of ministers.

Of course, this need not imply that the legislative arena matters *only* for intra-coalition politics. The same legislative institutions that allow cabinet parties to scrutinize and amend legislative initiatives may also empower opposition parties. However, opposition parties are likely to be more constrained in taking advantage of this resource. Especially where they face a majority government, they are typically not in a position to force change simply because government parties, at least where they are united, are able to ignore the opposition's wishes. The empirical analysis presented in Chapters 5 and 6 suggests strongly that the legislative influence of opposition parties facing majority governments is limited, even in strong committee systems.

Opposition parties facing a *minority* government may find themselves in a stronger position since such governments must rely on outside support to implement their legislative program. Especially identifiable, formal support parties may therefore have some leverage to influence policy. While such parties—which typically negotiate a formal agreement with the government and pledge consistent support across issues (Strøm, 1990*b*)—do not sit at the cabinet table, the government is not in a position to ignore their claims in the same way it can ignore "ordinary" opposition parties. Consequently, it would not be surprising if formal support parties use the legislative process to enforce the agreement they have reached with the cabinet. Empirically, the analysis we have presented does not allow a direct evaluation of this argument. The minority governments in our sample—most of which come from Denmark—relied on "ad hoc" support, rather than on agreements with formal support parties (Strøm, 1990*b*; Damgaard, 1992). However, formal support arrangements are quite common in other countries with a tradition of minority government, including Norway and Sweden. As Strøm (1990*b*) has argued forcefully, strong legislative institutions in these countries may provide such parties considerable influence over policy. This would be an interesting avenue for future research.

7.1 THE ORIGINS OF LEGISLATIVE INSTITUTIONS

Because strong legislative institutions play a role in solving intra-coalition monitoring problems, political parties that expect to be frequent participants in coalition government have incentives to maintain strong legislative institutions where they exist and to create them where they are absent. Legislative institutions should be, at least in part, endogenous to the prevalence of coalition government. An ideal test case for evaluating this expectation would be a polity with a history of single-party governments operating under weak legislative institutions that undergoes a dramatic and permanent shift to coalition government. Once coalition government becomes an established practice, do government parties attempt to strengthen legislative institutions? Several pieces of evidence suggest that the answer to this question is "yes."

For most of the post-war period, single-party government was the norm in Irish politics. Until 1989, the dominant party in the Irish political system, Fianna Fáil, explicitly rejected the possibility of coalition, instead preferring to form single-party governments when it was able to do so (Laver, 1992; Mitchell, 2000). Although there were brief periods of coalition before the late 1980s, usually between Fine Gael and the Labour Party, single-party government dominated the political landscape. Beginning with the 1989 election, this situation changed drastically as Fianna Fáil dropped its resistance to the idea of multiparty government and went into coalition with the Progressive Democrats. Since then, Ireland has experienced coalitions after every subsequent election. Multiparty government is now the expected (and accepted) outcome of the government formation process. As we pointed out in Chapter 3, one response to this change was a gradual strengthening of the legislative committee system. Following the 2002 election, the coalition of Fianna Fáil and the Progressive Democrats created a system of thirteen select committees with jurisdictions that closely correspond to those of government ministries. It remains to be seen whether Irish committees will ever have the influence enjoyed by their counterparts in Denmark, Germany, and the Netherlands (see, e.g., Gallagher, 2005), but unquestionably, Ireland now features the strongest committee system in its history.

In New Zealand, the change in legislative institutions was tied even more closely to the rise of coalition governance. Until 1996, parliament was elected under a first-past-the-post electoral system, which (predictably) produced single-party majority governments. Since 1996, parliament has been elected through proportional representation rules. No party has been able to win a parliamentary majority since, and coalition government has become the norm. Hand-in-hand with the rise of coalition governments, legislative committees have been strengthened to provide more opportunity for the serious scrutiny and amendment of government bills (McLeay, 2008). The change in the power and influence of legislative committees has been drastic. In 1991, Sir Geoffrey Palmer, having served in parliament for eleven years, and as prime minister for one year, offered the following assessment of parliament's role in the legislative process:

> Each week MPs of the governing party met in caucus and in secret settled their policy. Once adopted, all members were obliged to vote for it in Parliament. Parliament became a rubber stamp—it determined nothing. It was just a talking shop. The positions were pre-determined elsewhere and the control just about total, to an extent still not possible in the United Kingdom. (Ganley, 2001: 81)

Writing in 2001, following the transition to coalition governance and the legislative reforms of the mid-1990s, Ganley (2001: 89) offered a radically different view of the impact of parliamentary committees:

> New Zealand's select committees ... have considerable legislative influence. Not only do they play an important tidying role that inevitably comes with close scrutiny of bills; they also bring about important changes to legislation. In addition to direct changes made to the draft bill the committee reports back to the House, Governments are prompted to draft their own changes in response to issues arising from select committees' hearings of evidence. Through their inquiries, committees also bring pressure on Governments to initiate legislative change. This inevitably gives rise to another question: why is the New Zealand committee system so influential? Part of the answer must be electoral system change. With the change to the mixed-member system of proportional representation (MMP) has come a large parliament (120 rather than 99 members), a wider spectrum of parties and a complete overhaul of Standing Orders. All of these have helped strengthen the committees.

The Irish and New Zealand experiences are suggestive—in both cases, historically weak legislative institutions were strengthened. Of course, this does not necessarily imply that these institutions were changed *because* of the rise of coalition politics, but it is consistent with a conscious choice of legislative institutions to resolve the tensions of coalition governance.

It is important not to overstate the extent to which legislative institutions are created in response to the demands of coalition. While it is natural to expect that parties confronting the need to police the coalition bargain will find it advantageous to create strong legislative institutions, their ability to do so is not unconstrained. Internal legislative structures can be changed by simple majority rule in many parliaments. But legal and constitutional constraints can pose significant obstacles in others. In France, for example, the constitution of the Fifth Republic limits the number of legislative committees to six, and constitutional amendments require parliamentary supermajorities or a popular referendum—a high bar that makes changing legislative institutions a challenge.[1]

[1] Notably, the constitutional restriction on the number of committees in France was introduced as part of President de Gaulle's constitutional reforms in 1958, which were designed precisely to weaken the legislative branch (Williams, 1968; Huber, 1996).

In addition to legal and constitutional constraints, widely shared public understanding of what is politically legitimate (which is, at least in part, a product of historical tradition and experience) imposes political constraints. Attempts to manipulate or change political institutions may be politically costly for parties if doing so is perceived as an illegitimate manipulation of the "rules of the game" (for an elaboration of this argument, see Weingast 1997). As an example, consider the number of justices of the US Supreme Court. Although, in principle, Congressional majorities are free to change this number (with the support of the President) by simple majority rule, attempts to do so are likely to incur a significant public backlash that makes it next to impossible politically to pursue such a strategy (Leuchtenburg, 1996; Friedman, 2009). To the extent that parties face similar constraints in attempting to reform long-standing parliamentary procedures, legislative reforms—even where parties desire them—may be prohibitively costly.

7.2 IMPLICATIONS FOR OTHER SETTINGS

One important question is how well the argument of this book "travels." What are the implications for coalitions and parliaments in settings other than the five democracies we have investigated? In one sense, the answer is simple. Stated abstractly, three features define the policymaking problem we have addressed: (*a*) there are several policymaking actors, and compromise among them is desirable or necessary, (*b*) there is a need to delegate to a subset of actors in creating policy to implement those compromises, and (*c*) the actors are held to account separately by their constituencies. It is the combination of the three elements—compromise, delegation, and competition—that is critical: The pressures created by separate accountability generate the threat that delegation will be abused to undermine compromise agreements.

What does this suggest for the broader implications of the argument? Most obviously, the argument applies to situations of coalition governance beyond the five countries in our study. More surprising, perhaps, is that it has implications for single-party governments, which can be subject to similar pressures. As a number of scholars have argued, large parties are vehicles for achieving compromise among different interests (Rogowski and Kayser, 2002; Bawn and Rosenbluth, 2006; Linzer and Rogowski, 2008). The key difference is that such parties achieve *within* the party what is achieved *across* parties in coalition governments. One important consequence of this is that the third crucial element of our story—electoral competition—is (largely) missing: The various interests all compete under the same party label. Indeed, as Bawn and Rosenbluth (2006) have argued, this lack of electoral competition among factions within parties is critical, because it facilitates the enforcement of compromise agreements (in their particular application, fiscal restraint) that is much harder to achieve when compromises must be constructed across parties that compete separately.

There is, however, a caveat. The advantage that large parties enjoy in constructing viable compromises among competing factions is reduced when an electoral system facilitates competition among factions *within* the same party. Consider, for example, the case of Japan. Until 1996, Japanese elections were held under a single non-transferable vote electoral system, which made competition among factions of the same party (such as the dominant Liberal Democratic Party [LDP]) possible because voters had to choose between party candidates. In such a setting, even if one party is able to secure an overall majority, the dynamics we identify for coalition government can emerge among factions of the dominant party. Different interests within the party compete against one another electorally, and keeping tabs on ministers associated with other factions becomes critical for each faction. For example, Thies (2001) has demonstrated that just as competing coalition parties make use of the appointment of JMs to "shadow" hostile ministers, factions within the LDP appear to have used JMs in the same way.

In contrast, single-party governments operating in an environment that allows cohesive party control over elections—which reduces the ability of voters to choose among candidates affiliated with different factions of the same party—are much less likely to be afflicted by the threats of delegation. Such electoral systems reduce the position-taking incentives of policymakers significantly. As a result, implementation of compromise agreements that are reached within the party becomes much less problematic. Those charged with implementation face few reasons to undermine the agreement. Indeed, given central party control in the electoral process (over nominations, access to party lists, and ordering on the list), they may expect that significant "drift" would have detrimental consequences for their careers.

7.3 COALITIONS AND THE QUALITY OF DEMOCRACY

In closing, it is useful to consider the normative implications of the argument and the evidence we have presented. In many, if not most, of the world's democracies, coalition government is the norm. Public policy is made by multiple parties who share government power, rather than by a single party. Is the distinction between single-party and coalition government normatively relevant? Do the different types of governments have implications for the *quality* of democratic governance, broadly conceived? In other words, does one type of government perform better in terms of representing citizen preferences? This is a significant question, and one that has been the subject of vigorous debate among scholars.

A central dividing line in this debate is a disagreement over the implications of the fact that coalition government breaks the direct connection between citizen vote choice and the composition of the cabinet. Even in political systems characterized by coalition government, votes are, of course, not irrelevant to government formation. But their impact is indirect: Votes determine the distribution of parliamentary seats, which in turn influence the odds that particular coalitions will form. But the governing coalition that emerges out of inter-party bargaining is (usually) not directly determined by the election outcome.[2] As a result, political systems that encourage multi-party governance reduce the ability of citizens to choose their government directly.

Indeed, we can trace the impact of these arrangements empirically. As Powell (2000: 48) has shown, in majoritarian (i.e., single-party government) systems, there is a clear relationship between electoral outcomes and government participation: Incumbents who do not lose or gain votes are highly likely to remain in office, while those who lose votes are likely to be replaced. In proportional systems that tend to feature coalition government, the relationship is present (Powell, 2000; Martin and Stevenson, 2010) but not nearly as strong, with incumbents maintaining office at higher rates even in the face of electoral losses. In short, it appears easier to "throw the rascals out" under single-party government (Riker, 1982). As Pinto-Duschinsky (1999: 119), a vehement critic of PR electoral systems, argues (writing in 1999):

> Under PR, sitting governments are rarely sent packing. When they are dismissed, it is even more rarely as the direct result of an election but more often as a consequence of post-election bargaining between political party leaders. Since the formation of the Federal German Republic in 1949, no election has ever caused the ousting of the sitting government. There have been two changes of governing party in the past 48 years—in 1909 and 1982. On both occasions, the alternation of power has resulted not from the voters but from a decision by the small Free Democrat Party about which of the main parties to back . . .

A second, closely related normative challenge for coalition governance is tied to the need for compromise. To the extent that coalition government requires compromise, it obscures what Powell has termed "clarity of responsibility." As he explains (Powell, 2000: 51):

> If all the resources necessary for policy making are controlled by a unified, identifiable set of elected officials, it will be easy for citizens to perceive accurately that those officials are responsible for the policies made. On the

[2] One exception is the rare case in which parties form pre-electoral coalitions, whereby they announce to voters that they intend to form a government if they jointly receive sufficient seats to do so. Such arrangements obviously increase the certainty that voters have about the ultimate implications of their vote for government. Nevertheless, even in these cases, there is room for inter-party bargaining when no pre-electoral coalition achieves a parliamentary majority. See Golder (2006) for a detailed treatment.

> other hand, if the resources necessary for policy making are dispersed into the control of numerous groups and individuals, citizens cannot identify who is responsible for policies.... But because the parties [in a coalition] ran against each other and made individual policy proposals before forming a government, it may be difficult to attribute responsibility within a government made up of competitors, who can blame each other for failures.

That is, citizens face a difficult challenge in attributing praise or blame for government policy when confronted by coalition government. If they are dissatisfied with a particular policy choice, who is properly to blame? Did the party they identify with work vigorously to press the party's (and constituents') concerns, but was forced by the realities of coalition governance to make concessions to its coalition partners? In short, is the policy, unpalatable though it may be, the best that could be hoped for? Or did the party simply kowtow to the preferences of its coalition partners? This challenge is made worse by the fact that parties are likely to blame their coalition partners for any perceived government failures. Under single-party governments, voters normally do not face such uncertainties. Especially in "majoritarian," Westminster-style political systems, accountability is typically crystal-clear. For those who, like Riker (1982), believe that "accountability" in this sense is critical to democratic performance, strong single-party government (and the institutions that favor it) are thus much preferable to multiparty government. Highly accountable governments that must fear the verdict of voters will work diligently to represent the preferences of citizens accurately.

Ironically, some of the most powerful competing arguments that tout the advantages of coalition governance *also* take the necessity of compromise as their springboard. It is in the context of these arguments that the findings of this book take on central significance. Instead of focusing on democratic procedure, these arguments focus more directly on the qualities of the governments that form, and on the relationship between the preferences of governments and citizens, broadly understood. How well do the preferences of governments reflect the preferences of citizens in practice? How responsive are government preferences to changes in the preferences of citizens?

Empirically, such an investigation raises significant difficulties: How do we understand citizen and government preferences at a conceptual level? Even if we can agree on a conceptual definition, how can these concepts be measured empirically? Fortunately, we do not need to address these thorny issues here. For current purposes, it is sufficient to consider the approaches that have been developed in the literature. Arguably the most influential approach focuses on the correspondence between citizen and government preferences as measured on ideological scales that estimate citizen and policymaker preferences (Powell and Vanberg, 2000; Kim *et al.*, 2010).

A central finding in this literature is that proportional representation electoral systems do better in achieving congruence between governments and citizens than single-member district electoral systems. As Powell (2000: 229) concludes in perhaps the most extensive treatment of preference correspondence between citizens and governments:

> Even though correspondence between median citizen and policymaker should be a criterion of citizen influence especially valued in the majoritarian vision, it was the processes associated with proportionality that created the best correspondence.

A primary explanation for the better performance of proportional systems in generating correspondence, or congruence, relates directly to the distinction between coalition and single-party government. Political systems that encourage single-party government are much more sensitive in their quality of representation to the correspondence of a single, specific party to citizen preferences. If, for whatever reason, a party that deviates significantly from the median citizen forms a government, correspondence is poor.[3] On the other hand, coalition governments tend to be much less sensitive to the position of individual parties—precisely because they are based on compromise agreements among the participating parties. The moderate positions that emerge out of coalition governance tend, at least on average, to approximate the position of the median citizen better than the position of a single-party government (Powell, 2000: 246).

Our purpose is not to resolve this normative debate, or even to take a side. However, our argument, and the evidence we have presented, speak directly to a key empirical problem at its core. The normative appeal of the proportional vision—of which coalition governance is a critical component—rests in large part on the claim that coalition government results in more meaningful, and more centrist, policy compromise than single-party government. Proponents of the "proportional vision" argue that the reduction in direct citizen influence over government choice and the lack of accountability in coalition government are outweighed by its desirable policy consequences. At least on average, citizens are better represented, proponents argue, by the compromises inherent in coalition government.

It is with respect to this final link that the findings of this book are central. The fundamental assumption underneath the "congruence" literature is that coalition governments implement policies that correspond to compromise agreements among the parties that participate in coalition. But as we (and others) have argued, it is by no means obvious that coalition governments are in a position to implement such compromises. The dual threats of delegation and electoral competition must be contained if multiparty governance is to deliver on this promise. The

[3] Theoretically, such divergence between the median citizen and parties should be constrained, given the logic of the median voter theorem (Hotelling, 1929). However, a number of empirical complications, including the threat of third-party entry and the need to mobilize supporters, tend to limit convergence of parties.

good news is that there are mechanisms available—including strong legislative institutions—that allow them to do so.

7.4 SUMMING UP

Where does all of this leave us? Traditional accounts of coalition government in parliamentary systems ascribe rather limited influence to citizens in the political process. Citizens are generally restricted to casting a vote for a parliamentary party. These directly elected legislators, in turn, are assumed to exercise limited influence. Instead, traditional accounts imbue ministers (and their parties) with primary influence over policies under their jurisdiction. As a result, citizen votes are "diluted." Even if the party favored by a voter is included in a governing coalition, the party is able to exercise influence only in those areas under the jurisdiction of its ministers. In other areas, the party is largely powerless. The account we have offered here challenges this conclusion. A detailed analysis of the legislative process across five contemporary parliamentary systems leaves little doubt that—at least where legislative institutions are strong—parliament plays a central role in drafting and shaping policy. Coalition parties are able to successfully challenge and police the policies proposed by their partners, and they do so within the legislative arena. As a result, citizen votes exercise a more direct influence than often assumed: Voters elect legislators who have a central role in policymaking, and this influence extends to policy areas *beyond* the immediate ministerial control of their parties. While strong parliaments may not hold governments accountable in the sense of classic visions of democratic control of executive power, they are central to the task of policing the coalition bargain. They provide an institutional solution that allows coalition partners with divergent preferences to govern jointly.

Bibliography

Anderweg, Rudy B. and Wilma Bakema. 1994. "The Netherlands: Ministers and Cabinet Policy." In *Cabinet Ministers and Parliamentary Government*, eds. Michael Laver and Kenneth Shepsle. Cambridge: Cambridge University Press.

—— Galen A. Irwin. 2005. *Governance and Politics of the Netherlands*. 2nd ed. New York: Palgrave Macmillan.

—— Lia Nijzink. 1995. "Beyond the Two-Body Image: Relations between Ministers and MPs." In *Parliaments and Majority Rule in Western Europe*, ed. Herbert Döring. New York: St. Martin's Press.

—— Arco Timmermans. 2008. "Conflict Management in Coalition Government." In *Cabinets and Coalition Bargaining: The Democratic Life Cycle in Western Europe*, eds. Kaare Strøm, Wolfgang C. Müller and Torbjörn Bergman. Oxford: Oxford University Press.

Bagehot, Walter. 1872. *The English Constitution*. Oxford: Oxford University Press.

Bawn, Kathleen and Frances Rosenbluth. 2006. "Coalition Parties vs. Coalitions of Parties: How Electoral Agency Shapes the Political Logic of Costs and Benefits." *American Journal of Political Science* 50(2): 251–66.

Benoit, Kenneth and Alex Baturo. N.d. "National Party Competition and Support for European Integration." Working Paper. Trinity College, University of Dublin.

—— Michael Laver. 2006. *Party Policy in Modern Democracies*. London: Routledge.

Box-Steffensmeier, Janet M. and Bradford S. Jones. 2004. *Event History Modeling: A Guide for Social Scientists*. Cambridge: Cambridge University Press.

Bryce, James. 1921. *Modern Democracies*. New York: Macmillan Company.

Buchanan, James M. and Gordon Tullock. 1962. *The Calculus of Consent: Logical Foundations of Constitutional Democracy*. Ann Arbor: University of Michigan Press.

Carroll, Royce and Gary W. Cox. 2010. "Shadowing Ministers: Monitoring Partners in Coalition Governments." *Comparative Political Studies*, Forthcoming. Available at SSRN: http://ssrn.com/abstract=1157615

Cattell, R.B. 1966. "The Scree Test for the Number of Factors." *Multivariate Behavioral Research* 1:245–76.

Chubb, Basil. 1982. *The Government and Politics of Ireland*. 3rd ed. Stanford, CA: Stanford University Press.

Collett, D. 1994. *Modelling Survival Data in Medical Research*. London: Chapman and Hall.

Cox, Gary W. 1987. *The Efficient Secret: The Cabinet and the Development of Political Parties in Victorian England*. Cambridge: Cambridge University Press.

—— 1997. *Making Votes Count*. Cambridge: Cambridge University Press.

Cox, D.R. and E.J. Snell. 1968. "A General Definition of Residuals (with Discussion)." *Journal of the Royal Statistical Society B* 30:248–75.

Damgaard, Erik. 1992. "Denmark: Experiences in Parliamentary Government." In *Parliamentary Change in the Nordic Countries*, ed. Erik Damgaard. Oslo: Scandinavian University Press.

Diermeier, Daniel and Randolph T. Stevenson. 2000. "Cabinet Terminations and Critical Events." *American Political Science Review* 94(3):627–40.

Dinan, Des. 1986. "Constitution and Parliament." In *Politics and Society in Contemporary Ireland*, eds. Brian Girvin and Roland Sturm. Aldershot: Gower.

Döring, Herbert, ed. 1995. *Parliaments and Majority Rule in Western Europe*. New York: St. Martin's Press.

Epstein, David and Sharyn O'Halloran. 1994. "Administrative Procedures, Information, and Agency Discretion." *American Journal of Political Science* 38:697–722.

——— 1999. *Delegating Powers: A Transaction Cost Politics Approach to Policy Making under Separate Powers*. Cambridge: Cambridge University Press.

Fine Gael. 1980. "Reform of the Dáil: Fine Gael Policy on Reform of the Dáil." Policy paper.

Francis, Wayne L. 1982. "Legislative Committee Systems, Optimal Committee Size, and the Costs of Decision Making." *Journal of Politics* 44(3):822–37.

Friedman, Barry. 2009. *The Will of the People*. New York: Farrar, Straus, and Giroux.

Gallagher, Michael. 2005. "Parliament." In *Politics in the Republic of Ireland*, eds. John Coakley and Michael Gallagher. 4th ed. New York: Routledge.

—— Michael Laver and Peter Mair. 2005. *Representative Government in Modern Europe: Institutions, Parties, and Governments*. 4th ed. New York: McGraw-Hill.

Gamm, Gerald and John Huber. 2002. "Legislatures as Political Institutions: Beyond the Contemporary Congress." In *Political Science: State of the Discipline*, eds. Ira Katznelson and Helen V. Milner. New York: Norton.

Ganley, Marcus. 2001. "Select Committees and their Role in Keeping Parliament Relevant: Do New Zealand Select Committees Make a Difference?" *Australasian Parliamentary Review: Journal of the Australasian Study of Parliament Group* 16(2):81–90.

Gilligan, Thomas and Keith Krehbiel. 1989. "Asymmetric Information and Legislative Rules with a Heterogeneous Committee." *American Journal of Political Science* 33(2):459–90.

Golder, Sona. 2006. *The Logic of Pre-Electoral Coalition Formation*. Columbus, OH: Ohio State University Press.

Hallerberg, Mark, Rolf Rainer Strauch and Jürgen von Hagen. 2009. *Fiscal Governance in Europe*. Cambridge: Cambridge University Press.

Harfst, Philipp and Kai-Uwe Schnapp. 2003. "Instrumente Parlamentarischer Kontrolle der Exekutive in Westlichen Demokratien." Discussion Paper sp iv 2003-201. Wissenschaftszentrum Berlin für Sozialforschung (WZB).

Heller, William B. 2001. "Making Policy Stick: Why the Government Gets What it Wants in Multiparty Parliaments." *American Journal of Political Science* 45(4):780–98.

Hooghe, Bakker, Brigevich, de Vries, Edwards, Marks, Rovny and Steenbergen. 2010. "Reliability and Validity of Measuring Party Positions: The Chapel Hill Expert Surveys of 2002 and 2006." *European Journal of Political Research* 49(5): 687–703.

Hotelling, Harold. 1929. "Stability in Competition." *The Economic Journal* 39(153): 41–57.

Hougaard, Philip. 2000. *Analysis of Multivariate Survival Data*. New York: Springer-Verlag.

Huber, John D. 1992. "Restrictive Legislative Procedures in France and the United States." *American Political Science Review* 86(3):675–87.

—— 1996. *Rationalizing Parliament: Legislative Institutions and Party Politics in France*. Cambridge: Cambridge University Press.

Huber, John D. and Charles R. Shipan. 2002. *Deliberate Discretion: The Institutional Foundations of Bureaucratic Autonomy*. Cambridge: Cambridge University Press.

Hughes, Ian, Paula Clancy, Codagh Harris and David Beetham. 2006. *Power to the People? Assessing Democracy in Ireland*. Dublin: TASC.

Janda, Kenneth, Robert Harmel, Christine Edens and Patricia Goff. 1995. "Changes in Party Identity." *Party Politics* 1(2):171–96.

Jenny, Marcelo and Wolfgang C. Müller. 1995. "Presidents of Parliament: Neutral Chairmen or Assets of the Majority?" In *Parliaments and Majority Rule in Western Europe*, ed. Herbert Döring. New York: St. Martin's Press.

Kim, Dong-Hun and Gerhard Loewenberg. 2005. "Committees in Coalition Governments." *Comparative Political Studies* 38(9):1104–29.

Kim, HeeMin, G. Bingham Powell and Richard C. Fording. 2010. "Electoral Systems, Party Systems, and Substantive Representation: An Analysis of Distortion in Western Democracies." *Comparative Politics* 42(2):167–85.

King, Gary. 1989. *Unifying Political Methodology: The Likelihood Theory of Statistical Inference*. Cambridge: Cambridge University Press.

—— James E. Alt, Nancy E. Burns and Michael Laver. 1990. "A Unified Model of Cabinet Dissolution in Parliamentary Democracies." *American Journal of Political Science* 34(3):846–71.

—— M. Tomz and J. Wittenberg. 2000. "Making the Most of Statistical Analyses: Improving Interpretation and Presentation." *American Journal of Political Science* 44(2): 347–61.

Klein, John P. and Melvin L. Moeschberger. 1997. *Survival Analysis: Techniques for Censored and Truncated Data*. New York: Springer-Verlag.

Krehbiel, Keith. 1991. *Information and Legislative Organization*. Ann Arbor, MI: University of Michigan Press.

LaPalombara, Joseph. 1974. *Politics within Nations*. Englewood Cliffs, NJ: Prentice-Hall.

Laver, M. J. 1992. "Coalition and Party Policy in Ireland." In *Party Policy and Government Coalitions*, eds. M.J. Laver and Ian Budge. New York: St. Martin's Press.

—— W. Ben Hunt. 1992. *Policy and Party Competition*. New York: Routledge.

—— Norman Schofield. 1990. *Multiparty Government: The Politics of Coalition in Europe*. Oxford: Oxford University Press.

—— Kenneth Shepsle, eds. 1994. *Cabinet Ministers and Parliamentary Government*. Cambridge: Cambridge University Press.

—— —— 1996. *Making and Breaking Governments: Cabinets and Legislatures in Parliamentary Democracies*. Cambridge: Cambridge University Press.

Lees, John D. and Malcolm Shaw. 1979. "Introduction." In *Committees in Legislatures: A Comparative Analysis*, eds. John D. Lees and Malcolm Shaw. Durham, NC: Duke University Press (Chapter Introduction).

Leuchtenburg, William E. 1996. *The Supreme Court Reborn*. New York: Oxford University Press.

Lijphart, Arend. 1984. *Democracies: Patterns of Majoritarian and Consensus Government in Twenty-One Democracies*. New Haven CT: Yale University Press.

—— 1999. *Patterns of Democracy*. New Haven CT: Yale University Press.

Linzer, Drew and Ronald Rogowski. 2008. "Lower Prices: The Impact of Majoritarian Systems in Democracies Around the World." *The Journal of Politics* 70:17–27.

Loewenberg, Gerhard. 1967. *Parliament in the German Political System*. Ithaca, NY: Cornell University Press.

—— Samuel C. Patterson. 1979. *Comparing Legislatures*. Boston: Little Brown.

Luebbert, Gregory. 1986. *Comparative Democracy: Policy Making and Governing Coalitions in Europe and Israel*. New York: Columbia University Press.

MacCarthaigh, Muiris. 2005. *Accountability in Irish Parliamentary Politics*. Dublin: Institute of Public Administration.

Madron, Thomas William. 1969. *Small Group Methods and the Study of Politics*. Evanston, IL: Northwestern University Press.

Martin, Lanny W. and Georg Vanberg. 2003. "Wasting Time? The Impact of Ideology and Size on Delay in Coalition Formation." *British Journal of Political Science* 33:323–32.

———— 2004. "Policing the Bargain: Coalition Government and Parliamentary Scrutiny." *American Journal of Political Science* 48(1):13–27.

———— 2005. "Coalition Policymaking and Legislative Review." *American Political Science Review* 99:93–106.

———— 2008. "Coalition Government and Political Communication." *Political Research Quarterly* 61:502–16.

—— Randolph T. Stevenson. 2001. "Government Formation in Parliamentary Democracies." *American Journal of Political Science* 45(1):33–50.

———— 2010. "The Conditional Impact of Incumbency on Government Formation." *American Political Science Review* 104(3):503–18.

Mattson, Ingvar and Kaare Strøm. 1995. "Parliamentary Committees." In *Parliaments and Majority Rule in Western Europe*, ed. Herbert Döring. New York: St. Martin's Press.

Mayhew, David R. 1974. *Congress: The Electoral Connection*. New Haven, CT: Yale University Press.

McLeay, Elizabeth. 2008. "Parliamentary Committees in New Zealand: A House Continuously Reforming Itself?" Paper presented at the Australasian Study of Parliament Group Conference 2008.

Meguid, Bonnie M. 2008. *Party Competition between Unequals: Strategies and Electoral Fortunes in Western Europe*. Cambridge: Cambridge University Press.

Mezey, Michael L. 1979. *Comparative Legislatures*. Durham, NC: Duke University Press.

—— 1993. "Legislatures: Individual Purpose and Institutional Performance." In *Political Science: The State of the Discipline II*, ed. Ada W. Finifter. Washington, DC: American Political Science Association.

—— David M. Olson, eds. 1991. *Legislatures in the Policy Process: The Dilemmas of Economic Policy*. Cambridge: Cambridge University Press.

Mitchell, Paul. 2000. "Ireland: From Single-Party to Coalition Rule." In *Coalition Governments in Western Europe*, eds. Wolfgang C. Müller and Kaare Strøm. Oxford: Oxford University Press.

—— 2003. "Ireland: 'O What a Tangled Web . . .'—Delegation, Accountability, and Executive Power." In *Delegation and Accountability in Parliamentary Democracies*, eds. Kaare Strøm, Wolfgang C. Müller and Torbjörn Bergman. Oxford: Oxford University Press.

Müller, Wolfgang C. and Kaare Strøm. 1999. *Policy, Office, or Votes? How Political Parties in Western Europe Make Hard Decisions*. Cambridge: Cambridge University Press.

Müller, Wolfgang C. and Kaare Strøm, eds. 2000. *Coalition Governments in Western Europe*. Oxford: Oxford University Press.

——— 2008. "Coalition Agreements and Cabinet Governance." In *Cabinets and Coalition Bargaining: The Democratic Life Cycle in Western Europe*, eds. Kaare Strøm, Wolfgang C. Müller and Torbjörn Bergman. Oxford: Oxford University Press.

Murphy, Mary C. 2006. "Reform of Dáil Éireann: The Dynamics of Parliamentary Change." *Parliamentary Affairs* 59(3):437–53.

Norton, Philip, ed. 1998. *Parliaments and Governments in Western Europe*. London: Frank Cass.

Paterson, William E. and David Southern. 1991. *Governing Germany*. Oxford: Basil Blackwell Ltd.

Pinto-Duschinsky, Michael. 1999. "Send the Rascals Packing: Defects of Proportional Representation and the Virtues of the Westminster Model." *Representation* 36(2): 117–26.

Polsby, Nelson W. 1975. "Legislatures." In *Handbook of Political Science*, eds. Fred I. Greenstein and Nelson Polsby. Reading, MA: Addison-Wesley.

Powell, G. Bingham. 2000. *Elections as Instruments of Democracy: Majoritarian and Proportional Views*. New Haven, CT: Yale University Press.

Powell, G. Bingham, Jr. and Georg S. Vanberg. 2000. "Election Laws, Disproportionality and Median Correspondence: Implications for Two Visions of Democracy." *British Journal of Political Science* 30(3):383–411.
URL: http://www.jstor.org/stable/194001

Riker, William. 1982. *Liberalism against Populism*. San Francisco, CA: W.H. Freeman.

Rogowski, Ronald and Mark Kayser. 2002. "Majoritarian Electoral Systems and Consumer Power: Price-Level Evidence from OECD Countries." *American Journal of Political Science* 46(3):526–39.

Strøm, Kaare. 1984. "Minority Governments in Parliamentary Democracies." *Comparative Political Studies* 17(2):199–227.

—— 1990a. "A Behavioral Theory of Competitive Political Parties." *American Journal of Political Science* 34(2):565–98.

—— 1990b. *Minority Government and Majority Rule*. Cambridge: Cambridge University Press.

—— Wolfgang Müller and Torbjörn Bergman, eds. 2008. *Cabinets and Coalition Bargaining: The Democratic Life Cycle in Western Europe*. Oxford: Oxford University Press.

—— Benjamin Nyblade. 2007. "Coalition Theory and Government Formation." In *The Oxford Handbook of Comparative Politics*, eds. Carlos Boix and Susan C. Stokes. Oxford: Oxford University Press.

Thiébault, Jean-Louis. 1994. "The Political Autonomy of Cabinet Ministers in the French Fifth Republic." In *Cabinet Ministers and Parliamentary Government*, eds. Michael Laver and Kenneth Shepsle. Cambridge: Cambridge University Press.

Thies, Michael F. 2001. "Keeping Tabs on Partners: The Logic of Delegation in Coalition Governments." *American Journal of Political Science* 45(3):580–98.

Verba, Sidney. 1961. *Small Groups and Political Behavior: A Study of Leadership*. Princeton, NJ: Princeton University Press.

Verzichelli, Luca. 2008. "Portfolio Allocation." In *Cabinets and Coalition Bargaining: The Democratic Life Cycle in Western Europe*, eds. Kaare Strøm, Wolfgang C. Müller and Torbjörn Bergman. Oxford: Oxford University Press.

Volkens, Andrea. 2001. "Manifesto Research Since 1979: From Reliability to Validity." In *Estimating the Policy Positions of Political Actors*, ed. Michael Laver. London: Routledge.

Ward, Alan J. 1994. *The Irish Constitutional Tradition: Responsible Government and Modern Ireland, 1782–1992*. Washington, DC: The Catholic University of America Press.

Warwick, Paul V. 1994. *Government Survival in Parliamentary Democracies*. Cambridge: Cambridge University Press.

—— James N. Druckman. 2001. "Portfolio Salience and the Proportionality of Payoffs in Coalition Governments." *British Journal of Political Science* 31(4):627–49.

Weingast, Barry. 1997. "The Political Foundations of Democracy and the Rule of Law." *American Political Science Review* 91(2):245–63.

Wheare, K.C. 1963. *Legislatures*. New York: Oxford University Press.

Williams, Philip. 1968. *The French Parliament: Politics in the Fifth Republic*. New York: Praeger.

Wright, Vincent. 1989. *The Government and Politics of France*. 3rd ed. New York: Holmes and Meier Publishers.

Index

Made in the USA
Lexington, KY
29 May 2014